Chicken Soup for the Soul.

Count Your Blessings

Sandy
I count my day
Blessings every day
that you are in my
life, and that we
are blessed with all
that we could wish
for in life.
Count your blessings
every day for they
are plentiful.
all My Love!
Jim

Chicken Soup for the Soul: Count Your Blessings
101 Stories of Gratitude, Fortitude, and Silver Linings
Jack Canfield, Mark Victor Hansen, Amy Newmark, Laura Robinson, Elizabeth Bryan

Published by Chicken Soup for the Soul Publishing, LLC   www.chickensoup.com

The publisher gratefully acknowledges the many publishers and individuals who granted Chicken Soup for the Soul permission to reprint the cited material.

Front cover, back cover, and interior illustration courtesy of iStockphoto.com/Pony-art. Back cover photo courtesy iStockphoto.com/CapturedNuance.

Cover and Interior Design & Layout by Pneuma Books, LLC
For more info on Pneuma Books, visit www.pneumabooks.com

Distributed to the booktrade by Simon & Schuster. SAN: 200-2442

Publisher's Cataloging-in-Publication Data
(Prepared by The Donohue Group)

Chicken soup for the soul : count your blessings : 101 stories of gratitude, fortitude, and silver linings / [compiled by] Jack Canfield ... [et al.].

    p. ; cm.

ISBN: 978-1-935096-42-9

1. Gratitude--Literary collections. 2. Gratitude--Anecdotes. 3. Fortitude--Literary collections. 4. Fortitude--Anecdotes. 5. Conduct of life--Literary collections. 6. Conduct of life--Anecdotes. I. Canfield, Jack, 1944- II. Title: Count your blessings

PN6071.G73 C45 2009
810.8/02/0353   2009935581

PRINTED IN THE UNITED STATES OF AMERICA

3 9082 13942 8737   ∞free paper

18 17 16 15 14 13 12 11 10   04 05 06 07 08 09 10

Chicken Soup for the Soul®
Count Your Blessings

101 Stories of Gratitude, Fortitude, and Silver Linings

Jack Canfield
Mark Victor Hansen
Amy Newmark
Laura Robinson
Elizabeth Bryan

Chicken Soup for the Soul Publishing, LLC
Cos Cob, CT

Contents

❶
~Expressing Gratitude~

❷
~Back to Basics~

❸

~Recovering from Adversity~

❹

~Silver Linings~

❺

~The Joy of Giving~

❻

~Attitude Is Everything~

❼

~I've Got What I Need~

8

~Thank My Lucky Stars~

9

~A New Perspective~

10

~Having Faith~

Introduction

A few months ago, we published *Chicken Soup for the Soul: Tough Times, Tough People*, our book on people overcoming adversity. Many of our writers stressed how happy they are now, despite lower incomes, smaller homes, and simpler lifestyles. Many wrote about the new lives they have come to accept and enjoy after chronic illness, accidents, losing loved ones, or other non-economic challenges. Some were victims of a crime, some watched their houses burn down, and some are living with incurable illnesses or disabilities.

Many wrote about finding inner strength, support from friends, marriages strengthening in the face of adversity, and rediscovering the joys of their families. They wrote about the silver linings they found in their troubles and the many blessings in their lives. We had so many fabulous stories about "counting your blessings" that we decided to make this companion volume to *Tough Times* and to do it with the assistance of Laura Robinson and Elizabeth Bryan, whose amazing sagas you will read in this book.

When we needed a few more stories to finish this book, we sent an e-mail to our past contributors, letting them know what we needed and giving them only two weeks to submit. We received almost 2,000 submissions in those two weeks, a record number of daily submissions for a single book. The tremendous interest in this topic tells us we struck a chord—it seems that we are all reassessing our lives and our needs, thinking about what really matters to us, and realizing how good things really are.

These inspirational stories remind us that each day holds something to be thankful for—whether it is having the sun shine or putting food on the table. Power outages and storms, health scares and illnesses, job woes and financial problems, housing challenges and family worries test us all. But there is always a silver lining, and the pride and self-esteem that come from meeting a challenge are always empowering and invigorating.

In this book you will read stories about how to express gratitude, whether it is by making lists, reaching out to thank people, or just approaching each day with a positive attitude. You'll read about families who have gone back to basics, and are so much happier with their new focus on what really matters. You'll read inspirational stories about people who have recovered from horrific injuries or illnesses, and the lessons they have learned. We have some "wow" stories about silver linings, good fortune, and lucky coincidences that happened to people in the middle of their struggles. You will gain a new perspective on life as you read this book, and we are sure that it will put a spring in your step as you reflect on the many blessings in your own life.

I tip my hat to all of you readers. I know that the stories in this book mirror your own experiences, and that our writers reflect the fortitude, resilience, and joy that you all show in your daily lives. Your strength, your good humor, and your generosity in the face of adversity are a great inspiration to all of us.

~Amy Newmark
Publisher, Chicken Soup for the Soul

Accidental
Blessings

Coincidence is God's way of remaining anonymous.
~Albert Einstein

Behind every book, every movie and every work of art exists a "how we got here story." Some are brief, and some are long, but regardless, there is always a journey. Typically, journeys are fraught with ups and downs, strung together by some odd series of coincidences that later take on some greater meaning. They are also usually full of reasons to be grateful that we can't always see at the time. But if we examine any of life's stories, even the ones defined by huge challenge, there really are silver linings on every cloud—better known as "blessings-in-disguise."

The story of how *Chicken Soup for the Soul: Count Your Blessings* came to be is no exception. It began with me as I woke up, pinned underneath my silver Ford Escort at 5:30 A.M. on July 3rd, 1981. The tire was holding me down by my hair and the sleeve of my white peasant blouse that I had put on the evening before. At nineteen years of age, I had no idea that I wouldn't live forever; nor would I have believed it if anyone had told me so. I had fallen asleep while driving with my two best friends in the car, under no influence other than exhaustion. There, underneath that tire, my entire world changed.

I had no pain, as my body was in shock. What I did have was a strange numbness in both of my legs. I wanted very badly to get up, walk away, and explain to my parents that I hadn't meant to dent the car. Because I was under a tire on the passenger's side, my only vantage point was to turn my head to the right and look underneath the vehicle through to the road. I could hear my friends' faraway voices calling for help—but all I could see were their two sets of legs, running in the middle of the parkway.

Seeing those two sets of running legs crystallized the purest moment of gratitude that I had ever experienced. In that singular moment, I understood two things: I was alive, and my two best friends had not been hurt—I was grateful.

As the paramedics lifted the car off my body, the lack of feeling in my thighs quickly turned to blinding pain. I had severely fractured both of my femurs, several ribs and my nose. I was lucky, although that is not how my parents felt when they got the 6:00 A.M. call that I had been in an accident. All they heard before driving the thirty miles to the ER was "Your daughter was alive when we put her in the ambulance."

For my parents, history was repeating itself in the form of a nightmare. Thirty-eight years and eleven days earlier on June 22nd, 1953, they had flipped their convertible, driving from New York to Virginia on their honeymoon. Like me, my twenty-five-year-old father had been pinned under the car, fractured a femur and broken some ribs. He'd sustained other serious internal injuries that made his recovery in 1953 much more challenging than mine. My mother couldn't help but question: How could the same accident be happening again; what was the reason?

I had heard about my parents' accident my entire life—how they had nearly died together after just being married, how my grandmother had moved in with the local postman so that she could care for them daily, and how the only way my mother knew my father was alive was by hearing his screams each morning as the orderlies turned him over in bed. Now, it was all happening to me.

My own first days in the hospital were a blur of intensive care, being strung up in traction, and all kinds of theories about my treatment and my fate. My parents barely left my side—their own experience in the hospital had left them terrified that something even worse might happen if I were left alone. On the fifth day, I woke up with a slight fever and a piercing pain in my back. The nurse placated me, saying I had probably pulled a muscle when I lifted myself up in my bed with the traction bar. By midday the pain was excruciating, my fever was rising and breathing had become difficult. The overworked staff was nowhere to be found when I began coughing up clots of blood, but my mother was right there. I heard her in the hallway, demanding that somebody bring me oxygen. She insisted that I was having a pulmonary embolism, and if they didn't help me soon, I would die.

My mother knew this because of a "coincidence"—only two days before, she'd read someone's firsthand account of having an embolism. And there I was, having one, right before her eyes.

It was hours before the doctor came, confirming my mother's fears. If I survived the night, the odds were that I would probably live. For me, the pain had become so unbearable that I no longer cared. My father spent the night whispering softly to me, trying to assuage the pain as I drifted in and out of consciousness. When I next opened my eyes, the sun was filtering through the hospital blinds and my parents were still sitting in chairs beside my bed. We'd come through it together.

In the space of one week, my world had gone from predictable and safe to "all bets are off." Would I walk again? Would my legs ever be right? Would my lung heal from the embolism? Thoughts like these dominated the minds of everyone in my immediate world. Yet, something else was stirring inside me. I was a young woman faced with the possibility of being handicapped for life, and somehow, I was *grateful*.

I had "woken up" under that car in more ways than one. No matter what the doctors said that was ambiguous, overwhelming or frightening, I heard another voice—one that kept reminding me that *I was still here*. My friends weren't injured, we had insurance, and my family had come together as never before to help me heal. Yes—I had moments filled with anger, fear and self-pity. But as my recovery continued, my gratitude grew to such a degree that I began to understand: there was a much bigger reason that I had survived.

Three months later I was discharged from the hospital in a full body cast. The joy of my homecoming was eclipsed by sorrow; one day earlier, my adoring grandfather had suddenly died. My grandmother moved into our home, and sat vigil by my bed, just as she had done thirty-eight years before with my parents.

In March of the following year, I took my first steps with no crutches, walkers or braces. My legs were miraculously the same length, and would eventually run anywhere life would take me. Things that I had taken for granted, like sitting on the toilet alone or getting dressed without help, had become momentous occasions. My parents and I had bonded in a way that I could never have imagined, and I had become incredibly thankful for waking up each day. I had glimpsed Life's Big Picture, and while my mother will say she didn't need to go through it twice to understand the lesson, I felt truly blessed.

I also knew that it was part of my path in life to somehow share what I had learned.

Fast forward to July 3rd, 2009 — *exactly twenty-eight years to the day* that I woke up underneath the tire of my car, I was getting much different news about my future. After months of typical contractual back and forths, all the terms of our agreement with Chicken Soup for the Soul Publishing had been settled — on the anniversary of my accident. Was this even possible? My business partner Laura and I would be co-authoring this book, and launching the *Chicken Soup for the Soul: Count Your Blessings* board game for the 2009 holiday season — my life had come full circle. And now I would have the opportunity to share my feelings of gratitude with a large audience of *Chicken Soup for the Soul* readers — what an incredible way to spread the message and share the gift of my accident.

When I considered the entire journey from my parents' story to my own, and what was now happening with this project, beginning on this magical date, the undeniable synchronicities confirmed what I already felt in my heart — there really are no "coincidences."

Talk about counting your blessings.

~Elizabeth Bryan

From Balderdash
to Blessings

Life is the game that must be played.
~Edwin Arlington Robinson

I often say I've been selling laughter for twenty years... but it hasn't always been funny!

My name is Laura Robinson and I am one of the co-authors of this book and the co-inventor of *Balderdash*, the classic bluffing game that has sold millions of copies all over the world. *Balderdash* is based on an old parlor game my family started playing when I was twelve years old—we all just called it "Dictionary." Everyone loved it and I made them all play every chance I got. It was so creative and funny and fun—all the elements that to me, make up a great game.

In my early twenties, I had a close friend who invested in *Trivial Pursuit*. He was making bundles of money, and I thought, as did many people, "Hey, why don't I make a game?" With a partner, I created a prototype for that dictionary game we loved to play—my mom suggested we call it "Balderdash"—and we went looking for a license. Not sure if it was beginner's luck or just that the game was so fabulous, but we got a deal with our first meeting. The whole process was remarkably fast—from inception of the idea to product on the shelves was under a year, but it was one very intense year. We basically worked around the clock, and did everything ourselves, researching words, finalizing packaging, making prototypes, procuring trademarks, doing the deal... the list goes on.

Luckily, *Balderdash* rose to the top fairly quickly. We made fantastic radio commercials that really helped with sales. I actually *dreamt* the characters and the script the night before we produced the spots. The games sold out their first run, and the stores were taking orders and creating waiting lists of customers. It took a while but the climb was fairly steady. In my hometown of Toronto there is a strong "weekend culture"—people get out of town, winter and summer, to ski or to go to cottages in the beautiful lake regions north of the city. This demographic really embraced the game and helped us gain recognition and word of mouth.

We hit a bit of a roadblock when we first took the game into the States by picking the wrong company to distribute and we were almost discontinued. Eventually, *Balderdash* was picked up by the right large U.S. company, which made the game a hit in the mass market. They produced some hilarious television commercials as promotion, Howard Stern even played a version of it on his radio show and the game was officially "on the map." We branched out into many other countries, and millions of people worldwide have loved playing the game. I am so happy and grateful to have made an impact on families everywhere, helping them laugh and spend quality time together!

Many years later, through Rachel Naples, a friend I'd known for years, I was introduced to Elizabeth Bryan—an artist, designer and writer who was midway through a book proposal called *Embracing Divorce*. Elizabeth and Rachel were both newly divorced and Rachel was also working on a book proposal; they decided to join forces and Rachel thought it would be a great idea to create a board game to go with it.

The three of us sat down in Rachel's backyard to create the game, and *spontaneous combustion* occurred. Before we knew it, the *Embracing Divorce* game had practically invented itself. Part of the game logic centered around the idea of counting your blessings by collecting plastic jewelry "charms" that had things written on them like love, hope and giving. By the end of the game, each player would have made a "count your blessings" charm bracelet.

I flew back to Toronto, where my family and I were living. Later that night, Elizabeth called me with the idea to make *real* charm bracelets and sell them. Coincidently, I had a close contact at QVC, the U.S. home shopping channel, who was looking for new products to take on the network. Before any of us could blink, we were on the air, selling out our newly developed "Count Your Blessings" jewelry. We still had the game about divorce in the queue, so I pulled out the stops and the three of us headed to meet Phil Jackson, then president of the games division of Mattel. Phil and his team loved the game, but felt that they could not sell a game about divorce to their mainstream audience. I heard myself saying that we "really intended to make a whole suite of games and products, all under the umbrella of 'Count Your Blessings.'" Phil replied, "Now, that could be big!"

Recognizing the potential of the brand, Rachel, Elizabeth, and I applied to trademark the phrase "Count Your Blessings" across several categories, and by some miracle the marks registered. It was clear the message was meant to be shared. The three of us worked tirelessly for several years trying to build the brand.

Elizabeth and I also licensed the rights from Franklin Covey to create a wonderful family game inspired by *The 7 Habits of Highly Effective People* and truly counted our blessings every day that Rachel had put us together.

The world of game inventing had changed dramatically in the twenty years since *Balderdash*. Along the *7 Habits* journey, our first choice in manufacturers turned us down, and our second choice completely changed development teams at the onset of negotiations. A huge blessing-in-disguise appeared right then and there when game company number two introduced us to Family Games America, which ultimately became the publisher for *both* our games.

It seemed that doing games on a grand scale today would take great perseverance and belief in your mission—Elizabeth and I were both determined and committed to share "good message" games with people and families everywhere, and we weren't about to give up.

In December of 2008, I got a call that would connect me to the management of Chicken Soup for the Soul to discuss a game, and

Elizabeth suggested we pitch "Count Your Blessings." We hopped a plane to Connecticut and from the moment we walked into the Chicken Soup for the Soul office, we knew our game had found a home.

The wonderful team at Chicken Soup for the Soul had always wanted to do a book called *Chicken Soup for the Soul: Count Your Blessings*; in fact they already had the title in their line-up. They had been gathering stories for a book called *Chicken Soup for the Soul: Tough Times, Tough People* and the submissions had been pouring in—ironically *filled* with the phrase "count your blessings." It seemed that our joining forces was destined.

We created a new, updated version of the *Count Your Blessings* game, further inspired by Chicken Soup for the Soul. Our experience and journey over the previous year and our wonderful synergies allowed us to take our renamed *Chicken Soup for the Soul: Count Your Blessings* game to a new level of content and design.

I may not always be laughing as I create games that make others laugh. But I am learning and re-learning how to be grateful for the process and the "journey," which is a wonderful gift, all on its own. In getting our games done, we've come up against many obstacles that seemed like the end; delays and dead ends that always turned out to be huge blessings-in-disguise. More than anything else, I have personally learned to trust that amidst the chaos, inside of every cloud, there really is a silver lining.

It's amazing to think that I would still be here making games, twenty years after inventing *Balderdash*. I count my blessings that I can share my work with the Chicken Soup for the Soul audience and continue making people everywhere laugh and connect for many decades to come.

Gratefully,

~Laura Robinson

Chapter 1

Count Your Blessings

Expressing Gratitude

I can no other answer make, but, thanks, and thanks.

~William Shakespeare

The Blessing Sheet

Gratitude unlocks the fullness of life.
~Melody Beattie

The recession hit early in Florida—some newspapers called our state Ground Zero. My husband, Curt, lost his executive job in construction in August of 2007. Somehow we had deluded ourselves that he would make it through the next round of cuts, but when he called me and whispered, "I'm gone," I knew our dream had ended.

A year later, I couldn't believe how much our lives had changed. We no longer threw whatever we wanted into the grocery cart. I used coupons to buy toilet paper. New clothes were something I fingered on the sales rack when I convinced myself that window shopping could be fun—but it never was. Getting the mail was the highlight of our day along with watching *Jeopardy!* at seven and *Wheel of Fortune* afterward.

"I don't know how long we can hold out unless one of us makes some money." My husband tipped his head back and let out another long sigh. I echoed it in my own head. I hadn't worked outside the home in years. After sending his résumé out for hundreds of jobs with no luck, we decided Curt should open his own business and take whatever work he could find.

"I'll start sending mine out tomorrow. I'll get something," I assured him. But I had already scanned the job postings for positions with my experience. They were as limited as the construction field he left.

"When we get down to $10,000, we'll put the house on the market."

"We can't move back north—there's nothing for you there anymore." I was sick of this conversation. Each day hung on us like the weights at the gym we used to attend. I fled the room and hugged my knees to my chest in my bedroom chair. Life was as ugly as the smears on our windows. How much longer could we hold up without eventually hating each other or the world?

I grabbed the phone when it rang beside me and answered on the first ring.

"It's Kelly. Are you doing alright today? You don't sound so good." I smiled as I heard the voice of my best friend from back home. She'd sent card after card hoping to encourage our lagging spirits.

"I keep thinking about what might happen to us." I shared my fears about foreclosure and bankruptcy and ending up on the streets homeless. Before long I was blubbering into the phone like a newborn baby. "I just want to give up."

I heard her sharp intake of breath. "Do this. Take a blank sheet of paper and post it on your refrigerator. I want you to write down at least one thing each day that is good. I don't care if it is as insignificant as you ate three meals—put it down. You need to focus on the positive, because good things are still happening, you just can't see them now."

I didn't understand how a piece of paper would help. I knew Curt wouldn't write anything down and it would all be on me. "I'll give it a try," I promised.

The next day I twirled the pen in my hand as I stood in front of my refrigerator. I'd told Curt about Kelly's idea and he'd only nodded. But I had to start somewhere. NO BILLS TODAY, I wrote. When I pulled my hand away, I felt an unfamiliar sensation—one I hadn't felt in a long time—gratitude. I smiled.

The next day, I added two more blessings to my list—we walked for half an hour and my back didn't hurt. When I got a card in the mail, I posted about it too. Before long, my list filled two pages. But I knew Kelly was onto something the day my husband reminded me to write down some good news.

The other day, six months later, I cleaned off the top of my refrigerator and discovered the blessing sheets I'd tossed there after my husband had found temporary work. Last week he was laid off again. I read through my scribbled list, then reached for a clean sheet of paper. I couldn't wait to fill the sheets again.

~Terri Tiffany

Counting Laps

H2O: two parts Heart and one part Obsession.
~Author Unknown

In 2002 my dad, brother, sister and I bought a small condo in Florida. Being faint-of-pocketbook, my quarter-share took most of my retirement money, but I live by the principle that you should follow your dreams while you're still awake. Besides, I was born in Tallahassee just two months after the big war ended and I've always thought God intended for me to be a Floridian, even though my folks moved back to their home state of Illinois three weeks after my birth and I'd lived up north, mostly in Wisconsin, ever since.

At any rate, I was happier than a flower-lover in a field full of orchids every time I got to stay at the family condo. Florida captured my heart. No matter how many times I made the trip, I was thrilled to arrive in sun, sand, sea, surf and swimming pool country.

Two years later, after visiting the sunny south at least five times, I sold my home in Wisconsin and bought a condo in the building right next to the one where our family condo is. My building is directly across the street from the big luxurious swimming pool. Heaven on earth!

The large condo pool is next to the Intracoastal Waterway, one street away from the Gulf of Mexico. Now, I swim almost every day of my life. Sometimes twice a day. And each time I'm at the pool, I'm actually in the water, unlike most people who sit in the lounge chairs reading, talking or sleeping. Not me. I go to the pool to swim, and

I'm often in the water for an hour and a half or two hours at a time, swimming leisurely laps.

The problem with swimming laps is keeping track. My mind wanders. Oh, look, there's a dolphin jumping out of the Intracoastal! Or three or four condo friends jump in the pool to cool off and we gab each time I reach the shallow end. Or perhaps a pelican, seagull, heron or egret swoops by to my delight when I'm doing the backstroke and I lose track of my lap count.

My cousin Meta has one solution for keeping track of laps. She walks around her one-eighth mile circular driveway out in the country every morning twenty-four times with her neighbor. Meta has a large coffee can on the driveway that holds twenty-four small pebbles. When they start walking she puts the pebbles in her coat pocket and drops one in the can each time they go around. As these two women chat about everything under their Cincinnati sky, they know exactly when they've finished their three miles.

But at the swimming pool there's no place in my swimsuit for thirty pebbles. The solution came one day when I was feeling especially joyful about being in that pool under a robin egg blue sky on a glorious 80-degree Florida day. I started thinking about all my blessings. That's it! I thought. I'll think about specific blessings that have particular importance in my life and that have significance to the number of lap I'm on.

ONE: The amazing, warm, wonderful sun. What a blessing! For twenty-four years in Wisconsin I froze every winter. Now I'm swimming outdoors every day all year long thanks to that one glorious, magnificent sun. Side stroke, breaststroke, crawl.

TWO: On this lap I think about how fortunate I am to have my dear friend Jack who lives in the condo fifty-seven steps from my own. We've been together as a twosome, a wonderful couple since 2004. Two people whose hearts are together and who both love to swim for exercise.

THREE: Lap number three is about the work I do, work I love. Three part-time freelance jobs, instead of one monumental stressful one. I write, I speak, I paint jars. I make a little money with each, enough to survive. Lots of freedom. Breast stroke, frog kick.

FOUR: My four children, two daughters, two sons. Children who have filled my life with joy, sometimes angst. But, oh, the blessings of having children. As I butterfly kick my way to the other end of the pool, I think about each child. Jeanne, an art professor in California. Julia, working on her master's degree in Wisconsin while raising her three children as a single parent. Michael's busy life in Ohio with his wonderful wife and three beautiful redheaded children. Andrew, following his dreams working for a company in the sports field in California. Four interesting lives. Suddenly that lap is finished.

FIVE: I wonder what I'm thankful for that has a number five connected to it? Sometimes it's hard to come up with something for a certain number. One day in the pool I recalled that I have five pair of sandals in my condo closet. The next day as I did the side stroke up the pool and down, I thought about the tasty five-bean salad recipe I made and the five friends who ate it.

SIX: Six days of the week that we do water aerobics in the pool. Each morning at 9 A.M. one of the half-dozen CDs of great water aerobics instruction is played at our neighborhood pool, and Monday through Saturday, Jack and I and any number of friends and neighbors jump in the pool and exercise for forty or fifty minutes. Six days a week. What a great workout!

SEVEN: The seven seas. As a swimmer I pass the time back-stroking during lap seven by recalling all the wonderful places I've swam. Atlantic Ocean, Pacific Ocean, the aqua blue Caribbean, Gulf of Mexico, the warm waters off Kauai, Oahu, and the big island of Hawaii. I'm thankful for the seven seas, the oceans, rivers, lakes, and ponds. Thankful for water.

EIGHT: Eight grandchildren: Hailey, Casey, Riley, Hannah, Zachary, Chloe, Adeline and Ethan. I love lap number eight best. Imagine the fun of thinking about the antics of eight little people who are tied so tightly to your heartstrings that sometimes you think you'll just burst from happiness.

NINE: The first thing that came to mind when I hit number nine lap, was "nine lives" as in the number cats are supposed to have. Sometimes when my friends Wally and Shirley are on vacation I get to take care of their cats.

TEN: This is the place in my lap swimming where I examine my conscience. The Ten Commandments come in handy for this one. I run through them all trying to decide if I've blown it and whether or not I need to apologize to anyone for anything.

Sometimes I only do ten laps in the pool. Sometimes twenty. Now that I've figured out how to keep track of the count, my pool time takes on a life of its own. Every day emerge I from that pool a new person... blessings counted, conscience examined, life evaluated, attitude adjusted, and exercise completed.

Jump in! The water's perfect!

~Patricia Lorenz

"You Are a Lucky Person"

Luck affects everything. Let your hook always be cast;
in the stream where you least expect it there will be a fish.
~Ovid

"Y ou were in an automobile accident."

The date was June 22nd, 1953. I was twenty-one years old, a recent college graduate and a new bride just one day earlier. I woke up in a hospital bed with no memory about how I'd gotten there. I was told that my husband and I, on the first day of our honeymoon, had been involved in a terrible collision with the car owned by a doctor at the county hospital—the only one within a hundred miles—in a place called Nassawadox, Virginia.

The details were related to me later, when I was fully conscious. I had been driving our convertible with the top down. According to the police report, something had happened, and our car swerved towards a telephone pole and then across the road into the opposite lane, where it was hit by an oncoming car. The convertible was overturned, I was thrown out, and my husband was pinned beneath it. I later learned that a cardiologist, on his way to the hospital, had stopped at the scene of the accident and taken my husband to the hospital in his car, thereby saving his life.

My injuries, other than a concussion and various cuts and bruises, consisted of a broken pelvis, for which I was told I would have to remain on bed rest. My twenty-six-year-old husband had suffered major injuries, among which were a crushed hip, broken ribs, and a broken femur. He was rapidly losing blood, and during the first twenty-four hours was given at least twelve blood transfusions. After being stabilized, he was put in traction in a room down the hall. His doctor was a young Nassawadox resident who had done an internal medicine internship in Boston—Dr. Milton Kellam. There was no orthopedic surgeon on staff at this one-hundred-bed hospital.

My parents arrived in Virginia the next day. "Why," I questioned them, "why did this happen to me? I haven't lived long enough to do anything bad. I have always been a good person. Why am I being punished?"

"You are a lucky person," my mother said. "You could have been brought to the hospital a widow. You will be all right. Your husband will be all right. I will stay here with both of you until you are well and can go home. Don't cry. You are fortunate to be alive."

Her mantra was the same for the next two and a half months—"You are lucky to have survived—another might have been killed. Don't cry—be thankful."

It was difficult, at first, to follow my mother's directions and feel grateful as events progressed. Unable to sustain the traction, my husband was encased in a body cast from his armpits to his knees. It became a daily 5:00 A.M. ritual for him to be turned in order to prevent pneumonia. The pain he endured was excruciating, and he would cry out in agony.

So, I would awaken every day at 5:00 A.M. to listen for his cries—this became the only way I knew he had survived the night.

We fell into a routine, my mother, my husband, the doctors and I. There was nowhere to stay in the immediate area, but fortunately, the local postmaster and his wife had offered my mother a place to stay. My father had to return to work, so he could only visit on the weekends. Each morning the postmaster drove my mother to the hospital and each evening he returned to take her to her room. She would put me on a stretcher and wheel me to my husband's room, where I would remain for most of the day. There was a big leather chair in the corner where she sat, vigilant for every gesture or need from either of us. To otherwise occupy herself, she started knitting. No one knew what it was supposed to be—it was gray, it was lengthy—a sweater? An afghan? We never found out and it never mattered.

Within a few weeks another complication arose: my husband had severe abdominal pain. Late one evening Dr. Kellam approached me, saying, "Dena, we're going to operate on Sonny tonight. His white count is very elevated. We don't know what's wrong, but something is and we must find it or he will not last the night." I was horrified. At 5 feet 11 inches Sonny had dropped down to less than 120 pounds and he was so weak. How would he survive major abdominal surgery—in a cast!

The doctor cut a hole in the cast, did exploratory surgery, found a gallbladder that was about to rupture, and removed it. Once again my mother, who had remained in the hospital with Dr. Kellam the entire night, reminded me of our good fortune—to have such a wonderful doctor who was so caring, so competent. By this time, he and everyone else were calling her "Mama!" She tended to my husband as she would have to a child of her own, watching every movement, showering him with affection. With the doctor's consent, she even used the hospital kitchen to prepare food that he would eat.

The summer weeks passed, I was able to sit and then walk, and finally the time to leave the hospital arrived in early September. The difficult process of rehabilitation began.

After several years of financial and physical duress, Sonny and I prospered, had three children, and settled into raising a family. Our accident became a bad memory that we seldom discussed. Now, go forward to July 3, 1981. Our oldest child, Marjorie, was married with a baby. Our son Jon was in medical school, and Elizabeth, nineteen years old, was our youngest. Tall, slim and beautiful with thick curly blond hair, Elizabeth was always happy, always optimistic. She went out for the evening with two friends, and called me at 4:00 A.M. to tell me not to worry, she was on her way home. I remember telling her, "Why would I worry? I was asleep!"

At 6:00 A.M. the phone rang again. It was the state police. There had been a bad accident and the driver, Elizabeth, had been taken to the hospital. "How is she?" The reply, "She was alive when we put her in the ambulance." Her two friends were unhurt.

An air of unreality enveloped my husband and me. Another accident? How could that happen to us? We arrived at the hospital and were taken into ICU to see our daughter, who had sustained major injuries after falling asleep at the wheel, swerving into a tree, and being thrown from the car. She had been pinned under the car just as Sonny had been so many years before. She had two fractured femurs, and broken ribs, just like Sonny, and a broken nose. She would be hospitalized for an indefinite time—the parallels were chilling. As soon as possible the attending doctor planned to operate on one leg and insert a metal rod. The other would remain in traction until it was healed enough for Elizabeth to be put in a full body cast.

The July days passed slowly. I took my mother's place in the hospital, arriving early in the morning and leaving in the evening after the night nurse came. My husband stopped to see Elizabeth every morning on his way to work and every night before coming home. Marjorie came daily with the baby, and Jon came in between classes. The staff marveled at the family devotion; Elizabeth was never alone.

I, however, had become quite depressed. It was difficult to function. How could I survive another life and death situation? Why was I fated to endure this trauma twice? I remember weeping in my husband's arms—I just couldn't go on, I told him. "You can and you will," he replied. "You have to be strong, just as you were before. We are fortunate that Elizabeth is alive and will someday be all right. She needs your strength and courage just as we needed Mama's. Perhaps our accident was meant to teach us how to cope with this one. Everything happens for a reason."

I drew strength from his words. Until the morning I walked into her room and realized she was struggling for breath. "Mom, I am spitting up blood, and it's hard to breathe." I had just finished a book about a woman who, after surgery, had a pulmonary embolism and described it graphically. Immediately, I realized the same thing was happening to Elizabeth and ran to the nurse, calling frantically,

"Get oxygen. My daughter is having trouble breathing. I think she is having a pulmonary embolism!"

"We're busy now. She probably had some internal injuries. It takes a while to set up the oxygen."

"It doesn't take a while to die. You get that oxygen right now!" I yelled.

She got the oxygen. It was, as I had diagnosed, an embolism, from which she could have died. From that moment on, I went home only to eat, shower, and return. The summer passed, and in the late fall we planned to take our daughter home in a full body cast.

The day before what should have been a happy event, my dear father died very suddenly. I remember my son's meeting me at the foot of the driveway to tell me what happened. I had no more tears to shed. Elizabeth's day of celebration became a day of mourning for my father. Although a nurse came on a daily basis when I went back to work, my mother sat silently in the corner of Elizabeth's room watching over her, as she had watched my husband and me, so many years earlier.

A strong bond had developed among us; I marveled at Elizabeth's courage and determination to heal, return to college and graduate with her class. My only fear at this point concerned the possibility that, like her father, she would recover with one leg shorter than the other. When the cast came off, and Dr. Salzar measured her legs, they were the same, and I wept in appreciation for the gifts that had been given to me: the lives of my beloved husband and child.

When I look back, I think that perhaps my husband was right and everything does happen for a reason. My mother and father gave us strength to go on after our accident, and it was from their example that we did the same for our daughter. I cannot say that I am glad for the time we suffered and the pain we all endured but I can say that these experiences filled me with a sense of deep gratitude that I might otherwise never have known.

~Dena Slater

4

The Blessing Bowl

For today and its blessings,
I owe the world an attitude of gratitude.
~Anonymous

My daughter's first birthday. I was thrilled that we were celebrating a year of her life but saddened at how hard this year had been. We had spent sixty-one days in the hospital, battled seizures and infections, two Flight for Life helicopter rides, numerous 911 calls and late-night trips in the ambulance. My daughter Samantha was a sick little girl and we were still searching for a diagnosis. Her first year had been tumultuous at best.

To honor Samantha's first year, I had asked people to bring a trinket, a stone, a poem, something that brought peace or felt good to them — their blessings for her. I found a simple bowl given to me by my great-grandmother; a bowl for her blessings... her blessing bowl.

I found my contribution to the bowl in my garden. Many times I have set my fragile daughter on the soft dirt hoping something might soak up. Grow, thrive, baby girl; take an example from the zucchinis.

I snipped a bloom from the lily I planted the summer my husband and I were married. The bloom was a buttery yellow with three soft petals; Samantha, my husband and myself. I held a bit of the hearty earth in my hand to form a hard clump and added it to the bowl. My offerings were simple but they represented growth, hope, and my little family; nothing could be more precious.

Samantha woke up on her own at precisely 4:00, when the

party was going to start. She's on so many anti-seizure meds that fully waking her up can take about an hour. Yet today she was lucid and playing in her crib; ready to go for her party. I put her in a blue dress with yellow daisies. I had been saving that dress. I was waiting for her to be big enough, waiting for that first year. The blue brought out her red hair. I placed her tiny tortoise-shell glasses on her nose and laughed to myself. She was absolutely the most precious thing on earth.

Grandparents, aunts, uncles, cousins filed in and kissed Samantha. Wine bottles were uncorked; hummus and brie were laid out on the table. The mood was festive as everyone toasted to Samantha's health.

As the evening progressed and the dinner plates were cleared away, it was time for our blessing bowl "ceremony." Samantha was still awake, babbling to her grandma and seizure-free. I felt an enormous weight lift off my shoulders.

I brought out my great-grandmother's bowl and set it in front of our family, studying the faces in front of me. I thought of what a long haul it's been for everyone — the sleepless nights, the worried phone calls, the private tears cried away from the hospital, all for our daughter. I felt overwhelmed with gratitude.

I cleared my throat and thanked my family for being there. I reached into the bowl and pulled out my blessings for Samantha — the earth and our flower.

I passed the bowl onto my grandmother, Samantha's great-grandmother. She pulled out a silver bell in the shape of an angel, "because Samantha is our angel." When my talkative grandma gets emotional, she is a lady of little words. She passed the bowl onto one of Samantha's grandmas.

She pulled out a perfect sand dollar she found on a California beach. "I chose a sand dollar because it comes from the ocean. The ocean is a beautiful, constant, volatile source of life. The surface can be calm or stormy but we never really see what is going on below. And there is a whole different world below. This reminds me of Samantha;

we don't really know what's going on underneath the surface but there is a beautiful world full of life."

My aunt pulled out a small silver heart. "I have carried this heart with me for twenty years and it has brought me good luck all of these years. Samantha, I now hand it onto you."

She passed the bowl to my sister-in-law who presented a prayer for health and longevity from a Buddhist temple in Hong Kong.

My mother had also chosen shells. The first was a perfect brown and white spiral I had found years ago during a family vacation in Florida. The second was from Tahiti, another beautiful, smooth shell, chosen thousands of miles away years before Samantha was even born.

My dad was next. He had a small stuffed dog dressed in a karate uniform. When you pressed the dog's stomach it yelled out "HY YA!" It reminded him of how Samantha continues to fight.

The last trinket in the bowl was a jade necklace from Hong Kong. My sister-in-law is from China and went home for a visit in May. Her mother gave her the necklace to give to Samantha for good luck. Thirty-four years ago, her son wore the necklace for good health and safety during his babyhood. The span of people loving and praying for Samantha had traveled thousands of miles.

I lit her single candle, overwhelmed that this beautiful little girl was a part of my life, and that she had fought so hard to stay a part of our lives.

Samantha's dad helped her blow out the candle. We fed her frosting and pieces of mushy cake which she smashed between her fingers and toes.

The night came to an end. I finally got my rowdy daughter to sleep. I wandered through the house remembering the night. I took the lily out of the bowl and placed it in our big family bible to be pressed for safe keeping. The bible belonged to my grandfather, who passed away over a decade ago. As I thumbed through the pages, I found a red rose, perfectly pressed between the passages. I don't know the origin, but I put it in the bowl. It was my grandfather's wish, his blessing for Samantha.

We have asked so much from our families, friends, and people we don't know. They have spent countless hours in the hospital, brought meals, coffees, contacted other family members, held and loved Samantha, prayed, sent jade pendants from Hong Kong. How do you give that back?

Gratitude, I thought. I am grateful for my daughter's pink cheeks, for every breath she takes, for a seizure-free birthday. I am grateful for family and friends who would give their silver heart for the blessing bowl.

Someday I will repay the world for their acts of kindness to our family. I will make meals for someone else. I will send their family good wishes for good health and visit the hospital with coffee and fresh brownies. Right now I can only reflect on the joy of the night and be grateful.

~Heather Simms Schichtel

5

A Little Bird Told Me

Faith sees the invisible, believes the incredible and receives the impossible.
~Author Unknown

I am sitting in the movie theater with my husband and tears are welling up in my eyes. We are watching *About Schmidt* with Jack Nicholson. It's the scene where a colleague is looking at a photo of Jack's daughter on his desk and says, "She's beautiful, does she live close by?" Jack responds, "She's the apple of my eye. I think about her every day. She's 3,000 miles away, in California, but it's okay—I see her a couple of times a year."

In the darkened theater, my husband glances over at me and whispers, "Honey what's wrong?" Tears are streaming down my cheeks now, and I choke out the words, "We have to move back to Canada. I have to be with my Dad."

I had always been the apple of *my* daddy's eye, and I knew that he was thinking of me every day, many times a day. I grew up in Toronto, Canada, but had moved to Los Angeles to be an actress. I was enjoying a successful career, had found an amazing group of friends and loved L.A. But I missed my family so much, and they missed me. I had been living in California for fifteen years. I had gotten married, and had two wonderful children. And even though we always came home for Christmas, and my parents came to see us in the spring, it never felt like enough. I had watched both my husband and my best friend lose their dad and mom, respectively. I saw how devastating that had been for them. My husband had been planning to go on a trip with his dad for years—they never got to do it. My best friend got a call that her mom was in I.C.U., raced to the hospital to be with her, but did not make it there in time.

The secondhand experience of those losses became a huge blessing in my life.

My dad was having health issues and a voice in my head had been getting louder and louder: it was telling me that time might be running low for him. Nothing was technically life-threatening, but my "daughter's intuition" was on high alert, and I was listening. And I am so grateful that I was, because in that moment, in that movie, I made the decision to totally re-route my life... and, thankfully, my husband and kids supported my decision and happily came along on the adventure with me.

We moved back the summer of 2003. Instead of seeing my parents twice a year, we started to see them every week. We all had so many great times together. My dad came to see my son play hockey, played cards with my daughter, and he and I would go out for breakfast a lot—that was one of our favorite things to do. We did all the simple little things there isn't time for when visits are rushed or pressured and you are trying to fit a million things into one week's vacation.

I wanted to be there for my dad, and I was. I wanted to have my kids get to know him, and they did. Most of all, as crazy as it seemed, and as hard as it was for me to leave my friends and life, I followed my heart, and for that I will always be grateful.

Because, after four and a half years, it happened. My dad went into the hospital for simple issues with circulation and one night, in front of my eyes, he had a massive heart attack and the next morning he died.

I was shocked, bereft and confused—but I was there.

I did not get the dreaded phone call in the middle of the night. Did not have to fly home and experience all the guilt and regrets that would have gone along with losing him and not being present. I had played that scenario out in my mind, and had done something about it before it happened.

Cut to the day of my dad's funeral. I was brushing my teeth, staring at myself in the mirror in the daze that comes at such a time. Drained, beyond tired, and cried-out, I caught a little movement out of the corner of my eye. A bird was sitting in the middle of the tree outside the bathroom window. I walked over to the window, turned the crank and opened it. I thought the bird might fly away at the sound—but it didn't. In fact, it never moved a feather and kept its eyes glued to mine. Suddenly, the world went very quiet, and everything distilled down to the bird and the tree and me. And in that moment, I knew it was my dad, coming to tell me he was okay, and that I would be okay. I felt my deep sorrow lift a little and the bird and I stayed there, our eyes locked on each other for a long time. I finally had to turn away, and when I looked back a split second later, the tree was empty.

Later that week, I was telling the story to a dear friend. She asked me, "What kind of bird was it?" "A robin," I said, "but he had grey feathers, which is unusual. I don't know why, but I felt like it was my dad." My friend grabbed my hand and said, "A robin? Laura, your last name is *Robin*son."

And there was one more piece to the story. I got an e-mail from another friend who had been quite close to my dad. She said she had asked a year or so earlier, that when he died, he would send her a sign, and then send the same one to me. My dad had agreed. She was writing to ask me if I had had any "signs" since his passing.

I wrote back and told her my robin story. She immediately replied, "I am covered in shivers right now, because the sign your dad and I agreed upon was a *red bird*. There was a cardinal on my deck yesterday. He stared at me for ten minutes. I'm sure it was your dad!" I understood then, without a shadow of a doubt that my dad had come to me, was watching over me and would continue to.

It's always so hard to lose a beloved parent, but what I am grateful for is that I do not have to live with regret: regret that I had moved so far away, that there hadn't been enough time to be together and to reconnect again after all those years. At the funeral, I said that I knew I had been unconditionally loved every minute of my life. I feel so lucky to have had that blessing.

I miss him every day but I have peace in my heart... and a little bird on my shoulder.

~Laura Robinson

6

Resilience

Man never made any material as resilient as the human spirit.
~Bern Williams

Shortly after my husband Ken's diagnosis of kidney failure, we were told the only way to extend his life would be an organ transplant. In the meantime, regular dialysis treatments were to begin immediately. Our "new normal" began with the surgical placement of a port in his chest, and just hours after the surgery, my husband went directly to his first "dialysis run." That heart-wrenching first day of dialysis was the only time I ever saw my heroic husband weep. Just three weeks later, Thanksgiving Day happened to be a dialysis day, so instead of the usual big family gathering, our family of three chose a simple meal at home accompanied by a simple prayer of thanks, "Thank you dear God for time together."

In the weeks following, our perspective and our emotions swung from high to low like a pendulum almost daily. While the situation we faced pulled us together as a family, it drained our time and our energy. One possibility that kept us buoyed was the hope of an organ transplant. Suddenly, making memories with family and friends compelled us to set aside the trivial in favor of somehow emotionally extending our life together.

The phone call with news of a kidney match finally came in the early morning hours one snowy December day. The university hospital several hours away meant we needed to leave immediately, and despite a blizzard we arrived at the hospital by mid-morning. While Ken was being prepped for surgery, a nurse brought in a Styrofoam box bearing large orange letters that spelled, "Human Organ for Transplant." They literally put the kidney, in what looked like a cooler for a six-pack of pop, on the foot of the bed! With shock and suppressed giggles, Ken and I looked at the box and then at each other.

With comical disbelief, I sputtered, "Do you believe this!" A very sobering event was lightened by the sweet sound of my husband's chuckling. The laughter we shared was a precious gift before they wheeled him to surgery. A few hours after our kiss and saying, "See ya soon," the kidney had been transplanted and immediately began producing urine.

That Christmas was one of the most wonderful of any I remember. Our son, David, was home from college, Ken was still recovering, and every other day there was a snow storm. The gratitude in our huddled hearts rivaled the warmth in our fireplace. We spent many weeks in a perpetual state of awe. Our future together had been restored because of an organ donation. To this day, our family is mindful of the fact that because someone else's life had ended, Ken's could continue. We never take for granted our ability to celebrate an extended future together. Somewhere an organ donor's family is grieving an empty place at their family gatherings, and every time my husband swallows his medication or has blood drawn, we humbly remember that.

Ken's doctors told us that the chances of him rejecting the transplant will remain slim as long as he continues to take his medications at precise intervals. Blood samples collected every other month for the rest of his life will continue to be monitored for signs of rejection by the University of Michigan and Mayo Clinic. Gratefully we reflect on the network of a caring medical staff, family and friends who continue to surround us, and we now seek opportunities to walk alongside others going through devastation. Rebounding from life's tremendous challenges requires resilience, but oft times, resilience requires some assistance. Offering and receiving.

~Linda Tabbert as told to Debbie Harrell

7

Other People's Beds

Travel and change of place impart new vigor to the mind.
~Seneca

Fourteen years ago, after my husband Mort died, I spent my summers living in other people's houses, traveling to places where, by invitation, I found myself in a mountain house in Virginia, a lakeside house in Maine, a clapboard cottage at the foot of the Berkshires, and a musty-scented dwelling on Fire Island, overlooking the sea. It was a summer of social gatherings; cocktails at sunset on verandas that spilled over the edge of lush gardens with flowers exploding in color against a pink and orange sky, where finding a patch of cloud was a startling, unwelcome intrusion on an otherwise perfect afternoon.

The rest of the year I worked hard, teaching my classes, meeting my weekly column deadlines and working on my next novel. Friends had offered their homes as healing retreats after the death of my husband. And so, still numb from my loss, I took them up on their offers. I packed an overnight bag and headed off, feeling emotionally wobbly and slightly off-balance.

"You'll stay with us," my Virginia friends implored. "We won't take no for an answer. June in Virginia is lovely."

Other friends who own a summer house in Maine asked me to join them in August.

"Houses are meant to be shared," my Lenox, Massachusetts, friends told me in July. "You can hear the music of Tanglewood from our terrace."

Listening to Mozart waft through the crisp evening air was hard to resist.

Then, there was Fire Island where my children spent their summers. I had an open invitation. Before I knew it, I was filling a suitcase with summer clothes and easing into the role of the rotating houseguest, spending time with my gallery of friends, who introduced me to the rhythm of their summertime lives and the myriad of activities that went along with it.

All that summer, I hiked high up into the hills of the Blue Ridge Mountains to commune with nature and its animal inhabitants, some of which, obviously sensing my reticence, had the good sense to leave me alone. A garter snake slithered by me as I leaned up against a tree trying to regain my composure. My usual stash of bottled water was replaced by fresh water from mountain streams. Here, all pretenses were dropped.

Similarly, the Maine trails whose silence was stirred by bird sounds and rustlings gave way to a silver lake shining in the sun, punctuated with little boats against a landscape of green and purple mountains, providing postcard-perfect settings at every turn.

Fire Island was damp and overcast when the ferry delivered me into the arms of my squealing grandchildren. The afternoon threatened rain as I trekked the beaches and watched as streaks of sunlight tried hard to work their way through the storm clouds. Fire Island is beautiful in any season, and when the winds became fierce, we found seclusion indoors, alternating between games of *Trivial Pursuit* with the adults and *Chutes and Ladders* with Andrew and Caroline. One afternoon, I found myself engrossed in play while the parents took leave and put me in charge of four children all under the age of seven. By 5 P.M. I was exhausted. I took them all for treats. We ate ice cream in the rain.

And then there were the naps, where we retired to our respective rooms without the pressure of schedules or the cacophonous ring of telephones or television sets blasting annoying commercials. Reclining on other people's beds to finish a book seemed at once both comforting and strange. Sleeping on sheets that bore no resemblance to my own—pillows that didn't caress my head exactly right, were unfamiliar to my touch yet oddly inviting. Blankets smelled differently, and mattresses, unaccustomed to my body's contour, dipped and peaked as I tried to find a spot that felt secure under me. These were constant reminders I was not home. Once again, the tug of my loss gnawed at me at every turn.

But, friends and family filled the void of loneliness and provided solace during those difficult times. I moved among them all, enjoying their food and partaking of their hospitality. I was grateful that my grieving was accepted, and that I was being nurtured. I did not need to put on airs. Those yellow summer afternoon, filled with light banter and conversation, warmed my soul.

"Do you prefer cold lobster or leftover poached salmon?" were the most difficult decisions of the day. Invitations to take the boat out for a spin, run into town or walk a mile up the road to the general store was about as complicated as it got. It was a time of borrowed books, smearing sun block over a child's shoulders, dining al fresco, and skinny dipping in the lake in the black of night.

And then, like an unexpected intruder, the winds began kicking up earlier than usual. Sweaters replaced halter tops and the first subtle whisper of autumn was felt. Thoughts of new beginnings took hold as summer began to wane. It was time to put away the porch furniture and throw an extra blanket on the bed at night.

And so, I officially bade a fond farewell to those summers: to sand in my shoes, damp hair that curled exactly right when exposed to sea air, and to the sounds of motorboats putt-putting me to sleep. My legs bore a slight coating of suntan. Mosquito bites were reminders that we lingered too long on open patios. Children's voices echoing in the evening air still reverberated in my ears: "Can't we stay outside and play a little longer?" Mental snapshots of my grandchildren jumping the waves and building sandcastles, eating corn on the cob, and catching fireflies in discarded jelly jars filled my memory bank for months to come.

Lying in other people's beds reminded me I was not alone. Loss had been buffered by a season of friends, and I had a chance to begin to heal. But, in the end, it was my bed that knew me best. Nothing could replace the lure of familiarity. Arriving home, my cat, Annabelle, curled up next to me, and feeling safe, dared to close her eyes. She had traveled with me, but only now, like I, felt at home. A faint hint of my favorite shampoo's aroma now lingered on my pillow. I ate crackers in bed (my late-husband's pet peeve and I giggle at the thought of his disapproval) without the fear of getting crumbs on other people's blankets.

2008: Another summer had come and gone. I am re-married now and home in our house, Mark's and mine: the place of intimacy, where I can relax and be completely myself. I stretch and curl up in all the right spots, as I drift off to sleep on an early December night, recalling the bittersweet memories of summers past, and all the future summers spread out before us, yet to be lived.

~Judith Marks-White

We Didn't Know

My cancer scare changed my life. I'm grateful for every new,
healthy day I have. It has helped me prioritize my life.
~Olivia Newton-John

"When you feel up to it, we'll get two claw-foot bathtubs, put them in the backyard, climb in and hold hands. Then we'll give you a Cialis pill and see what happens," I said, referring to that television commercial where the couple looks longingly into each other's eyes.

"That's not funny," my husband deadpanned.

Throughout this whole thing, I've tried to maintain a sense of humor. Richard was now a cancer patient. And his cancer was in his prostate.

Before the diagnosis, Richard had endured tests that made him increasingly uncomfortable. "Why do they have to mess around down there?" he fumed. A few years ago, blood work indicated his PSA level was elevated. The doctor said he probably had an enlarged prostate. Then his PSA level spiked. "I need to have a biopsy," Richard said. I could hear the trepidation in his voice.

"That doesn't surprise me. You get up every few hours to go to the bathroom." I had a feeling the doctor suspected something.

A week after the biopsy, Richard phoned. "The bad news is I have cancer, the good news is it's treatable."

I expected it, I think more than he did, but it was still a blow.

"I can't have cancer," he almost shouted through the phone. "I take good care of myself. I go for all my checkups. I get my blood work done. How can this happen to me?"

"Honey, we'll deal with it. Don't panic." I put all the reassurance I could muster into my voice. "You'll be fine."

"You have to come with me to a consultation."

"I'll be right beside you."

In the doctor's office, my strong, 200-pound-plus husband looked like he was going to collapse. I asked most of the questions and cataloged in my mind all the answers. "Okay," the doctor began, "this is what we're dealing with." He showed us a chart of Richard's elevated levels. "The prostate is three times the size it should be and one quadrant shows an aggressive cell."

Radiation was an option. That would zap the prostate and the cells but the downside was that it was so close to other tissues that could also be damaged. Surgery would remove the entire prostate with minimal chance of damaging surrounding tissue.

I asked the big question. "What's the downside of surgery?"

The doctor looked directly at Richard. "You may have loss of manly function."

Richard turned white as a piece of paper.

I thought I'd have to carry him out of the doctor's office. "That's not important to me." I took his hand in mine. "Let's get rid of the cancer. We'll cross that bridge later."

The doctor said to let him know what we decide.

"What's happening to my body?" Richard asked when we were home. He was perfectly healthy, except for the cancer that he could not see and could not feel.

I tried to lighten the mood. "Honey, you can live without your prostate."

A hangdog look accompanied his next words. "I won't be a man anymore."

"Yes, you will." But I could tell he wasn't convinced.

It was difficult to relate to Richard about a part of the body a woman doesn't have. Girlfriends discuss details of childbirth, episiotomies, sitz baths, and those unsightly stretch marks. We talk to each other about heavy bleeding, hormone changes, mood swings and hot flashes. But ask a man about his nether-region and he'll shut you down like a light switch. Heaven knows Richard wasn't used to his private parts being probed and poked.

The next morning on the way to work I called my best friend. "It finally hit me that he has cancer," I told her. "But for him, it's not just that he has cancer—it's where the cancer is."

Richard opted for surgery. He came home from the hospital with a catheter to drain urine, a tube running from the incision to drain his wound, and staples from his groin to his belly button. We inched to the bathroom to empty the bag, then inched our way back to his comfy recliner. That's when we looked at each other and said, "Where are we going to hang it?"

"I've got it!" I said, and grabbed the fireplace tools, removed them from their standing holder, and hung the bag on that. "Perfect."

A few days later, the stomach tube was removed, a week later the staples, and two weeks after that the catheter. During all this, I was his nurse, trying to keep up his spirits, read the instructions for his care, and take him back and forth to doctor's visits. We had lots of time to talk, and talk we did. About how blessed we were that they caught it early, and how much worse it could have been.

We feel a little bit stronger since the diagnosis, a lot wiser, and thankful for each and every day we have together. Richard will need to be tested periodically, now that he's someone who has had cancer. But he came through the hard part. We both did. And the tests so far have shown no recurrence.

And those two claw-foot bathtubs? We didn't need them; but if we ever do, I plan to crack open a bottle of wine and make a toast to the joy of life. We didn't know fighting cancer would bring us closer, in ways we could have never imagined.

~Isabella Gianni as told to B.J. Taylor

Flooded with Blessings

If pregnancy were a book they would cut the last two chapters.
~Nora Ephron, Heartburn, 1983

We began 1983 as a young couple full of happiness. We had just purchased a new home after learning that we had a baby on the way and were excited to be moving and starting a family. The baby was due in September and we thought we had plenty of time to move into the new house and set up a nursery. Our new home was completed toward the end of March and we were completely moved in by the end of the month.

It was a fun and exciting time. We had rented previously and were looking forward to having lots more space. Our excitement came to a halt the following month when extreme weather brought a flood to the area. We were located near the Amite River and we woke up one morning to find water covering the floor throughout our new home.

We soon learned that the river had overflowed its banks, and the water had crossed a highway and coursed through the woods to our subdivision and into our new home and those of our neighbors. I was four months pregnant and still going through the "very tired" phase of pregnancy. There wasn't much that I could do to help clean up the mess.

Damage to our home was minimal, and we counted our blessings that it wasn't worse. There was just enough water to thoroughly saturate the carpet, but not to damage the baseboards and walls.

Since we had just moved in, our contractor was gracious enough to help us out. He sent someone over with a commercial vacuum to start drying out the carpet. He also hired a professional to come in and chemically treat the carpets so that they would not mold or mildew. When this job was completed, the carpet looked brand new and you couldn't tell that it had been saturated and under water the day before.

We counted our blessings, added flood insurance to our insurance policy and went on with life. After all, we were expecting our first baby!

Several months later, in August, we were again fighting a flood. This time we had excessive rain for several days and nights and the drainage system just couldn't keep up with the amount of rainfall. We hoped and prayed that our home would be spared, but it wasn't. This time we had about a foot of water in our home. I can remember watching water being pumped out of a low window in the den with a sump pump.

I was only a month away from my due date this time, had the nursery all ready for the baby and was not in any physical or emotional condition to deal with a house with one foot of water in it. We had a long road ahead of us concerning repairs. The carpets all needed to be ripped out, furniture needed to be moved around, ruined belongings thrown away and the walls repaired. We would not only be starting over on so many levels, but we were now without a nursery and only a month away from delivery!

My parents brought their travel trailer over for us to stay in while getting the house back in order and cleaned up. We had all the basics that we needed in the trailer and were adjusting to the cramped quarters fairly well. It was quite cozy!

Toward the end of August, I woke up having pretty strong labor pains. We waited to see if this was a false alarm, but they continued so we headed to the hospital. Of course, after being admitted to the hospital the pains disappeared and we were sent home to our little travel trailer.

The following week I developed a pinched nerve which made

walking very difficult and painful. I was beyond ready to have this baby at this point. Finally the big day arrived and we were blessed with a beautiful baby girl. She was completely healthy and once again I thanked God for my blessings. We brought our new baby home from the hospital and back to our house. My husband had gotten the essential things like our bedroom, kitchen and nursery back in place. We just didn't have any flooring since the carpet had been ripped out and the insurance settlement had not yet arrived.

This was a very trying time for us, especially for me since I was pregnant and had to go through the house flooding not once, but twice. My emotions went up and down like a roller coaster during my first pregnancy with all the excitement and added trauma. I learned that my faith in God would help me through trying times and that he also doesn't give you more than you can handle. We survived!

~Karen H. Gros

Don't Take Away My Coffee

Starbucks represents something beyond a cup of coffee.
~Howard Schultz

They're threatening to close my favorite coffee shop.

The economy is weakening, and people are losing their jobs. But they can't close my coffee shop. I listen to the national and local news channels. I understand budgets, dollars and severance pay. Every morning when I get ready for work, I pray that the next morning I'll still have a job. I want to get ready for work every Monday through Friday.

But they can't close my coffee shop.

Eight years ago, I sat in front of a judge and listened to her end my marriage. It wasn't what I had envisioned when I walked down the aisle in my white dress. But it happened, and as a middle-of-the-demographics woman, I was suddenly thrust back into the marketplace. I worked three jobs, saved every possible penny and finished raising my son.

One of the things that kept me going was my goal to someday be able to afford a drink at the coffee shop. I watched other people going in those hallowed doors and coming out with smiles on their faces. They seemed to have no problems, no financial concerns. Surely none of them worked three jobs like me and saved every scrap of food for leftovers. They carried Styrofoam cups filled with mocha, caramel or some other type of sugary foam. Some lucky guys and gals carried metal cups with the coffee shop brand on them. How I wanted one of those cups! How I longed to be part of the gang!

As the calendar months in my planner flipped over, I continued to work various jobs. Two years passed, and life was still in the survival mode. Then one day, a co-worker noticed that my birthday was coming. "What do you want?" he asked.

It was too easy. "My love language is coffee."

On my birthday, I opened his card and saw the answer to my dream—a gift card with the coffee shop logo. You would think that I might have scurried out of the office during my lunch hour to gobble that coveted drink. But I had waited too long for this goal to hurry happiness.

I planned the right moment: a Saturday morning when I didn't have to work. My son was at band practice. I was alone and geared for joy. After fixing my hair and putting on my best make-up, I drove carefully across town. Slowly, savoring each ray of happiness—I parked and walked toward the door with the coffee logo on the front.

Once inside, my senses exploded into overload. Brownies beckoned from glass cases. Those coveted metal cups gleamed from a corner shelf. And the menu—rows and rows of delightful possibilities. I would choose wisely, and make my gift card last.

"I'll have a small chocolate something," I told the young man behind the counter.

"A tall mocha?" he asked.

Did I sound like a rookie at this game? Probably. No doubt this polite young man was laughing inside. I didn't care.

"Yes, that's right," I said, squaring my shoulders like a sudden expert. "A tall mocha."

My treasure and I sat on a tweed sofa while I slowly sipped. Nothing I had tasted previously in my entire fifty-plus years gave me such pleasure. I pulled a novel from my purse and read about a faraway place, imagining myself there, with another tall mocha—or maybe the largest size, whatever that was called. I pretended I had all the time in the world and was as rich as all the people who kept opening that door and ordering their favorite drinks.

During the next few months, I carved out special outings at my coffee shop. Each time, I tried a different drink. By the time I had used up my gift card, I had a relationship with chai latte, hazelnut and a delightful pumpkin spice. But that first mocha still remained the favorite.

Now that my son is raised and I'm working only two jobs, I visit my coffee shop more often. I still ask for those gift cards on my birthday or at Christmas. Last year I saved enough coins to buy myself one of those treasured cups. It sits on my desk at work, but I don't always drink from it. Sometimes I just stare at it and say a prayer of thanks that I'm finally out of the hole.

You see, they can't close my coffee shop. We all need a place to find hope.

~Rebecca Jay

11

Healing Toxin

We have no right to ask when sorrow comes,
"Why did this happen to me?" unless we ask the same question
for every moment of happiness that comes our way.
~Author Unknown

When she was four months old, our daughter Eva got sick for the first time. The doctor thought that it was just a cold. But Eva became more silent and still as the hours passed. We called another doctor and he told us it was probably a bad virus and that she would be fine. "That's how babies fight these things," he said. "They just shut down until they fix the problem."

Two days later, our baby was not only "shut down" but almost gone.

Running to the ER wasn't easy. It was late at night, and one of us had to stay with our two-year-old son. We decided that my husband would go with Eva. I am from Argentina and moved to the U.S. when I was twenty-eight. English is not my first language, and it was important that every word in that exchange with doctors was understood right away. After the longest hour of my life, my husband called. "You should come right away. This is serious." My knees were weak, but in a flash I left my son in the care of good neighbors and rushed to the ER.

When I got there, I saw my baby daughter lying on a stretcher, now completely limp and barely conscious. She was making a soft, weak sound. I didn't cry or ask many questions; I was shocked. I just watched as if standing in the eye of a hurricane of white and blue scrubs.

During our first night at the hospital, my husband and I looked into each other's eyes in silence while holding this limp little baby. That night I memorized every single feature of her face. I would have given my own life in a second to secure hers. That night, my husband's hug felt like a life preserver.

The next day we were transferred to a bigger hospital where they hoped doctors could figure out what was happening to her. She was steadily getting worse. Eventually she was completely paralyzed. Gradually, inexplicably, she was fading away.

We decided to call family, and from all of those phone calls I only remember the voices of my parents asking, "How serious is this?" and my response, "You might not see her ever again."

Two days later, my mother came from across the world. She and a good friend took care of our son, Martín, while we were at the hospital. I always tried to make it home for Martín's bedtime and after kissing him good night, headed back to the intensive care unit.

We felt Eva's life slipping through our fingers. Would she survive? And if she survived, would there be disabilities?

Eventually somebody had an idea: botulism. Infant botulism, called an "orphan disease," is a rare paralytic illness caused by a nerve toxin that is produced by the bacterium Clostridium botulinum. All forms of botulism can be fatal and are considered medical emergencies. Botulism is very rare in infants; there are around eighty cases each year in the whole U.S. Even though botulism could be lethal, it doesn't have any long-term effects if it is overcome.

Given the other possible diagnoses, botulism was our best-case scenario. It was impossible for me to believe that she had botulism since she was exclusively breastfed. However, I was told later that the bacterium is in the air and soil, and medical science does not yet understand the factors that make one baby more susceptible than others to botulism spore germination.

There was no time to lose. Doctors decided to treat Eva for botulism even before the final results came back from the lab.

In the hallways of that hospital, I met other parents. From them I heard about transplants, neurological impediments, cancer, and post-surgery complications. I heard about parents' plans for organ donation if the worst happened.

Some of these children had been in intensive care for a long time. Others were "frequent flyers"—as their parents call them. They spend weeks at a time in the hospital and go home hoping that the next time they come for a checkup they won't end up staying.

My husband and I stood by Eva's sleeping body day and night, waiting for a sign of recovery. Days later, Eva started to react. One day she moved her fingers and toes. The next day she opened her eyes. In time, over many days of waiting and then receiving the confirmation that she did indeed have botulism, life clearly began to circulate through her whole body again. Eventually her eyes could fix on mine. She was holding on to life. She managed to smile, and that was when we knew she would return to normal. Some days later, her smiles brought life back to our hearts and for the first time I was able to sleep.

I still find an inexplicable peace when holding Eva. We still almost burst into tears when Martín kisses her forehead.

One friend whose daughter is a "frequent flyer" supported me greatly when Eva's hospitalization started. When I asked, "Why is this happening to us?" she replied, "Why wouldn't it happen to you? There are lots of people out there to whom these things happen all the time."

Some people live long lives, some don't. Instead of asking why, we are grateful for what we have. We also notice the good things that come to us during, and even because of, the worst of situations.

~Maria Victoria Espinosa-Peterson

Chapter 2

Count Your Blessings

Back to Basics

*I am beginning to learn that it is the sweet,
simple things of life which are the real ones after all.*

~Laura Ingalls Wilder

Opting for a Slower Pace

Life is really simple,
but we insist on making it complicated.
~Confucius

In the 1980s, my husband, David, and I married, bought a home, and began our careers. It wasn't long before a friend informed us we were "Young Upwardly-Mobile People" or "Yuppies." Who knew?

Then came the 1990s. Still childless, we were working from dawn to dusk and spending nights and weekends at the local amateur theater. It was a great life. That's when another friend told us we were, "Double Income No Kids" or "DINKs." It was news to us.

In the next few years, we went from double income-no kids to single income-three kids and began a whirlwind of diaper bags, minivans, and play groups. We decided I'd put my career on hold and be a full-time mom. After waiting so long to have a family, we wanted to do this thing right. Before we knew it, elementary school came along, and things really got hectic.

We signed up for gymnastics, soccer, Girl Scouts, T-ball, and karate. So much to do. So little time to do it all. There were art classes, French, and Suzuki violin.

A balanced dinner became nachos and a corn dog at the ballpark.

Some of our most meaningful conversations took place on our

street with David sitting in his car heading home from work and me in mine dashing off with the kids in another direction. "Dinner's in the microwave." Kiss. Kiss.

I suppose it was inevitable that I discovered I was, once again, an American cliché when yet another friend informed me I was a "Soccer Mom." I could live with that.

Then one day, I looked around and thought "What are we doing?"

We had three beautiful, healthy kids and everything we ever wanted. Yet the five of us hardly knew each other.

I'd put my career on hold to be a full-time mom and had become a full-time maniac. My schedule was worse than it had been when I was working. I couldn't remember a time when we'd had dinner around the table like a real family.

Was this what we were aiming for? No time for us to be a family, no time for our kids to be kids, to use their imaginations, to enjoy just doing nothing?

By trying to give our kids everything, what were we taking away from them?

After several late-night discussions and a lot of praying, David and I decided we wanted out of the minivan marathon. Secretly, I wondered if it'd be that easy.

When friends asked, "Do you want to carpool to karate?" or called, "See you at the ball field?" I took a deep breath and declared we were taking some time off.

As they raced past our front door, we stayed home and built birdhouses, baked cookies, read books in the hammock, and planted a vegetable garden. My kids made stuff. They painted. We took nature walks and wrote nonsense poems. Our river replaced the van as the place we were most likely to be found.

I had moments of panic when I thought of all my kids were missing. The twenty-first century was going on without us. Should we clamber to catch up? David and I lay awake at night second-guessing ourselves. Maybe we didn't have to cut out everything. Maybe just French, gymnastics, and...

Then I began to hear my friends complaining that no matter how much they did, their children were always bored. Meanwhile, my own kids made blanket forts, performed original plays, composed songs on the piano, taught tricks to the dog, wrote stories, and were anything but bored. They didn't ask for TV. They didn't ask to go anywhere. They were too busy just being kids.

Instead of rushing out of the office to meet me at the ballpark, David came home to a picnic dinner in the backyard. He and I began to remember why we'd married each other.

For once we were bucking the trend, and we'd never been happier.

I guess it had to happen and this past week it did. Much to my dismay, a friend informed us we are "minimalists," and that "minimalism" is the newest trend with American families.

It seems that even when we try to be pioneers we're destined to follow the crowd.

All I can say is, if kids having time to be kids and families having time to be families is a trend, then this is one time this former Yuppie, DINK, Soccer Mom is glad to be considered trendy.

~Mimi Greenwood Knight

13

No Longer Needed

We all have big changes in our lives
that are more or less a second chance.
~Harrison Ford

The ringing of the telephone greeted me as I walked into the house after another long, stressful week at the office. I tossed my purse on the kitchen counter and glanced at the caller ID screen on the phone. It was a call from the staffing company that sent me my paycheck for the last twenty years. With a sense of dread, I slowly picked up the receiver. The voice at the other end of the line informed me that today would be my last day on the job because my services were no longer needed. My inner strength trickled down to my toes and my heart beat faster as I cleared my throat and remembered to breathe.

I swallowed hard and said, "Are they going to hire another person to do my job?"

Her voice sounded a little too perky as she answered, "No. The company has been downsizing, and we are sorry, but they eliminated your position. However, you are eligible to receive severance pay, and please let us know if there is anything we can do to help."

I stumbled through the rest of the conversation trying to come up with good reasons for them to keep me—as if I could change her mind. After all, the office would still need someone to maintain department records, create correspondence, edit the newsletter and take care of numerous other tasks. I knew that it wasn't her decision, and in the end, all I could do was sigh and accept my fate.

I walked over to the mirror that decorates the living room wall. Hazel eyes with long, dark lashes stared back at me through gold, wire-rimmed glasses. There were a few wrinkles around my mouth, and the skin under my chin sagged a bit. A picture of a rooster's wattle popped into my head, and at that moment I felt like an old hen that had been booted out of the coop.

That life-changing day was also my wedding anniversary. Ken and I had been married for thirty-eight years. We were going out to dinner the next night to celebrate. Well, now we could also celebrate my early retirement. The problem was that I wasn't ready to retire and my income helped to defray the high cost of gas, food, and medication that we both needed. I felt betrayed. I worked hard for that company and gave them twenty good years of my life. In spite of that, I knew the company's new quest — to become a "big fish" in the trucking industry — called for restructuring. Experienced, dedicated employees were being trimmed like excess fat from a big, juicy steak. I always knew that sooner or later the cleaver would swing my way.

When Ken came home from work that evening, I gave him a big anniversary hug. I didn't know how to tell him the bad news, so I just blurted it out. "Happy anniversary, hon, and by the way, I was laid off today."

He looked a little stunned, and I thought I saw a few more strands of his salt-and-pepper hair turn gray. He raised his hand to his forehead. "Wow! You really know how to jazz up an occasion. Happy anniversary. Are you okay?"

"Yeah, I'm okay. At least I think I'm okay. Pinch me to make sure I'm not dreaming. No, wait... that might hurt."

Ken said, "For now, why don't you think of it as a well-deserved, long vacation. The weather will soon be warm, and you'll have a lot of time to work in your garden. We'll cut back on our expenses. We'll only go out to eat once a month and this year we'll spend our vacation at home — we'll find some good, inexpensive day trips to take. And, don't worry, I'm sure we can find more cuts to make in our budget."

"I think you're right," I said. "I'll bet I could trim our grocery bill by using the extra time to cook and not have to buy those expensive convenience foods."

So I filed for unemployment benefits and adopted Ken's strategy. I had to admit that it was easier to rise and shine in the morning without being rudely awakened by the urgent beeping of my alarm clock. I didn't miss sitting in traffic during early morning rush hour. I went grocery shopping on a weekday morning and enjoyed the ease of shopping without the pushy, annoying weekend crowd of people who block the aisles and stand right in front of the product I need to grab. I even bought a guidebook about North American feeder birds to help me identify the songbirds that come to my birdfeeder during the winter months.

All of a sudden, my world slowed down to a more enjoyable pace. I found time to dig in my garden, read, make daily entries in my journal, take an online writing class, and spend more quality time with my grandchildren. I discovered a new kind of happiness, and my fear of fading into oblivion dissolved. I am now eager to discover how the next chapter in my life will unfold, and since I can't travel back in time (and I'm not sure that I would want to) I will forge ahead and think positive. I may even crow a happy tune in the early morning hours.

~Helen Stein

14

Making a Home from Scratch

My home is not a place, it is people.
~Lois McMaster Bujold

Survivor, victim, refugee, evacuee—it doesn't really matter what they call you. Yesterday you had a place to live and today you have a pile of sticks and rubble, or a moonscape of ashes. Maybe you have credit cards and a healthy balance in your checkbook, or maybe you are living in poverty. The haves and have nots aren't too different anymore, not right now. Not when the place you call home is gone.

Can you picture yourself right now: one of the needy, one of the newly homeless? You are looking at what used to be your home, your neighborhood, your world, and maybe all you have left are the clothes on your back. No toothbrush, no bed, no socks or shoes. It's easy for me to picture that scene. It happened to me in October 1991. My home was one of three thousand destroyed by a fire that swept through the hills in Oakland, California.

Blocks and blocks of homes looked just like ours: barren lots, charred trees, foundations without houses to hold up, and chimneys standing sentry over many a scorched and lonely hearth.

Our insurance company required us to list everything we had lost in the fire, down to pots and pans and underwear, for a household of five: me, my husband, and our three kids, ages thirteen, ten and five. Making a list of replaceable things was easier than thinking about the precious items with more emotional value than monetary: the baby sweaters I had knitted for my daughter, secretly tucked away to be handed down one day; a growth chart, measuring the inches from toddler to teen; and old love letters, saved in a box for lonely afternoons. There were the everyday things that you reach for without thinking: a needle and thread; a bowl or a wooden spoon. And the special things: a black velvet dress, the good china, a gold watch from a beloved grandfather, a child's handprint in clay.

We moved to a rental house immediately after the fire, and quickly filled it with rented furniture. How would we make this place feel like home? Every home has its own look, feel, and smell. How would we create that again, when we did it without thinking before? For the sake of our children, we had to figure this out. Still reeling ourselves from the shock of having lost the home we had worked so hard to provide for our kids, we had to act and act fast. Our kids wanted to keep the mealtime and bedtime routines going, and we did too.

We began with the basics: beds, a place to gather for meals, books for bedtime reading, and music. A thoughtful friend gave us a gift certificate to a local bookstore. When my husband took the three kids to replace our copies of *Madeline*, *Winnie-the-Pooh*, and our favorite Shel Silverstein, he broke down in tears. He also went out right after the fire to replace his favorite music. "I miss my friends," he told the guy behind the counter. Once again, he could hear his beloved jazz, blues, and rock 'n' roll.

After a couple of washings with our familiar detergent, our new bedding and towels felt like our own. With new basic kitchen equipment, we began cooking when there was time, and the spaghetti sauce had the same aroma it always did. Every day we discovered things we didn't have that we needed immediately: pot holders, laundry baskets, a vacuum cleaner, scissors, tape, and a hundred other things. Nothing could be made from scratch without a shopping list: flour, sugar, eggs, vanilla, measuring spoons, bowls, and baking sheets. With a mixture of the new and the familiar, we began to create a small, safe cocoon in our temporary place.

My younger son, then only five, had taken his treasured blanket along when we evacuated our neighborhood. He could go to sleep peacefully in a new bed with new "Where's Waldo?" sheets because he had the familiar yellow quilt to hold next to his face. But my older son mourned the loss of his special "cat blanket," so we searched all over in an attempt to find the same fabrics: the pastel green flannel, the brown plaid, the midnight blue satin with tiny white stars. Two gifted friends collaborated and managed to recreate the beloved quilt for him—a family portrait of cats, curled up together in front of a window full of stars.

We decided to rebuild our home in the same space as the one we lost, although many of our neighbors didn't. The block was empty and barren for months. Slowly, we began planning a home that would remind us of the old one, but would have some new things too—our two boys wanted a "secret passage" between their rooms, and (shh-hhh) we were able to make one for them. It was exciting to watch the progress as the house took shape, but also bittersweet as we looked ahead to starting over with new neighbors. Construction noise and dust were the order of the day as we watched the old foundations make way for new houses.

In just over a year, we moved "back home." We took care during the rebuilding to visit often and walk around, becoming comfortable with the place we would live, even though it wasn't home yet. We acquired more of the things that would make our rebuilt house feel like home: pictures on the mantel, baking equipment for special treats, and more of our favorite books and movies.

Putting our new home together, book by book and picture by picture, taught us a valuable lesson. Our things did not define us. Losing our house and our neighborhood did not defeat us. Others lost their lives in the fire; we lost things that, for the most part, could be replaced. Even the kids knew the difference between being a victim and being a survivor: they were survivors all the way. We did the best we could to keep life normal for them, and it wasn't always easy. They saw us cry, but they also saw us make decisions and act. Our most important task was to make them feel that they were home, no matter where we were.

If anything, losing our home made us stronger as a family and allowed us to find untapped strengths in each other. For us, even in the aftermath of the fire, home was all of us together, curled up like the cats, in front of a window full of stars.

~Risa Nye

15

I Don't Want to Die!

There's no disaster that can't become a blessing...
~Richard Bach

"I don't want to die!" was all I could say, all I could think about. Nothing else mattered. No other thoughts intruded. I felt as if I was drowning and my husband was the life preserver I clung to.

"We'll beat this," he assured me, holding me tightly.

I heard the words, but the reality of the moment was just too terrible to accept. I wasn't old. I felt wonderful—except for the insidious cancer that had just been diagnosed. That news hit me like a blow to the heart, to the soul. This wasn't possible. It had to be a mistake.

At that time I was fifty, with my children raised, my husband moving up in his job and our finances finally stable. Life was good. I felt I was in the best physical shape of my life. I felt accomplished in my career. I felt—a lump in my breast.

"It can't be anything bad," I kept assuring myself, even as I kept that first, fateful doctor's appointment. Of course not. Those kinds of things happened to other people, not to me. There was nothing like it in my family history.

"How long has it been since your last mammogram?" the nurse asked as I sat there shivering, more from fear than from the chill in the air of the examination room.

"I don't know. Two years or so, I guess." At that time, the recommended interval between mammograms for women under fifty was every two years. Thankfully, that has now been changed to once a year after the age of forty.

"Well, we'll need to see the old films and I'll schedule you for a new series," the nurse said, so businesslike it seemed hardhearted. "Since they weren't taken here, you'll have to request them."

"The old X-rays? How do I do that?" My mind whirled and I wondered how I was going to function, let alone handle all the details alone. Why was I there by myself? Because, in my panic, I had decided to shelter my husband from the trauma until I was certain I was all right. I had not told him what was going on or what I feared. After all, I was still assuring myself that this threat was nothing but a figment of my overactive imagination.

The doctor entered the exam room. He glowered at me. "Why are you here?"

"I found a lump."

He checked the nurse's notes. "I see that. But why come to me? Why not see your regular doctor?" Still, he scowled as if I were annoying him.

There was something in his tone and in my own mental anguish that pushed me over the edge. He was young, yes, but that was no excuse for his attitude.

I blinked back tears and spoke my mind, raising my voice. "Do you know how hard it was to come here at all? Do you? My regular doctor wasn't in today and I said I needed to be seen urgently so they sent me to you. Do you want me to leave?" By this time I was weeping openly. I slid off the table while clutching the paper gown to my body. "I can go. I will go."

He seemed to come to his senses and looked truly surprised. He also apologized, more than once, and I got my cursory exam before leaving for the mammogram. When I did hear from my regular physician the following day, he also expressed empathy and explained that my mini-tirade had actually helped open his colleague's eyes.

That event, as unwelcome as it was, also taught me to stand up for myself. To ask for whatever I needed and to demand that my concerns be addressed. It was a new role for me, but it has become part of the advice I now pass on to other cancer patients. "This is your life. Your body," I say. "Take responsibility for your care."

Which brings me to the evening my husband brought me the bad news. I was away from home, attending a conference, and my husband, who was now aware of the tests that had been done, was to join me for the weekend.

I greeted him with a grin, then saw his expression. My jaw dropped. He reached for me. I think I may have said, "No," or maybe merely thought it.

"The doctor called," he said. "He gave me his home number so you can talk directly to him instead of having to wait till Monday morning."

Nothing else was said. I fell into my husband's arms, sobbing, "I don't want to die."

I don't really know how long we stood there together. Perhaps it wasn't long, but in my memory the scene stretches eternally because so much of what happened next is just a blur. I telephoned my regular physician and he explained what to expect next. He was patient with my confusion and I thanked him for giving me his home number, an act of unusual kindness that I remember to this day.

As I hung up, my husband asked, "What do you want to do now?"

The answer was easy. "All I want to do is go home."

No banquets, no speeches, or party atmosphere appealed to me as it had just a few minutes before. I wanted peace. Quiet. Home. And now, as I relive that day, I sit in the special place that was the ultimate result of my illness. You see, we both got a wake-up call that day. Jobs were no longer as important. Money and career advancement took a back seat to survival.

I had surgery, then chemotherapy, and seventeen years later I am cancer-free. I still get nervous from time to time, sure, but I have learned to live with that lingering uneasiness about my health and it has kept me aware of the narrow escape I had. That's not a bad thing, especially since I have been given many chances to reach out to others who are battling the same disease.

Through it all, I came to understand more about what really matters than I had in my whole adult life up to that point. Friends matter more. Family is paramount. Expressing my love and affection for everyone takes precedence over the many mundane tasks that had monopolized my previous hours on earth.

I still feel enormously blessed to have accidentally discovered that lump and to have survived to talk about it. Each day, each breath, each opportunity is an unimaginable gift.

Always remember that others have walked the same path that you are on, whether it was through illness or financial trials or other disastrous calamities.

You are not alone. Reach out. We're here to take your hand.

~Valerie Whisenand

16

The Sweetest Sight

While we try to teach our children all about life,
Our children teach us what life is all about.
~Angela Schwindt

I was in the most beautiful city in the world yet I only wanted to go home.

It had been an amazing week of travel for my husband and me—London and Paris—the trip of a lifetime. Months previously, when my husband Doug told me that he was hoping to attend a ministry conference in London, I told him there was no way he was going to Europe without me. We cashed in our frequent flyer miles, secured my in-laws to watch our two children, booked the most inexpensive hostel we could find and were off.

After navigating the subway system, we soaked up as much of London as we could, taking in sights that we had only ever seen courtesy of the Travel Channel; the Tower Bridge, Buckingham Palace, Big Ben, even original manuscripts by Jane Austen and sketches by da Vinci. We boarded the Eurostar and zoomed to Paris to cap off our adventure. As we exited a corner bakery, croissant in hand, the Eiffel Tower peeked out at us and we pinched ourselves. We toured the gothic Notre Dame and marveled at the brilliant stained glass of the round "Rose" windows. Unable to afford a fancy dinner, we bought fresh bread, cheese and fruit and nibbled away as we sat in the courtyard of the Louvre. We stood beneath the colossal Arc de Triomphe, the sculptured marbled angels towering above us. It was truly amazing.

On our last night in Paris, after witnessing the Eiffel Tower twinkle with hundreds of white lights while Parisians picnicked on the lawn, Doug found a payphone in a small pavilion and called home. It was midnight. We were sleepy but giddy.

"Bonjour," he chirped as his mother answered the phone back in Illinois. In mere seconds, my husband's face fell, his blithe expression suddenly somber. My heart immediately went into overdrive.

"What?" I said. "What's wrong?"

He shooed my question away with his hand and continued to listen. I began to silently pray. Oh God, Oh God, My kids my kids. A prayer of desperation. A prayer I hoped God could decipher. I had no idea what was going on, had no idea what to pray.

Finally, Doug covered the mouthpiece and whispered to me that Elijah, our seven-year-old, had fallen off his bike and broken his leg. I began to cry. Was it a bad break? Yes. Was he in pain? Yes. But he was okay. He had broken his leg. Just his leg. He was okay but we needed to get him to an orthopedic surgeon in our hometown as soon as possible.

As we walked back to our hotel, Paris suddenly lost its charm. I don't want to be here, I thought. I shouldn't be here, I should be home with my kids, with my son, and our flight didn't leave until the following afternoon. It wasn't soon enough.

The next day we made it as far as Cleveland only to discover that our flight to Chicago was delayed due to storms. I sat in the terminal with other disgruntled travelers, most of whom had not just endured a transatlantic flight, and couldn't help but overhear their conversations:

"I was supposed to be at a meeting tonight."

"We'll have to cancel our dinner plans."

"Better find a hotel and come back in the morning."

I sat and seethed, wanting to scream that none of their petty plans mattered—I needed to get home to my son. Had I been in my right mind I would have realized that everyone around me had a life too; they had their own problems and dilemmas, some probably more dire than mine. But in that moment I was completely myopic. I was an irrational, frightened mother who didn't understand why the plane couldn't just fly through the lightning bolts to get her home.

We finally got into Chicago at around three in the morning and I snuck a peek at both of my sleeping children, wanting and not wanting to wake them. There is nothing, nothing, nothing like the sight of your children after you've been separated. No cathedral, no great painting or famous landmark compares to the sight of their sweet faces.

For the rest of the summer and into the fall, Elijah was in a hip-to-toe cast. We took up jigsaw puzzles, read *James and the Giant Peach*, drew all over his plastered leg with markers and even hobbled to the beach and dug out a water hole for his good leg to soak in.

We told our kids all about the great cities of London and Paris, showed them our photographs and gave them the souvenirs we had bought for them. Yet the truth was, out of all the amazing sights we took in that summer, our favorites were the two little faces that greeted us at home.

~Rachel Allord

We Have It All

A successful marriage requires falling in love many times,
always with the same person.
~Mignon McLaughlin

We thought we had it all—a beautiful house, three healthy children and one more on the way, two cars, a couple of four-wheelers for entertainment—and we loved it. We spent money like it was going out of style. Then, the market turned and my husband's job as a bigwig at a construction company was gone. The company had declared bankruptcy and was closing down for good.

We both started looking for jobs right away, but there weren't any to be found. With each passing day our panic increased and we continued to work together in order to pull our family through. The more we pulled together, the closer we got. I felt feelings of adoration for my husband that I hadn't felt in years.

That's why it was so hard for me to watch him blame himself for our current situation. I knew that he had no control over the economy, however, he constantly degraded himself and his spirits sunk lower with each snide comment. I continually asked him to stop, but he seemed to want to punish himself for not having a job.

Finally, one afternoon I pulled him aside and said, "We have four healthy children and each other. That's what's important. That makes you a rich man."

"But what if we lose the house? They'll hate me—you'll hate me," he replied.

I smiled at him and put my hands on both sides of his face to make him look me in the eye. "If we live in a cardboard box on the empty lot across the street I will be happy — as long as I have you." I smiled again as I realized that I wasn't just saying it. Somehow, in all the struggling together I had found that deep abiding love for him that I had on the day we said "I do."

I could see relief wash through him as his shoulders and neck relaxed and the tension left his body. He held me close and we were able to talk and plan and dream together in a way that we hadn't in quite some time. It was a turning point for us as a couple and a family.

We are still struggling financially, but I consider us well-off because we have something that money can't buy and no one can take away from us.

~Christina Dymock

The Flag

You're the emblem of
The land I love.
The home of the free and the brave.
~George M. Cohan

itting on the beach, I find myself mesmerized by the waves crashing into the sand. My trance-like state is interrupted by my two-year-old son. He is pointing at an object in the distance.

"Flag," he says.

I am intrigued by his new observation, a stark contrast from his usual sightings of trucks, trains and planes. Where did he learn this new word? What does he find fascinating about the flag? Most likely, he is interested in the bright red, white and blue colors fluttering in the wind.

Soon he will learn what the colors, stripes and stars represent. The stars symbolizing the fifty states, the stripes signifying the original thirteen colonies and the colors indicating philosophical attributes — red for hardiness and valor, white for purity and innocence, and blue for vigilance, perseverance, and justice.

Later in life he will learn that the flag stands for democracy, freedom and equality. When he is finished with his social studies lessons, I will step in and impart my wisdom.

I will share with him the horrific tragedies this country has endured recently. Instead of focusing on the gory details, I will highlight stories about altruism and bravery. He will learn about people who gave their life in an attempt to rescue strangers from a building brought down by terrorism. He will learn about the people who opened their homes to strangers left homeless by a hurricane. He will learn about the schoolchildren who sent letters and care packages to strangers fighting for freedom in a foreign land.

"Flag," my son adamantly says again. Understandably, he wants to make sure I see it.

~Cheryl Maguire

19

My Half
of the Sheets

Your work is to discover your world
and then with all your heart give yourself to it.
~Buddha

Divorced. There I was, after fourteen years of being wildly in love with one person, desperately trying to fall asleep in a strange, rental home on my half of the sheets and pillow-cases. I never would have imagined this scenario, after so many years of thinking that *we'd be forever*. Not only was I a newly single mother of two little boys; I'd also learned days earlier that my soon-to-be ex-husband and I were about four million (*yes, million*) dollars in debt. My ex is a brilliantly talented entertainer, and the debt was some bizarre combination of bad investments, legal fees and incredible lack of foresight and responsibility on anyone's part.

This may sound naïve (and it was) but I had lived for fourteen years in the blissful glow of submissive love, allowing my man to lead the way. If he said finances were handled by the business manager and "not my role," I was happy to believe that the things I brought to our relationship had equal, if not more, importance. My eyes were shut firmly to the whole picture, and I ignored the occasional feeling in my gut that something was severely out of balance in my relationship. Ultimately, my lack of participation in our finances did not in any way absolve me from being accountable for the result. "Ignorance of finances" is no more an excuse than "ignorance of the law."

As an intelligent, educated grown woman, I was incredibly angry at myself for whatever role (albeit passive) that I had played in creating the whole mess. I felt so much guilt and shame. For years I had allowed being in love to override my own values, and now my children and I were paying the price. I had no idea how we would manage, and I was terrified. To make matters worse, my divorce was far from amicable. It seemed that the great love that my husband and I had shared had morphed into a greater degree of bitterness and resentment. He was furious; it didn't matter who left whom or why; on some level, I had abdicated the monarchy. The person to whom I had completely devoted myself was now my biggest adversary; my boys were devastated, and the divorce was overriding every part of my life.

The massive debt made me feel isolated from the rest of the world. I recalled years before having to use a wheelchair for a brief time after my car accident. Strangers either avoided my eyes or looked down on me with pity. Being broke brought back those same, dejected feelings of being an outcast. For me, whoever "knew" or whoever found out would either feel sorry for me or imagine me a huge failure. Once again, I felt handicapped; fear, shame and guilt colored all my thoughts and emotions.

I was blessed with incredibly supportive parents, and there was no time for self-pity: I needed to find work, fast. An artist by nature, my role as a full-time wife and mother had pretty much eclipsed my capacity to earn a living, and my prospects were slim. I was doing my best to keep my spirits up, but "my half of the sheets" posed a big problem, since I had to sleep on them every night. They represented "us," and no matter how hard I tried, I could not wash away the memories of the intimacy we'd shared lying between them. With bankruptcy looming in the foreground, I wasn't about to buy new bedding.

A funny thing about artists—when we can't afford something, our next resort is always an attempt to "make" that something ourselves. À la Scarlett O'Hara, I ripped my half of the sheets off the bed, throwing them into the washing machine with some Rit Dye that I'd picked up at Walgreens. By the time the spin cycle had spun, the sheets were transformed, along with a tiny piece of my sorrow. The pillowcases and the slipcovers off the sofa were next, and before I knew it, my refurbished furnishings would have made Martha Stewart proud.

Into the next load went an old suede jacket. The results were phenomenal—as I experimented with the cycle lengths and mixing different colors directly in the machine, I didn't know what I had, but I knew I had *something*. My parents loaned me a few hundred dollars, and I began dying different colored pieces of suede. The pieces became shawls and the shawls became skirts. Pretending to be on top of the world, I proudly wore my creations into all of the stores I had shopped in before going broke, and sold my one-of-a-kind skirts to every single buyer, right out of the gate. Before I knew it, celebrities all over Hollywood were wearing my designs, big resorts were selling my clothes, and I couldn't keep up with the demand.

It happened so quickly; in truth I had no more clue how to run a business than I did to manage finances. After a series of very poor choices in planning and partners, my fledgling business went bust. There I was—creative, determined, single... and now, *officially bankrupt*. I did my best to make sense of it all, so I could explain it to my sons. Our life was about to change dramatically yet again—while their father helped, his financial situation was worse than mine. The difference was that he had a career, and I had nothing.

When we lost our home and moved into a tiny apartment, it began dawning on me that having "nothing" really could mean having *everything*—it was up to me to decide. The cramped quarters meant that my boys and I were living on top of one another; it also meant we were together more. The fact that there was little money with which to buy new things meant more forts made out of cardboard in our tiny living room, and more little friends sleeping inside of them. The lack of closets meant I could give everything we no longer used to families who had even less. My business had failed miserably, but through that experience I had tapped into some innate marketing skills that brought me steady consulting work. After long days with little pay, my sons and I played cards, watched cartoons, made brownies and ate the batter. We played outside and started making weekly trips to the library, where we took out books instead of buying them. Slowly, but surely, our lives became uncluttered and unencumbered.

I began to notice my sons' becoming much more appreciative—because we no longer had very much, they took better care of everything. They were also developing a whole new level of respect for me. I had always been the stay-at-home mom; now my boys saw me working all hours to support our household as I navigated a full-time job and various entrepreneurial endeavors. They watched as I fell down, and cheered when I got up. My sons became my biggest fans. They saw me cry, they heard me yell; I was no longer "perfect" and they loved me all the more. They witnessed my own parents' rallying to our side, they brainstormed crazy ideas with me and earned their allowance by helping to clean up the constant mess we inevitably made in our simple, creative household.

At my consulting job, I was learning how to manage a budget—for the first time in my life. I excelled at Excel, although there were still many times my heart pounded as my debit card was declined, I slowly learned to apply my new financial skills to my personal life. At forty-two years of age, I was growing up. My compensation was small but, my education was huge. As my new life unfolded, I began to forgive myself. With each tiny victory, and every moment with my sons, my guilt and shame transformed into gratitude for the new life I was creating. To my own amazement, I began to see my divorce and bankruptcy as a gift. Once again, my parents encouraged and supported me in ways I could never have dreamed of. While my heart ached over the loss of love, I had found gratitude for the wonderful years I had shared with my ex, and I was grateful to him for giving me children. I was learning accountability, living according to my own truths and values, and most importantly, my boys and I had become a tight-knit team.

The blessings in disguise that resulted from this time in my life continue revealing themselves to this day. Had I not experienced "my half of the sheets," I would never have understood that "nothing" can mean "everything."

~Elizabeth Bryan

A Valentine's Day to Remember

*When you look at your life
the greatest happiness are family happinesses.*
~Dr. Joyce Brothers

Not long ago, my wife and I shared our tenth Valentine's Day together, a day when I typically reflect on how lucky I am to have found the perfect soul mate. A day to express gratitude to the fates for bringing me a love usually reserved only for movies and Air Supply songs. A day every year that I do whatever is necessary to show her how much I truly care.

Though normally a well-planned and romantic day for us, this year's version marked a dramatic change. At first glance, there could be only one word for it—failure.

Unlike prior years, there was no romantic dinner or picnic lunch. Flowers would not be delivered on the big day. There were no chocolates or candies. No small jewelry store boxes were placed on the dresser. There was no necklace, no bracelet, no ring. No limousines, no movie tickets, and no concerts were arranged. There was no homemade CD of "our" songs. There was no romantic poem hidden under her cereal bowl, professing my undying love.

There was nothing. Well, almost nothing.

There was a road trip—though not the kind of road trip we would have voluntarily embarked upon. The trip was not to the beach, the mountains, or any such getaway. No, this road trip was to the office of a UCLA doctor—a pediatric specialist. We needed answers, and we needed them quickly.

Only a week had passed since the first ripple began to rock our calm and quiet lives. A passing observation during our eighteen-month-old son's routine checkup led to a blood test. An odd collection of contradictory data led to a more extensive blood test, then another, the results of which merely led to more questions. A brain MRI was immediately scheduled.

Doctors and nurses did their best to maintain a calm demeanor, but the hastiness and urgency of their actions belied their efforts to convince us these tests were merely precautionary. All the while, our little boy remained blissfully unaware that his parents were scared out of their minds.

Because of the conflicting nature of initial test results, the doctor opted to conduct an extensive and comprehensive investigation. During the course of the day, we found ourselves shuttling to radiologists, phlebotomists, and other specialists. Most of the day hovered in a narrow realm between surrealism and automatism. Through all the evaluations, we made every attempt to make the afternoon as normal and calm as possible for the little one.

Valentine's Day cards were exchanged in the carpool lane of the 405 Freeway. The picnic lunch was replaced by a drive-thru window in the shadow of the hospital. Small, token gifts were swapped in the radiologist's waiting room.

Amazing how quickly your reality can change, and how dramatically your priorities shift in such a brief period of time. There were no "I hope she likes my gift" concerns. Instead, thoughts were restricted to "I hope my baby is okay."

On Valentine's Days of the past, I would be thankful for on-time flower deliveries or timely dinner reservations. This year, I was grateful for funny nurses that made my son laugh, laboratories that were willing to push back lunch breaks, and a boss willing to let a worried Daddy off work only a few weeks into his new job.

I was thankful for phlebotomists who miraculously managed to find the small vein on the arm of a screaming baby, on their very first attempt. I was thankful for doctors who believe in attacking a problem head-on, refusing to accept a "wait-and-see" position. I was thankful for professionals who made me feel as though my son were the most important patient on their daily schedule.

After a chaotic and tense afternoon, we were all finally able to return home. As the sun began to set on an excruciatingly long day, at about the time most couples were settling in at their romantic dinners, my wife and I lay sprawled on the sofa doing our best to put the day in perspective. Clearly, this would be a Valentine's Day that we would never forget as long as we live. There was relief that the day was over, and apprehension at not knowing what lay ahead.

There was also an unexpected moment of clarity. It occurred to me that the "commercial" aspects of the holiday are inherently meaningless. The flowers, candies, and other gifts that have become the norm every February 14th are not the reason for the holiday; they are merely symbols of it.

In the end, maybe Valentine's Day should be about spending a day with the people you love most in the world. It should be about doing everything in your power to calm a crying baby. It should be about a husband and wife recommitting themselves to the "home" team, and knowing neither one of us could survive without the other. It should be about re-evaluating your priorities, and making certain you are never too busy to be with your family.

And if Valentine's Day really is about all of these things, perhaps the day was not a failure after all. Maybe, just maybe, it was my most successful Valentine's Day yet.

~Rob L. Berry

This Is the Life!

Life holds so many simple blessings,
each day bringing its own individual wonder.
~John McLeod

I buckled in Cody, wedged a Slushee between his legs, and powered up the truck. Cody laced his fingers behind his head, heaved a big sigh, and said, "This is the life!"

A profound statement for such small pleasures. Time alone with Mom, combined with a Slushee, were apparently the recipe of happiness to my six-year-old.

I recalled the times when I experienced such moments, these wellings-up, a rush of love to the heart.

On our way home from a camping trip one time, my husband suddenly pulled the truck onto the shoulder and with the engine idling, slid out, skipped to my side, and opened my door with great ceremony.

"What's going on?" I asked.

"I need to show you something."

He pulled me to the front of the cab, wrapped his arms around my middle from behind, and there on the side of the highway proceeded to do a show-and-tell of all the constellations in the cloudless midnight sky.

Wellings-up happen when we least expected them.

Cody came up to us one day and said, "I have a great idea! Let's send balloons to God!"

And so we inflated four balloons — one from each child — wrote

"I ♥ you, God!" on each one, then watched them drift away. That is, until our neighbor's tree snagged them. I think God got the message anyway. I envisioned Him having a welling-up of His own.

En route to Open House at their school one evening, our second eldest, Ethan, was giddy with anticipation of this particular outing. After we parked, we were spilling out of the car when Ethan proclaimed, "I love Cody! I love Matthew! I love Madison! I love Daddy!"

He looked up at me and added, "I even love you, too!"

For one Halloween, we invited ghouls and goblins to roast hot dogs and marshmallows over an open fire under the watchful eye of a full harvest moon. While gazing into the hypnotic fire, one of the parents sighed and said, "Now this is the life!"

I glanced across the street to our home, a fixer-upper that dared us to finish it. We'd been without a kitchen for eight years, the balcony on the upper story was in the midst of being converted into a third bedroom to accommodate our growing family, and the bottom story was a construction zone. The kids bathed in an antique German child's tub, which also doubled as a kitchen sink. We liked to joke that our grandkids would be completing our perennial fixer-upper for us at the rate it was going. We often dreamed, too, of Ty Pennington and the *Extreme Makeover* crew coming to our rescue.

In spite of it all, our kids seemed blind to their home's shortcomings. On more than one occasion, they've shouted, "I love this house!"

Many people have questioned our sanity over the years, wondering why the progress on our house continues at a snail's pace. One overriding factor—raising kids—usurped the majority of our money, time, and attention.

And one might say we were too wrapped up in producing welling-up moments like this. I squeezed my husband's hand, watching our kids in Halloween costumes spearing marshmallows with antique extendable forks.

Then I concurred quietly with the parent's observation, "Yep, this is the life."

Think about it. Think about the things that give you a welling-up and make you want to declare out loud, "This is the life!"

Then say it!

~Jennifer Oliver

Chapter 3

Count Your Blessings

Recovering from Adversity

*Life's ups and downs provide windows of opportunity
to determine your values and goals.
Think of using all obstacles as stepping stones
to build the life you want.*

~Marsha Sinetar

Victor Not Victim

Turn your wounds into wisdom.
~Oprah Winfrey

I guess we never truly know how tough we are until really tough times peck at our heels and dominate our souls. Sure, everyone has trials and difficulties. Trials and difficulties are a natural part of living, but sometimes those trials are so enormous that we can become disoriented, disillusioned, downright depressed, and caught up in a web of inactivity.

I grew up in a very dysfunctional and abusive family, and I quickly had to learn to either sink or swim. Even though my childhood was an extremely difficult period, I have come to understand that it really did prepare me to face adult difficulties straight up. I learned early on in my life that no matter what happens to me, it is my attitude about what happens to me which either makes me or breaks me.

I know the economy is as bad as it has been in decades, and I also know many people are downright scared about what their future holds. I have heard some people say they just don't know what they are going to do, and I tell them that when tough times come in my life, I just have to work harder for positive results. I use the fear and negative energy my trials produce to work harder for a positive solution. My parents did not conquer me and neither will my problems.

I was diagnosed with colon cancer in June 2003, and talk about a very tough period in my life. I was devastated and I was scared, and I certainly had many sleepless nights praying to God for strength and to help me beat this thing. But I also took charge and sought out the best surgeon and oncologist I could find. I then double-checked their recommendations with yet other physicians to make sure I was doing the right thing before I underwent major surgery. I had a positive outcome from that surgery, and the pathologists indicated that all of the cancer had been removed. They told me that I had no worries, and to go and have a good life.

But the cancer did return in November of 2004, and I was completely devastated once again. I endured another six-hour surgery, followed by chemotherapy treatments. It took me months to recover from these procedures. My body was so weak and I thought the chemo fatigue would never end, but I took one day at a time and I finally returned to my normal life again. I fought all of the negative thoughts I had during this time, determined that cancer was not going to take me.

I have been cancer-free for over four years now, but recently had to undergo major spinal fusion surgery, with the addition of plates and screws to hold my spine stable and secure. But, hey, these are the medical cards I have been dealt in my life, so I will play them the best way I know how. I refuse to be a victim in all of these health issues. Instead, I choose to be a victor. I truly believe these problems have made me a stronger and better person. They have taught me to be more compassionate for other people, especially those who are sick. And I certainly have a much deeper appreciation for life on a daily basis, and for the love and companionship of my dear family.

Yes, there are rough economic times out there, the job market is unstable, and it is getting very difficult to make ends meet. But so what if I have to do with a little less? So what if my retirement plan is worth forty percent less than it was at this time last year? I am just very grateful I still have my life, and I am also very grateful for how much closer my family and I have grown as a result of my health issues. That is worth much more than a large stock portfolio.

~LaVerne Otis

My Super Bowl Highlight

*Without the illness I would never have been forced to
re-evaluate my life and my career.*
~Lance Armstrong

Superstar cyclist Lance Armstrong's world was famously turned upside down on Oct. 2, 1996, the day he was diagnosed with cancer. Now a survivor, he celebrates 10/2 as the moment his life changed unexpectedly for the better.

I have my own 10/2 — as, I believe, do most of us — on 1/26. That was the date of Super Bowl XXXVII in San Diego in 2003, which I covered as a newspaper sports columnist. A few hours after the Tampa Bay Buccaneers turned the Oakland Raiders into twisted, total wreckage, 48-21, an uninsured drunk driver did the same to my Honda Accord.

Police estimated that he was flying at 65 miles per hour on a downtown street at about 11 P.M. before ramming my car as I waited to make a right-hand turn. The impact was so violent that the driver's seat was ripped off its bolts. When my wife called the towing company, she was offered condolences; the worker couldn't believe I hadn't been killed.

"You're a very lucky man," one of the police officers told me after he finished documenting the accident scene.

Lucky, indeed. According to the National Highway Traffic

Safety Administration, 17,602 people were killed in alcohol-related accidents in 2006, about the same number as in 2003.

Still, luck is relative. I suffered a ruptured disk in my neck and underwent a two-hour operation called an "anterior cervical discectomy and fusion five-six with iliac graft." Translation: The neurosurgeon sliced open my neck from the front, delicately removed the damaged disk between my fifth and sixth vertebrae without damaging the spinal cord, used a power saw to cut a wedge of bone from my pelvis and then shoe-horned this slice of bone between the two vertebrae to allow them to fuse together.

The surgery left a three-inch scar running across my Adam's apple that allows me to honestly tell people who ask about it, "Oh, it's from an old Super Bowl injury." Unfortunately, I had nerve damage that proved irreversible. Now, six years later, my left thumb and fingers remain numb and slightly uncoordinated. I found that hunching over a keyboard in a cramped press box was tortuous after about an hour.

All the same, I look back on 1/26 as a blessing.

For starters, it forced me to leave a job I loved too much to leave on my own. Sportswriting had me away from home too many nights a week, almost every weekend and most holidays. Yes, I miss the press box, but in return I have not missed so much more. My wife and I recently celebrated our silver wedding anniversary on the correct date, not the nearest night with no game. Instead of covering the Lakers or Dodgers, I attended every performance of two plays my daughter wrote in high school. I have not missed a single one of my son's high school and college cross-country or track meets. I wouldn't trade the Super Bowl, Final Four and Olympics for that.

Sports are still part of my life. I write for magazines and am working on a book that includes words of wisdom from athletes I have interviewed over the years. Olympic track champion Jackie Joyner-Kersee, for instance, who shared, "When you have hard times or low moments, that just makes the good times more valuable and special." Or UCLA basketball Coach John Wooden's adage, "Make each day your masterpiece." And of course, Armstrong, who told me:

"My philosophy is to never waste another day thinking about tomorrow or next week or next year. Cancer taught me that today is all I have. I want to live today like there is no tomorrow."

I didn't fully appreciate these insights before having my life spun around by a drunk driver.

Sure, there are times when my fingers feel like they are on fire and I fall into self-pity. I sometimes curse the drunk driver who rear-ended me because my neck aches 24/7. I had to "retire" from playing men's rec-center basketball and give up tennis. Still, I was lucky. I completed a marathon (3 hours, 18 minutes) two years after the accident, and I didn't have to do it in the wheelchair division; this year I've qualified to run in the Boston Marathon.

As much as I lost because of a drunk driver—a portion of my health, my dream job, income—at least it wasn't my life. As much as I lost, I have gained much more—such as the perspective that Lance Armstrong's 10/2 and my 1/26 and so many people's 9/11 should make each of us realize that our days are numbered.

~Woody Woodburn

Floating Bones

The difficulties, hardships and trials of life... are positive blessings.
They knit the muscles more firmly, and teach self-reliance.
~William Matthews

I have hip dysplasia. I bet I know what you're thinking: "Isn't that what dogs get?" Yeah, it is. Me and the dogs. Basically, my thigh bones don't fit well into my hip sockets, so I've got pain, cartilage damage, and arthritis. Being human instead of hound, however, I insist to my husband that I don't need to be put to sleep.

My doctor suggests periacetabular osteotomy surgery on my right hip, the one more damaged. The operation, more complex than hip replacement, will sculpt and reposition my bones, which are then held in place by metal pins. After finding an experienced surgeon and clearing it with insurance, I agree.

I feel okay about it until the big day. I talk to intake nurses, a physician's assistant, the anesthesiologist, and my surgeon, all of whom have this unsettling habit: they ask me why I'm there. Shouldn't they know?

"What are we doing today?" the surgeon asks me. I try not to panic. I've been told this is a hospital safety measure—if everyone involved in my care asks me why I think I'm there, and I keep giving the same answer, then apparently, that's what they're going to do. It doesn't occur to me until later that I should have answered, "liposuction."

Still, everything goes well, and the surgery is a success. After a week in the hospital, I am discharged with instructions not to use my right leg at all for six weeks. Back home, getting around is tough. One night, sitting on the sofa, I place my right hand on my walker and my left hand on the armrest. I try to push myself up to a standing position on my good left leg, but I can't. Struggling and straining, I fall backward onto the couch.

"Clackety clack!" I freeze, petrified. Have I broken myself? I've fallen only a couple of feet, back onto a squishy sofa, but the noise was terrifying. I remember the dire warnings of my surgeon: if I'm not careful, I may cause the metal pins holding my bones together to slip, and then the entire ordeal might have to be repeated. I do the only logical thing: cry hysterically, then page the surgeon.

A physician's assistant calls me back. As I tearfully describe what happened, she assures me it would take a much more serious fall to dislodge the pins.

"What about the clacking noise?" I ask, sniffling and red-nosed. "It sounded awful!"

"Well, you have to understand that the bones aren't set yet," she says. "They're just sort of floating around in there, and they're going to bump into each other for a while until they heal."

She assures me I'll be okay, so I thank her and hang up. Then I think, Um, wait. Floating bones?

When I tell my best friend, Kate, she laughs. "She's probably making that up," Kate says, "standing around with the other P.A.'s, snickering and telling them, 'Yeah, I told her her bones were floating around in her body and she bought it!' They're probably all laughing, telling their friends."

Okay, Kate has a point, but hey, blind faith in my P.A. is better than dwelling on the alternatives.

Side effects plague me after surgery, but the worst one is helplessness. You see, I'm a doer. Someone who gets things accomplished. Okay, actually, I'm just a control freak. The sticky incision that isn't healing, the blood clots bloating my calf, the blisters under the medical tape—all that is nothing compared to watching my summertime garden get devoured by weeds. The garden, the house, my waistline—it's all going to pot. I have a supportive husband who brings me homemade food and helps me get around, but tidying and weeding aren't his thing. Hence, the hours staring out my window plotting the demise of the dandelions I am convinced must be mortifying the neighbors.

I do get out occasionally. I have a wheelchair, and sometimes I get wheeled to the movies or out to dinner. It is in this scenario that I discover the joys of trying to use public restrooms while disabled. It's a comedy of errors.

My wheelchair is manual, chunky, and corners like a semi. I inadvertently crash into a trash can, knocking refuse across the room. I stare up at paper-towel dispensers I cannot reach, then pull myself up to wobble on one leg to grab what I can, worrying that people will think because I am sort of standing, I must be faking. Even the logistics of applying toilet seat covers seem overwhelming.

Generally, I'm fortunate enough to get others to open the bathroom door while I wheel myself into the room, but then I'm confronted with the challenge of correctly angling myself into the stall. The handicapped stalls that used to seem so spacious now appear akin to telephone booths. Ever tried to spin a wheelchair in a telephone booth?

One evening, I enter a bathroom stall and realize I have to spin. I cannot do this without knocking open the stall door. Straining to reach the latch, I shut the stall door again and survey my surroundings. I am going to have to sit perpendicularly on the toilet seat. This seems ridiculous, but somehow I maneuver myself into position, desperately thankful I have one good leg to help me. I huff and puff and finally get myself off the chair and atop my perch. It is then I watch in horror as the stall door slowly creaks open, the latch broken.

By the time I leave the bathroom, I am red-faced and sweaty, exhausted and embarrassed. I also have a profound respect for the disabled.

Three long months later, I am allowed to walk unassisted. My first attempt, I am told, is adorable. I wobble back and forth, holding my arms out for balance, looking like a toddler taking her first steps.

My husband generously resists whipping out the camera to capture the moment.

Over the next weeks, I practice walking, which doesn't hurt (unless I overdo it) but is still awkward. My center of gravity feels different on my right side than on my left. This weirds me out, but I am so busy taking out the trash, scrubbing the toilets, and driving myself to work that I'm too content to sweat it.

I have come away from this experience realizing that little things can make me happy if I just remember what blessings I have. It's so gratifying to walk and move without pain. Let me tell you, you've never seen a woman so thrilled to be cleaning out her garage. I cherish the now-strong left leg that helped me through this, and I appreciate my new right-side abilities. I'm not yet able to take long walks, hike nature trails, or even comfortably cross my leg, but that's okay. Even if I'm never fully up to speed again, my three months of helplessness were more than enough to make me infinitely thankful for what I can do—and that includes brandishing the cutest weed-free yard I've ever had.

~Alaina Smith

Turkey and Blessings

We should all get together and make a country
in which everybody can eat turkey whenever he pleases.
~Harry S Truman

December 24, 1974 was bleak and cold in Elko, Nevada, where I was living with my two small children. My husband was living with friends 300 miles west in Reno, where he was driving a taxicab to try to make ends meet after we had experienced financial disaster in the recession of 1974. I had been working as a nurse in the local hospital until I had to have knee surgery, the first of several over the years, and, after that, I was unable to work. As Christmas Eve dawned, there was no money to buy presents or to put food on the table. To make matters worse, the power had been off for about twelve hours after a winter storm tore down the lines.

In the middle of the afternoon, a neighbor appeared at the door with a plate of Christmas cookies for the children. A few hours later a couple of nurse friends from the hospital came by to check on me. When they heard about our empty pantry, they excused themselves and went to the hospital to obtain a frozen turkey like those the other hospital employees received earlier in the week as holiday presents. Because I was on sick leave, I didn't legally qualify for one.

Just as nightfall came, the front door opened and in came my husband, with a frozen pizza, bought with his recent cab fares. The pizza was cooked over the fireplace logs, and then about 9 P.M. the power came back on. The turkey was thawed, and the next day cooked and served, accompanied by Christmas cookies. By mid-afternoon on December 25th, we were a warm, full, and happy family. I cannot remember the menu for any other Christmas before or since, but I will never forget the one for 1974.

Early 1975 did not prove to be much better for us. By February of that year, my husband had moved out of our friends' home and into a room at the Rescue Mission in downtown Reno, where his window looked down on the soup kitchen. We had only one car between us, which he parked on the side of the street outside the Mission while he slept. Back in Elko, I had recovered enough from my knee surgery to again ride my bicycle to and from work, balancing my son on the seat behind me as I took him to day care. His sister joined him there later in the day after she got out of first grade. A teenage babysitter took them both to our home at supper time and kept them until my 3-11 shift at the hospital was over and I had biked home.

At about 2:30 one morning in March the phone by the side of my bed rang. It's never good news at that hour and when the voice announced that he was a police officer in a remote town in western Nevada, I expected to hear the worst possible news.

"Ma'am, I have a 1974 Ford registered to your name that has been abandoned outside a bar in Tonopah. Do you know anything about it?"

Yes, I told him, I knew it was our car but I had no idea why it was more than 200 miles away from Reno nor did I know where my husband, who was supposed to be sleeping in his room at the Mission, could be. By the time I found someone awake at the Mission who could check on my husband, I was frantic.

John turned up in his bed and we realized that the car had been stolen and driven until it was empty. Fortunately we had paid our insurance premiums and USAA provided us a rental car until ours could be repaired from the damage done when the thief had jimmied the ignition.

Reno was a pretty good place to be in 1975 if you were down and out, because the casinos offered good cheap food and some free entertainment. The children and I took a train there for Easter, staying together as a family at our friends' home while they visited family out of town. As the four of us sat in the dining room of the Nugget after enjoying the Easter buffet, I looked at John and we agreed that if our luck kept going in this direction we probably would be smarter to move back East where we could at least be within a day's drive of family and home cooking.

Two months later, we sold almost all our furniture and defaulted on the property in the country on which we had hoped to eventually build our dream home. We loaded our things in a trailer and started driving to Tennessee, staying first in a Motel 6 in Las Vegas, and then in other budget motels as we rode Interstate 40 across the country. The children thought it was a great adventure to eat cereal from plastic cups each morning and to roast hot dogs over fires in state parks for lunch. They said we were pioneers.

John and I didn't feel much like pioneers. Rather, we felt more like prisoners who had been freed and given a one-way bus ticket and a suit of clothes to get them started for the rest of their lives. We were homeless, unemployed, and depressed.

Then in a twenty-four-hour period, God intervened and we landed in Nashville where we found work, a furnished home to rent, an opportunity to go back to school, and people who cared about us. We have thrived here for the last thirty-five years. Times have not always been easy. In fact they are not easy now in 2009 when we are in our late sixties and have lost more than thirty percent of our retirement savings in this most recent recession. But we are luckier than many. We have never spent elaborately and we don't have major debt. We both have work that will probably continue for some time. We are healthier than many of our contemporaries. We have electric power most of the time. We have a roof over our heads and a mortgage we can pay. We have the strength that comes from facing adversity.

A few days before Christmas this year a neighbor brought us a plate of cookies. We ate takeout pizza in a warm kitchen with our grandchildren on Christmas Eve and had a turkey on the table for Christmas dinner. This time it was a legal turkey because the hospital where I now work gave all employees a bird for the holiday and I was not on sick leave. As I walked on my two artificial knees to the tent where the gifts were being distributed, I gave thanks for turkey and blessings.

~Ginger Manley

A Mother's Battle for Her Boys

I live for my sons. I would be lost without them.
~Princess Diana

When the doctors diagnosed me with multiple sclerosis, I was twenty-five years old. I was supposed to be in the prime of my life. Not to mention, I had three small boys, ages seven, five and two. My illness also put a big strain on my marriage. Sometimes I think it was actually harder on my family than it was on me. My boys didn't understand what happened to their mommy, my husband didn't know how to deal with it, and my parents were in denial.

I wasn't glad that I had MS, but it did explain some of the unusual things that had been going on with my body: numbness and tingling in my legs, blurred vision, lack of bowel and bladder control, and weakness and fatigue. My physical symptoms were difficult to manage, but my emotional state of mind was even worse. I had always been such an active mother. The boys filled my days with all kinds of activities, including going to the skating rink, the park, ball games and being room mother. When the MS flared up, this put a halt to some of these activities. For one thing, my vision seemed to be affected more than anything. When this would happen, I wasn't able to drive. During these times we couldn't even leave the house.

My boys wouldn't let me give up. I remember when my youngest son, Kyle, would come in my room in the mornings to wake me up. He would lightly pat me on the cheek, as he whispered, "Mama. Mama." When I opened my eyes, he would give me the sweetest smile. He would give me a little hug and then he'd pull back my covers and say, "Get up, Mama. I want some git-gits." Those words actually saved me. That little boy needed his Mama to make git-gits (biscuits). If I was using crutches, he would even hand them to me, to speed up the process a little. He was very persistent and he really liked his biscuits.

My friends and family were very supportive. Some of them brought over dinner for us or took my boys to school for me in the morning. Sometimes they even helped me with my housework.

Even though I learned to live with my sickness, and my boys adapted to it just fine, this whole thing really put a strain on my marriage. Some people have a hard time dealing with sickness. When I think back on it now, I really do understand; yet at the time, it didn't make any sense to me at all. Not only did I have to fight a terrible battle, but I had to deal with it on my own. Just a couple years after my diagnosis, my husband left us.

Trying to find a job was another obstacle I had to overcome. Since I was a stay-home mom for eleven years, I didn't have experience at anything except changing diapers. Unfortunately, that was not needed in the workplace. Finding a place to hire me with no experience was one thing, but having an illness that hurt my attendance record was a whole new issue. I wouldn't miss just a day or two; I would have to miss several days or weeks at a time when the MS flared up.

Somehow, I always found some kind of a job. I learned to keep my illness a secret until after I was hired. I felt like I had to work harder than everyone else, to compensate for my illness. It paid off most of the time. Many of the places worked with me and helped me through my bad times. I found that the smaller offices were much more tolerant.

One of the companies didn't have any patience with me at all. It was a big corporation and the first time I was out for a few days, my boss reprimanded me in front of everyone. He had no compassion at all. I cried in the bathroom and then I called a place that I had worked for before to see if I could come back. When they agreed, I gave my notice the next day. I didn't get paid enough to put up with that.

There were a certain number of things, of course, that I did have to put up with. There were mornings when I really struggled to get to work. By the time I got up, got myself ready, helped my boys get dressed and off to school, I was exhausted. Fighting the traffic and dealing with the aggravation at work was sometimes too overwhelming. Some days were a little more than I could handle. Each morning, when I got up and saw my boys' faces, it reminded me why I had to keep going. They kept me strong. I kept pushing myself.

As the boys got older, our lives became more and more hectic. There was baseball, football, hockey, basketball, band, choir, Boy Scouts, and I even served as room mother on my lunch hour when it was possible. I wanted my boys to have a good childhood, even though they had to deal with some unusual circumstances.

As I watched my boys grow up, I felt bad sometimes that they had to grow up faster than normal. However, I realize now, that it probably made them stronger. I am only about 5'3" and all of my sons are about six feet. Luckily, I had their respect, and they always looked out for me. There were some nights when I would come home after having a bad day at work, and my oldest son would actually pick me up, put me on the couch, and tell me, "I'm cooking dinner tonight and you're not getting off the couch." Then he would cook dinner and clean up afterward. He loved experimenting in the kitchen and he is a wonderful cook.

I remarried after my two older sons moved out. My husband is a wonderful man. He knew what he was up against when he married me. It hasn't been easy for him, I know, but he has still stood by me through some pretty rough times. My youngest son just moved out last year, so now it's just the two of us. My illness has progressed in the past few years. I have to give myself interferon shots three times a week and I am on disability now.

I wondered what would keep me going since my boys have

moved out. However, my family is growing now. Not only do I have my husband, but I have a daughter-in-law, two granddaughters, my other boys' girlfriends, and a puppy. My boys are still a big part of my life and they are still very protective of me. They also make me keep trying. We have come this far, so why would we give up now? We have too much to live for—we have each other; and that's a lot!

~Sherri A. Stanczak

One Step at a Time

*The first step towards getting somewhere is to decide
that you are not going to stay where you are.*
~John Pierpont Morgan

I magine a Type B person trying to be a Type A. That was me a year ago. There were assignments to finish, new computer programs to learn, invitations to accept, obligations to fulfill, problems to fix. No matter how many items I checked off my To Do list, it always seemed to get longer. I was feeling tired and stressed but was reluctant to let anything go, to say "no." Truthfully, I enjoyed most of these tasks but found myself using them as excuses to avoid dealing with some health issues and taking an honest look at my priorities.

My only nod in the health direction was an evening walk. I always feel better after a brisk constitutional. It's the exercise and endorphins, I know, but it's more than that. To me, walking means freedom—the comforting expectation that my legs will always be available to move me from place to place, one step at a time.

One morning in March, my husband Jerry and I decided to go on a four-mile hike. The coastal area had experienced heavy rains a month earlier and during the muddy days, off-road vehicles had torn up the landscape, turning the normally flat terrain into a labyrinth of dirt dunes. Now the mud had dried. As we navigated down one of the dunes on our way to the trail, my right foot slipped on a surface layer of loose, crumbly soil. I tried to regain my balance, but my foot had slipped too far. As I fell, I remember looking at my left leg, which hadn't moved and was bent at an odd angle. Then I heard the crack, felt the searing pain, and knew immediately that my leg was broken.

The days after my ambulance ride were a blur of hospitals, X-rays, tests, pain medications and surgery to install a titanium plate and ten screws that would hold together my shattered fibula and broken ankle bones. "It's the worst break I've ever seen," my doctor said. I was devastated and scared. "When can I walk again?" I wanted to know. "Four to six weeks," he replied. It sounded like a lifetime.

At first I was so weak from surgery I had a hard time adjusting to the crutches. The thought of falling terrified me. One evening, while Jerry was at work, our electricity went out. I sat in the dark, afraid to move, and obsessed about how helpless I would be if a burglar broke in. When our building elevator stopped working for several days, I agonized over how I would get down the stairs if a fire broke out.

Simple things I had taken for granted were now arduous tasks while balancing on crutches: washing, brushing my teeth and hair, fixing meals, even lowering myself to sit on the throne, then getting up again with a single leg that wasn't up to the challenge of lifting all my weight. Instead of a full cast, the doctor had immobilized my leg with a splint. "Be careful you don't bump or twist it," he told me, so I covered the bed with pillows and readjusted my position with every twinge, worried that I would misalign my bones during sleep.

Most of my time was spent either propped up in bed or in a living room recliner chair following doctor's orders to keep my swollen foot elevated. To reduce the need to move, I surrounded both spots with bottles of water, snacks, vitamins, books and other essentials.

Little by little, I adjusted to my new circumstances. Tall stools positioned at the bathroom sink and in the kitchen allowed me to sit whenever I needed to ease pressure on the remaining leg. A sturdy laundry hamper next to the commode enabled me to push myself into a standing position. Working the crutches built up my arm strength and I was able to maneuver more easily. I even started to enjoy discovering alternate ways to get things done. While my hands were occupied with the crutch handles, I could carry items from room to room in a fanny pack, or push larger, heavier objects along the carpet, between hops, using one rubber crutch tip. And I found the crutches to be handy arm extenders for plucking objects that were just beyond my reach. "You'll learn some new tricks on those crutches," a wise friend told me. She was right.

My husband immediately adapted to his new job as caregiver. Before leaving for work each morning, he fixed me a peanut butter and jelly sandwich for breakfast and refilled my water bottles. Evenings and weekends, he made simple meals and tended to all my needs. In the beginning, when I felt especially vulnerable, he lovingly bathed me, scrubbing my back and washing my hair. The bond between us deepened.

Friends also came to the rescue, fixing meals and offering support. Ironically, a friend living in another state had broken her leg and ankle just two months before my accident. She phoned every week, my guide on this unfamiliar journey, and we compared our common recuperation, sharing experiences, coping techniques and laughter about the predicament in which we found ourselves. The companionship lifted my spirits.

Weeks turned into months. The doctor had ordered physical therapy to increase the mobility of what he jokingly called my "bionic" leg, but I was still not permitted to walk. That made me reluctant to venture outside my apartment. There were times I feared that I would never be able to walk normally or without pain. To alleviate the worry and depression that set in, I knew I needed more exercise. But how? Then it dawned on me: bed exercises. Leg lifts, stomach crunches, hamstring stretches, muscling homemade weights. I must have looked like an overturned turtle, lying on my back amid the pillows, arms and legs flailing in the air.

After five months, I was allowed to take my first full-weight-bearing, tentative steps in hospital-prescribed footwear. The bulky, knee-length black boot made me look like a Star Wars storm trooper, but it reduced the pressure on healing bones and soft tissue. A month later, I slipped eagerly into my athletic shoes. My gait was awkward at first and I leaned on one crutch for balance. But with practice, the blood vessels, muscles, tendons and ligaments, damaged during surgery and withered from lack of use, gradually adjusted to the job demanded of them.

Now I'm walking comfortably. And there have been other improvements. I've had plenty of downtime to think about what's important to me. Allocating more time for healthy eating and exercise is at the top of my list, as is paying attention to my inner Type B voice. That means no longer accepting every invitation or taking on every task. I feel less harried, more at peace with myself. My body is healing and so is my spirit. I can honestly say I'm grateful for the physical and emotional challenges I was given to overcome. The experience made me stronger, more resilient and, I hope, wiser. My bionic leg and I look forward to striding confidently into the future, one step at a time.

~Jennifer Crites

28

One Second Changed My Life Forever

One of the secrets of life is to make stepping stones out of stumbling blocks.
~Jack Penn

As a little girl, I dreamed of owning a ranch with horses and marrying a wonderful man. I never dreamed my world would come to a crashing halt after a traumatic brain injury.

You see, I had to be a daredevil, riding the craziest horses, driving fast, always on the go. This time however, I pushed it too far. I had put a two-wheeled motorized scooter on the fastest setting I could. Next thing I knew, I was flying off the sidewalk. The machine had jumped the curb, hit the street and soared in the air with me still on it. Coming down, the machine was so heavy it thrust me head first onto the concrete street, cracking my head. Everything went twirling and into a blur; yet I didn't pass out. I went into shock. Thinking "I'm tough," I refused to go to the hospital. When I awoke the next day, I knew I was in trouble. When I spoke, I started with the end of the sentence and moved to the beginning of the sentence. My family rushed me to the emergency room, where they found a spot on my brain.

Sitting in the specialist's office while the doctor told my fiancé that I was not the same person he fell in love with was hard. He said that both the front and back of my brain had serious damage. Because of the severity of the damage, he said, I would never be the engineer I had been. He urged me to find jobs that required only one task at a time. I actually believed him. Taking a leave of absence from work, I started rehab.

My fiancé married me anyway. I told him that I would try my best to get "me" back. We bought that ranch I had always dreamed of, with beautiful horses, and settled in.

At first, I seemed normal. You wouldn't have noticed the subtle differences in my behavior unless you had lived with me. I "knew" without a shadow of doubt that I closed the horses' gates so they wouldn't get out. I saw myself actually closing the gates. A horse or two got out. You can guess who got in trouble. I knew I turned off the stove after cooking. I would talk about a memory and I would meld one from years before with one that happened recently. On it went. I soon found myself on my own because my husband would spend more time around friends and less with me.

I became suspicious of everyone. I thought people were talking about me, thinking I was weird, because that's how I felt. What was worse was no one could tell I had anything wrong with me on the outside until, under pressure, I started to stutter. I would say sentences backwards, and they would get distressed looks on their faces.

I became self-conscious about everything I said and did. I began isolating myself from everyone, alone in the house or outside with the horses. Even my family did not know how to deal with me. I went from being well-liked to being cold and distant. I started crying all the time. I felt as though I had lost my mind. I didn't understand what was happening to me. I was incredibly lonely and no one knew my pain.

As time passed, my husband and I fought constantly. I tried desperately to prove to him that I wasn't lying about closing things, opening things, hiding things... you name it.

Not being able to handle it anymore, I said a prayer. "God, I know he didn't know what he was getting into when he married me. Please tell me that I am not the lying person that he thinks I am. Tell me that I am worth something to someone, anyone, somewhere. Tell me that I am worth loving. Do you even care that I am literally stuck in here with my thoughts and I cannot get out? Do you see where I am? God, please save me and tell me what to do."

Collapsing on the bed, I heard a little voice in my head that simply said, "I want you to leave. Just leave. I want you to leave."

"But God, you don't want us to leave a marriage!" I retorted.

"His heart is hard, and I want you to leave. You have friends and I will supply everything you need."

"What friends?" No reply came.

There was no way I would leave without my horses. How could I afford to board huge animals on my minimum wage job? How would I pull this off? I decided it was better to obey and that is when the first miracle happened.

Old friends who I had distanced myself from a few years before offered to board my horses, free. That same day, another miracle occurred when an old colleague of mine said I could live with her for free until I got on my feet. Then, as if pre-planned, the third miracle arrived. Another old friend told me her husband was hiring at his office. The position was a perfect fit and paid more than enough for me to survive. Yes, just like that.

At my lowest point during this time, I had lost my dream home to foreclosure, been divorced, lost my stepdad to a rare disease, rushed to several hospitals for my mother's weak heart, battled creditors, lost a few jobs due to "mistakes," and I had put down my dear friend of more than fourteen years, my sweet dog, Nina.

Now, I manage an office. I successfully passed all four of the State Life and Health Insurance exams—which most people fail one or more times. My mom and I are best friends! I am at peace with myself while learning about the trials of head injuries and their impact on people's lives.

It is amazing when everything falls into place once you are back on the track you started. I believe there is a place in you that can overcome obstacles you cannot see past. There is hope; there is a promise. It might take some time, but you will get there.

I sure did.

~Susie Dinsmore

29

Never Lose Hope

The only disability in life is a bad attitude.
~Scott Hamilton

From a young age, I was intelligent and athletic and lived a pretty easy life, with my future full of trophies and awards. I met my true destiny at the age of thirteen as I lay on a soccer field, clinging desperately to my last shards of consciousness. Finally, I let go and tumbled into a world of darkness, leaving behind pandemonium as people struggled to help an unconscious girl who, just hours ago, had been perfectly healthy. Maybe if someone had warned me how drastically this was going to change my life I would've clung to my consciousness and made a miraculous recovery.

Three months later I was still spending most of my time in bed. I was in eighth grade at the time, and still had not returned to school. Most of my friends had become distant and doctors did not know what was wrong with me. Every day became more and more frustrating.

Eventually I returned to school on a part-time basis. Instead of getting the sympathy I expected, I received dirty looks and harsh rumors about how it was "all in my head." Things that were once easy for me became extremely difficult or altogether impossible. I could never concentrate on my schoolwork and the sports I'd once excelled at were completely out of the picture.

Somehow, I made it through the year and moved on to high school. Since my dreams of being a soccer and cross country star were ruined, I joined the drumline instead. I passed out at nearly every band practice and people were constantly complaining about always having to take care of me. Some people even tried to get me kicked off drumline. Luckily the band director stuck by my side. I think she knew how desperately I needed somewhere to belong. Still, I continued to be bullied and labeled as an "attention-seeker." I was even abandoned by the few friends I had left.

As I struggled through my health problems and loneliness I kept promising myself that things would get better, and eventually they did. I made friends with a few members of the drumline and even developed a crush on one of them. In my PE class I met a few nice girls who were on flagline, another section of the band. By the end of the year they convinced me to try out for flagline, and I made it! My crush also asked me out.

In my sophomore year, things began looking up. Most of the flagline girls understood that my sickness was real and they took good care of me whenever I passed out. My new boyfriend also helped care for me. Finally, I had an understanding group of friends and a boyfriend who loved and supported me through everything. Unfortunately, my struggle still wasn't over. In October, my health began deteriorating and I developed severe throat pain and lost my voice. Once again, I spent most of my time in bed and couldn't attend school, but this time I had friends to help me through it. In December, I still wasn't better and my doctor decided to send me to the Mayo Clinic in Minnesota in hopes that the doctors there would be able to solve the case that had puzzled every other doctor I'd seen.

After a week of testing, the Mayo doctors diagnosed me with a problem called POTS, postural orthostatic tachycardia syndrome. They were certain that the fatigue, headaches, passing out, brain fog (trouble concentrating), and other problems I'd been suffering from were not "in my head" and that I'd outgrow the sickness within a few years. They also determined that my throat pain and voice problem were caused by an inflamed nerve, which could be treated with medication.

It has been three months since my return from Mayo and my voice has made a full recovery. Although I still suffer from the many painful symptoms of POTS, I am extremely grateful to finally have a name for my illness. If it hadn't been for my family's perseverance in finding a doctor who could diagnose me, I'd still be wondering if my problem really was "in my head."

In the end, I'm glad that no one warned me what would happen if I let go of my consciousness. I may have lost the easy life of trophies and popularity that I used to have but right now I'm still happier than I've ever been before. I have new friends and an amazing boyfriend whom I never would have met if I hadn't been forced to quit sports and join band instead. I understand now that no one can be perfect, no matter how hard they try, and that strength isn't measured by how far we can run or how many pounds we can lift but instead by how we handle ourselves in the face of adversity. And, most importantly, I've learned to never lose hope because perseverance can get you through any situation, no matter how impossible it may seem.

~Carly Collins, age 15

Standard of Care

*Use your precious moments to live life fully
every single second of every single day.*
~Marcia Weider

I was lying in a hospital isolation room on a morphine pump—blood transfusions in one arm, a chemotherapy infusion in the other, and my insides packed up with long, burning radioactive rods. My vomiting had become so violent that I had filled up every container in the room. I called to the nurse for anything else to throw up in. She replied, "It's such a pain to come into your room."

Having stage III-B cervical cancer wasn't my fault, not that cancer ever really is anyone's "fault." Before I was diagnosed, I was a healthy, non-smoking registered dietitian, married to a pulmonary specialist. Being in the health care industry, I was especially diligent about my yearly pap smears, labs and everything else tagged as "preventative." But it wasn't enough. Somehow my pap smears hadn't been properly read—five times in a row.

My story begins in June 2002. I was happily breastfeeding my first baby and heading for my initial postpartum checkup. I had been seeing the same doctor for four years and completely trusted his care. For the first time in my life, the doctor called to let me know that my pap from my last checkup had come back abnormal, not to worry, that I should be re-tested. What I *wasn't* told was that the note on the lab report also read, "Cannot rule out serious lesion."

I followed instructions and had another pap. The doctor said that the results were perfectly normal; there were no cancerous cells. What I *wasn't* told was that my test was positive for a sexually transmitted disease. Having only been with my husband for the past eleven years, this information would have certainly raised my eyebrows. At the very least, if somehow I did have this disease, the "standard of care" would dictate treatment with antibiotics. Instead, hearing the words "normal pap" over the telephone, I breathed a sigh of relief and went on with my life.

In November, I became pregnant again and went to the doctor for my first trimester visit. I asked if I needed another pap along with the slew of standard first trimester tests, but the nurse said no, since there was a normal pap a few months earlier.

Around Christmas, I began experiencing lower back pain. By early February, it was excruciating, but my doctor could find no cause. I began making the rounds to all kinds of specialists from neurologists to orthopedists, but there seemed to be no justification for my suffering. The implication from the medical world was that I was an emotional, drug-seeking pregnant woman with a low threshold for pain. I was even referred to a therapist to help me "cope."

By the end of my second trimester, the pain had become so agonizing that I went on disability. I was seeing a pain management doctor who was trying to manage my pain with Class B narcotics, which barely took the edge off and mainly left me feeling "dopey." When I went for my twenty-six-week ultrasound, the doctor who performed it took one look at me and said, "Something is seriously wrong with you." This doctor had known me for many years, and just hearing him acknowledge that I wasn't out of my mind gave me vindication. He immediately ordered an MRI of my back, but the scan stopped above my cervix and did not image my pelvic area. Nothing abnormal was found.

By Mother's Day weekend, I was literally watching the clock to see when I could have my next round of medication. The baby wasn't due until July 23rd, and I didn't know how I could possibly endure that long. On May 14th I couldn't take it anymore. I was admitted to the hospital and learned that I was in pre-term labor. I was given medication to stop the contractions and hooked up to a morphine pump. The nurses rolled their eyes at me, believing that I was just some drug-seeking, crazy pregnant woman. From their perspective, there was no real reason for my suffering.

Five weeks into my hospital stay, at thirty-four weeks gestation, I went into labor again and had a C-Section. I was thanking God when my daughter Madeline was miraculously born healthy, but the pain was still there. About four weeks postpartum, I was still bleeding bright red blood. My doctor said this was "normal" after a C-section, but when he finally saw me in his office, he couldn't stop the bleeding. I had an emergency D&C and was hospitalized, this time for multiple blood transfusions. Finally, the bleeding abated and I was sent home.

Two weeks later, I was leaving for my post-surgical checkup with my OB-GYN when the phone rang. It was the office of an oncologist, whom I had never heard of or spoken to, calling me to schedule an appointment. When I asked the reason for calling, the voice on the other end replied, "Oh, you mean you don't know? You have Stage III-B cervical cancer."

The treatment was aggressive — eight cycles of chemotherapy, six weeks of external radiation, and the internal radiation described earlier. That procedure had to be repeated twice and was the worst experience of my life. When the doctor removed the internal packing at my bedside, I felt completely violated, as though my insides were being ripped out.

This treatment permanently damaged every private part of my body. As a result, I not only lost a kidney and needed a colostomy, but I now live with ongoing pain from the radiation damage.

After this horrific experience, my best friend prodded me to find out exactly what had been written on my "one" abnormal pap smear from the year before. To my amazement, my doctor's office refused to release my records. The medical assistant in my office requested my results from the lab and got a printout of all my pap reports from the past five years. My husband and I gave everything to a medical malpractice attorney who gathered all my records and sent them to the Director of Cervical Cancer at John Hopkins Medical Center.

The findings revealed that five of my paps had been misread beginning from 1998 through 2002. The first three had shown small, progressive changes, the fourth had indicated the need for a biopsy as the "standard of care" and the fifth turned out to not be my slide—the lab had actually mixed up my pap with someone else who had a sexually transmitted disease. It was also clear on my chart that my doctor had "doctored' his own comments to cover his tracks. There was no addendum, nothing official—just some scrawled writing circling his signature, stating that "patient refused biopsy." I was never told I needed one.

We filed a lawsuit—not for the money, but because someone needed to be accountable. We had to prevent this travesty from happening to anyone else. With our lawyer, we agreed to a very small settlement if I would get lifetime medical insurance, and the world-renowned hospital that was responsible would run a full page ad in the *Los Angeles Times* that said "if you had a pap smear between such and such dates you should have a follow-up pap smear because your results could be wrong." They refused, and we went to court. After a three-week trial, I was awarded millions of dollars for my pain and suffering. I would never collect most of my award because in the state of California, medical malpractice cases are capped at $250,000. It didn't matter; the trial served a much bigger, more important purpose for me—it was my therapy. I had tried for so long to be heard, to have someone believe me that something was wrong. Now, the truth had finally come out.

What I learned from my ordeal is that we must be our own advocates by taking health care into our own hands. I was no different than anyone else before I got sick. In fact, I even thought I had better medical care because I am married to a wonderful, caring doctor, and I am in the health care industry. Being your own advocate means not just calling for your test results, it means insisting on *seeing* your results and keeping a copy of all your own records. And, because women can be looked upon as being emotional, advocating also means paying attention to your instincts, no matter what you are told.

Finally, there is no single definition for the "standard of

care"—doctors are human, and capable of human error. They are also trained to treat disease; not necessarily to be proactive. That is *our* job.

Seven years have passed, and no one ever expressed sorrow or remorse for what happened to me—not the doctor, the lab or the hospital. But, I can honestly say that I no longer focus on my experience or the physical challenges with which I live. My experience gave me new insight into the miracle of simply being alive. I choose to share my message while devoting my life to my family and work. I am truly blessed with an amazing mother and the most loving and supportive husband that anyone could ask for. And, when I gaze into the eyes of my two incredible daughters, I only feel pure love and gratitude. Madeline and Gabrielle, this story is also for you. When you grow up, you will know that it was both of you and your father that gave me the strength to go on.

I completely love and embrace all aspects of my life, and I count my blessings for each precious day.

~Meg Werner Moreta

The Gift of Life

Life is what we make it,
always has been,
always will be.
~Grandma Moses

As I sat in a clinic room with my dad, the physician's assistant held a book open to a picture of the brain. Slowly, he explained I had an unidentifiable mass in my brain causing a condition known as hydrocephalus, or "water on the brain."

This mass appeared to be in the center of my brain and blocking the passageway where fluid should naturally drain. It caused my brain to swell, and, if left untreated, would cause death. For the past eight months, it had caused vomiting, unbearable headaches and enlarged pupils.

I would have to go to Duke University Hospital in Durham, North Carolina, tomorrow morning to see a brain tumor specialist.

The PA walked out, leaving my dad and me alone in the exam room. My initial thought was, "This guy is nuts!" But when I looked at my dad to confirm my impression, he was crying. I had seen my dad cry only twice before—once when my cousin Linda died, and once when he was watching a television show where a soldier from Vietnam was being buried.

The PA re-entered the exam room and handed my dad the manila envelope which contained my CT scans and other important paperwork.

As we walked out through the sliding glass doors, I kept quiet.

Dad seemed very upset and was doing everything he could to choke back tears. When we got into his truck, he picked up his cell phone to call my mom.

She wanted to know what on earth we had been doing because the CT scan was only supposed to take thirty minutes and we had been gone for hours. Dad told her the news was not good, but he would tell her everything shortly.

When we got home, I stepped slowly out of the truck and shut the heavy door gently. Dad grabbed the food he had gotten us for dinner and slammed the door on his side.

Inside, Mom was standing by the kitchen table. She hurried over and gave me a big hug. She held me for a minute or more, and I had no idea what to say.

I went to bed convinced an MRI at Duke would prove the PA wrong and I could go back to life the way I remembered it before the headaches. When my alarm sounded the next morning, I yearned to go back to sleep, but I slowly dragged myself out of bed and shut it off. I rifled through my chest of drawers, pulled some clothes out, and put them on.

I trudged down the steps and into the kitchen, where Mom and Dad were already dressed and waiting. The three of us went out to Mom's van and started the trip to Duke.

As I sat in the backseat, the van seemed to creep along, making the sixty-minute trip seem to last for days. My MRI was scheduled for 7:30 that morning, and I had to be there thirty minutes early to sign in.

When we finally arrived, I was anxious to get it over with. I figured the quicker I had the MRI, the faster they would find nothing was really wrong with me and I could go home.

Unfortunately, things did not quite work out that way. The MRI confirmed that the PA was right. There was a mass in my brain. It was a tumor big enough to cause swelling so severe that the neurologist on call said she had no idea how I was still alive, much less still conscious.

Six hours of brain surgery would be required to remove this

tumor. The neurologists debated whether to send me for emergency surgery or wait until the next morning. Finally, after lying on a gurney in the emergency room for fourteen hours, they decided I could wait until the next morning.

The smell of bacon woke me the following day. I knew I wasn't allowed to eat anything before surgery, but my stomach rumbled and I longed for something to eat. A nurse came in and told me that my neurologist had been called into emergency surgery and my surgery would be delayed. Two hours after that, the same nurse came back to tell me that yet another emergency surgery had come in and my neurologist would have to perform that operation before mine.

About lunch time, the shift changed and a different nurse came in and asked if I was ready. Considering that I never had any kind of surgery before, much less brain surgery, I was anything but ready. But I nodded. Several more nurses came in, raised my bed, unlocked it, turned it, and began to wheel me down the hall.

My mom walked along beside me, and I stared up at the ceiling wondering if Dad would make it to the hospital in time. He had gone home the night before to be with my younger brother, and I wanted to see him one last time before I went under.

Minutes before they took me into the operating room, Dad came running through the doors. I hugged both my parents the best I could, and then took a deep breath as the anesthesiologist wheeled me away.

Complications arose during my surgery. My neurologist told my parents the tumor was cancerous and it went deeper into my brain than he felt he could safely go. He didn't think I would ever wake up again. If I did wake from the surgery, the odds were not good. I would most likely be a vegetable for the rest of my life. For a week or so, it seemed as if initial predictions were going to come true.

When I finally did wake, I could not speak or really move. I could hear things perfectly—everything the doctors said around me, I could hear and I wanted to scream, "No! I'm here!" But I just couldn't.

The neurologist and other surgeons who performed my operation had no explanation as to why I couldn't speak, except that "A" and "B" in my brain had not reconnected properly. They even weren't entirely sure why I was still alive.

I had three more surgeries in the following three and a half weeks, and forty-four radiation treatments over an eight and a half week period.

Slowly, one word at the time, I did gain the ability to talk again. Countless hours of rehab taught me to sit, stand, and walk by myself.

It's six years later, and I'm now a student at a small southern college. While I do still have scar tissue where my tumor was, my cancer is in remission and I've recently decided to major in writing. Perhaps that time of speechlessness taught me the value of words. In fact, having cancer taught me quite a lot. Not the least of which is to be grateful for what I have. If I rush through life, I will miss all of the wonders given back to me.

It was one very important lesson for a sick fourteen-year-old to learn.

~Ashley Young, age 21

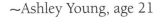

Count Your Blessings

Silver Linings

Was I deceived, or did a sable cloud
Turn forth her silver lining on the night?

~John Milton

The Unexpected Detour

*Nearly all the best things that came to me in life
have been unexpected, unplanned by me.*
~Carl Sandburg

On a warm June evening my husband and I, along with our little daughter, headed down the interstate in a worn-out van, pulling a pop-up camper behind us. It had been a long day, and we were anxious to reach our vacation destination in the Great Smoky Mountains. Just a couple more hours and we'd be in Chattanooga, where we planned to camp for the night, then head to Pigeon Forge the next morning.

Suddenly, my husband said, "You smell something?" He stared into the rear-view mirror, perplexed.

The tone of the question unsettled me. I sniffed, but didn't smell a thing.

"Smells like something's burning," he said. "I think we have a serious problem."

At the next rest area, Stan pulled out his tools and commenced diagnosing the problem. My daughter and I spread a quilt under a tree, where I quickly sank down with my misery.

"It's always something," I muttered under my breath. "Always something."

If only my husband had listened to me, we wouldn't be in this predicament. When the idea of a vacation first came up, I expressed deep concerns over taking such a long trip in a van with 200,000 miles under its hood. But, being the eternal optimist that he is, my husband's faith proved stronger than my doubts. And now, here we sat on the side of the road, a sad little bunch. So much for optimism.

Before long, Stan rounded the corner and gave the disturbing report. There was definitely an oil leak. A bad one, from all indications, but if we drove slowly and stopped to add oil every few miles, we should make it to the next town. We would spend the night there, then look for an auto shop tomorrow.

Heaving a sigh of surrender, I folded the quilt and crawled back into the van.

For what seemed like hours, we crept along the freeway in silence, stopping often to add oil. My mood plummeted with each miserable mile.

As darkness gathered at the windows, we came upon a place called Noccalula Falls Park and Campground, just outside Gadsden, Alabama. We registered at the office, set up camp, and fell into bed, exhausted.

In the morning, I rose to the wonderful smell of breakfast cooking. Peeking through the canvas flap, I saw my husband frying bacon in a skillet, four round eggs beside him.

I cracked the door an inch. "Whatcha doing?"

He smiled. "Making the best of a bad situation. Let's eat."

My amazing husband. Always rolling with the punches.

Over breakfast, Stan handed me some brochures. "I got these from the office," he said. "Looks like a neat place."

Still depressed, I nodded but wasn't interested.

"What I thought I would do," he said, "is take the van to the local dealership and see what the problem is. You know how that goes; I may be gone all day. But maybe we can do some sightseeing tomorrow."

I didn't say anything, but if I had, it would have been, "Have you lost your mind?" Sightseeing? It was the last thing I was in the mood to do, but I kept quiet.

We finished eating and I watched Mr. Optimistic drive off at a snail's pace, a trail of gray smoke following him.

How could he always take such things in stride? He really expected to enjoy our visit to this unexpected town. I, on the other hand, had no such intentions.

"Mom," my little daughter's sweet voice interrupted my dismal thoughts. "Can we go to the pool?"

"Sure, sweetie," I said, forcing a smile. "I'm right behind you." I could see the local paper's headline now: Distraught woman drowns herself in campsite pool.

Just about dusk, my husband drove up in a rental car. From the way he clumped into the camper, I knew it was bad news.

And it was. After a full day of waiting for a diagnosis, another full day was needed for repairs. The cost proved staggering. We discussed our payment options. None brought relief. Later, I climbed into bed, certain that this whole trip had been one giant mistake.

The next morning, despite my lingering gloom, we set out on a sightseeing excursion, trying not to think about why we were here. We discovered that Noccalula Falls Park and Campground, lying at the foot of the Appalachian Mountains, is both large and enchanting. A place of unspoiled natural beauty.

Not far from our campsite, we followed a sunny path to a stone monument of Noccalula, an Indian princess, poised as if about to jump from a ninety-foot cliff. Cold water swirled around her feet and rushed over the ridge, creating a spectacular waterfall.

Legend has it that Noccalula's father promised his daughter's hand in marriage to a member of an enemy tribe, in an effort to obtain peace. But the Indian maiden was in love with a man from her own tribe. Seeing no happy ending, she is said to have jumped to her death from this very cliff on the day she was to be married.

A few feet away, we took steep steps down into the cool gorge below the falls. As we navigated the slippery trail, I paused in a mossy clearing and looked up.

Out of the frothy spray of the waterfall, giant cedars and evergreens rose up like fluted columns and, overhead, yellow sunlight winked through a canopy of leafy branches. "Beautiful, isn't it?" Stan said.

"Yes," I said, suddenly mesmerized. "It is absolutely gorgeous."

After lunch, we hiked along a narrow trail that curved around magnificent pines, winding its way to the top of a straw-covered hill. Looking down to the valley below, I was captivated by the sight. Summer's sun lay in golden ribbons along the newly mown grass. Off in the distance, a cluster of children skipped among the shadows, their laughter rising and falling. The air was alive with the smells and sounds of summer. Breathing deeply, I sensed a lightness of heart, as if this were the place I should be.

As we gathered for supper that evening, we couldn't stop talking about the enjoyable day we had spent together, and the spectacular beauty that was ours for the taking. Had our trip stayed on course, we never would have seen this delightful place.

Noccalula Falls remains one of our all-time favorite places, and it was there I learned a valuable lesson: No matter where the road may take me, I won't let an unexpected detour spoil the day. Instead, I will follow its impulsive path to the sunlight and shadows just waiting to be discovered in serendipitous places.

~Dayle Allen Shockley

33

The Comfortable Living Checklist

Don't confuse having a career with having a life.
~Hillary Clinton

I found myself sailing through the economic crisis. Of course, I couldn't ignore the bad news shouting at me from every front, but on my front things were pretty comfortable. I was young, but I owned my home, and had a good job and no additional debt.

I must credit my parents with any monetary common sense I might have. If left to my own devices, I would have never understood the value of being debt-free over owning Louis Vuitton luggage, which I would most likely never use.

One beautiful day, I showed up for work, where I had just been promoted. I was right in the middle of training a new girl, when my boss asked to talk to me for a second. After that conversation, you can effectively cross "had a good job" off my comfortable living checklist. No warning. In fact, just the month before I had received my fifth Employee of the Month award. I was speechless and so was everyone else. Seven of us were cut from my department that day. Later, I would discover that there were thousands of cuts company-wide. I worked at a bank. A failing one.

For a week solid, I lay in bed. Blinds closed. Sweatpants on. I'm not even sure if I showered. I watched every movie I owned. Twice. My other recently unemployed and un-showered friends would come over and we'd lie in bed together, while eating chocolate and Doritos.

They were the only two things we could easily consume without exerting any effort. One week turned into a month. The depression that overcame me wasn't merely because of money, although as a single homeowner that was a concern. My depression was a combination of many different things.

When something like this happens to you, it's natural to ask why. I reviewed all my work accomplishments. I thought about how I had been a top performer every month since I had been hired and about how they gave me the highest rating of anyone on my review. What had I done wrong? What could I have done better? I had no performance problems, no warnings, and worst of all no clue.

The problem with this kind of worrying and speculation is that it will drive you mad. The truth is that sometimes we search for a logical explanation in a situation that can't be understood. The only way to move past it is to have confidence in the job you did as an employee and understand that you are a victim of an unfortunate circumstance. It doesn't make you any less of a person or undeserving of another job. It's a chapter closed and you must begin to write a new one.

Speaking of writing, with all of the extra time on my hands, I reunited with the long lost love of my life: writing. It has been the only thing I have loved to do for as long as I can remember. Unfortunately, we always tend to make time for everything except what we love. Funny how that works. Truth be told, I had hated my previous job. It stifled every bit of my creativity and left me mentally exhausted at the end of the day. Now that my mind was free from stress, I had so many creative ideas I couldn't even keep up with them.

I decided to pursue writing as an actual job, given the fact that finding employment in Illinois was pretty futile. I designed a website and applied for writing jobs. I started getting more and more clients. It occurred to me that with some hard work I might be able to make a living doing what I love. What in the world? Who does that? So there I was, three months after the sky caved in, thinking about how incredibly blessed I was. And how this never would have happened had I not lost my job.

I've learned two very important things from this bump in the road. The first thing is that all of the material stuff people go into debt for isn't worth a fraction of the peace of mind I feel at night, when my head hits the pillow and I know I'm debt-free. My car may very well have a piece of duct tape on the hood, but no one is going to take it away from me because I can't make my payment. The second thing I learned is that the old adage "everything happens for a reason" is true, even though we rarely believe this or get to see evidence of it. But it is true. And sometimes we get to see it.

~Britteny Elrick

34

A Tree Fell Through It

From a fallen tree, all make kindling.
~Spanish proverb

Brushing my teeth, I heard the scratching of what sounded like branches tickling the roof. I paused, wondering what it could be, given that no trees were close to our house. I attributed the sound to a stray branch that must have been flung onto our roof by Hurricane Isabel, which was blowing her way through our city in September 2003. Being pretty far inland, we were not too alarmed by this display of nature's fury.

Then I heard the faint sound of breaking glass. A split second later, the entire house shook. My husband and I stared at each other in frozen horror before bolting to check on our baby daughter asleep in her crib across the hall. The sound had jolted her awake—never had a cry sounded so sweet—and my husband gratefully snatched her up and darted back to the relative safety of our room.

Peeking down the darkened hallway, we could see remnants of our attic lying on the floor of our living room. After grabbing a few essentials, my husband ventured out, flipping on the hall light. We picked our way out of the house and into the still-raging hurricane.

My husband started the car while I hurried across the street to let a neighbor know we were okay and heading to a friend's home. Shaking but grateful to be alive, we drove away, skirting fallen trees and downed power lines.

The next morning, bright sunlight starkly displayed the storm's destruction. We returned home to see that a giant tulip poplar tree in the center of our yard had effectively split our house in two, crashing through our kitchen window with its long branches extending over the front of our house.

We had hoped to go inside to check on our cats, one of whom I had seen in the kitchen just moments before the tree fell, but we were uncertain of the house's stability. As we stood on the sidewalk gaping at the damage and wondering what to do, a local fire truck pulled up. The firefighters had heard about our house and informed us, with a note of awe, that our home had received the worst damage in the city. They volunteered to go inside to check for our cats, and we were thrilled when both felines were found unharmed, although plenty scared.

In the days and weeks that followed, we remembered the feeling of relief when we realized that everyone in our lives who mattered was unscathed—me, my husband, our daughter and even our two pets. We clung to that memory as we navigated the long and sometimes exhausting road to recovery.

Family, friends and neighbors—most of whom we hadn't yet met given that we had moved in only six months earlier—expressed amazement at our calmness throughout the ordeal. Words cannot fully express how utterly grateful we were to God that He had spared our lives. Yes, we lost many things: books, toys, furniture, dishes, computers, and a fridge and freezer full of food. But those things were replaceable. Our home was rebuilt better than before—and I even had the chance to make a few improvements during the reconstruction.

The damage inflicted by Hurricane Isabel—the costliest and deadliest hurricane in the 2003 Atlantic season—was temporary, but the opportunity to witness God's goodness in the midst of our trial is something we still cherish. When we meet neighbors for the first time, their eyes pop when they realize we live in "the house the tree fell through."

Every so often we pull out the photos of the tree's destruction and marvel at how blessed we were—and still are. Whenever we begin to feel ungrateful or unsatisfied with what we have, those photos and memories offer a reminder of how we came through that trial. Especially during this time of economic uncertainty, reflecting on our close call with that tree makes us all the more thankful for our lives and for the things that matter most.

~Sarah Hamaker

35

The Light at the End of the Tunnel

Sometimes that light at the end of the tunnel is a train.
~Charles Barkley

It came out of nowhere.

Barreling down the tracks with a will of its own, the unemployment train burst upon us with no warning.

"Honey, I just heard that Bill's shutting down the company on Friday."

It was Wednesday, July 5th. My husband and I had returned from a two-week vacation to Alaska on July 3rd. We'd timed the trip so we'd have the Fourth of July as a free day to recuperate from the time change and travel before he went to work.

This, however, had not been in our plans.

My heart dropped so far and so fast, it was a wonder I had enough blood flowing through my veins to hold me up. Joe was fifty-nine. Not a good age to lose a job, as he was ineligible for Medicare or Social Security. Since he'd suffered a minor stroke a few months before losing his job, we couldn't take a chance and go without health insurance.

I swallowed hard and attempted to provide the reassurance I knew my husband desperately needed to hear. "It will be all right. We have savings."

"Right."

Joe's effort to remain calm brought a quick smile as I hung up the phone. My husband's sense of humor and calm, steady, get-it-done attitude were among the many reasons I loved him. With thirty-four years of marriage under our belts, we complement each other. He sees most glasses half full. I see them half empty. That combination leaves us based in reality but willing to take chances—which makes for a healthy and always interesting partnership.

As the months of unemployment went by and our money dwindled, we each contributed in our own way.

I clipped coupons, followed sales, and learned all about cost-cutting. I found a local college that offered dental cleanings for a nominal fee, as a way to teach students. I also found other schools that offered everything from low-cost bakery items to haircuts. The library became our main source of entertainment, with books, DVDs, and a host of newspapers and other material related to job offerings. Joe became "Monsieur Joseph" and colored my hair.

To keep busy, we began housecleaning—sorting items we no longer needed into a pile and boxing them for a future yard sale. To stay active, we took walks. We played cards and games at night for fun. During nice weather, we often sat outside around dusk to listen to the birds. We even got up in the middle of the night to watch a meteor shower—something we couldn't have done when Joe was working.

Despite these measures, as our savings dwindled I grew more afraid. The cost for our health care was close to a thousand dollars a month. Joe was a disabled veteran with a bad back, so jobs requiring a lot of lifting or standing for long periods of time were out. And, as Joe worked in a dying industry (printing), jobs were scarce. When he did get an interview for an entry-level job, he was turned aside because hiring someone with his experience made most executives uncomfortable.

Never one to give up, Joe filled out any and all applications he could find.

We both depended on our faith in God to sustain us, but sometimes we wondered why he'd allowed this particular express train to hound us!

Nine months later, we received a call from the wife of a former minister we hadn't seen in years.

"I have an application on my desk. Is your husband looking for a job by any chance?"

As much as those words sounded like music to my ears, I knew the large home improvement store where she worked would turn down Joe with his medical problems.

"Yes, he is."

For a brief second, I thought about "forgetting" to mention his health situation, but I couldn't. We'd both been raised to stand behind our word and be honest.

"You do know he has a ten percent disability from the service and can't lift a lot," I said.

"That's okay. I know his character and his work ethic. Tell him to come in and take the pre-employment tests. If he passes, I think we have the perfect job for him."

Joe got the job (which didn't require as much standing and lifting) and is working there still.

Looking back now, the unemployment train we were sure would do us in actually taught us more than we could have imagined.

That speeding bullet just may have saved us.

My husband earns far less money now, but he has a ten-minute commute in light traffic. He earns far less money, but his stress level isn't as great, and we don't take our time or money for granted as much now.

The first February Joe was out of work, he painted me a Valentine's Day card and added a heartfelt sentiment. He didn't have the money to buy a traditional store greeting card, but love doesn't need expensive offerings.

No card has ever meant more to me.

This downward turn made us remember that the best things in life really are free.

It's been said the light at the end of the tunnel may be a train coming for you.

I agree.

But I think you have two choices when the unemployment train comes at you—you can allow it to run over you or you can grab hold and decide you are going to make the best of the ride and see where that metal monster takes you.

~Michele H. Lacina

36

Hurricane Rita and Her Silver Lining

A crisis is an opportunity riding the dangerous wind.
~Chinese proverb

I t was Thursday, September 22nd, and Rita had been upgraded to a Category 5 hurricane and was headed directly for Houston! My husband and I knew we needed to get out of town.

We had a full tank of gas, a cooler filled with water and food, a few suitcases, a Bible and reservations at a hotel in Kerrville — just a four-and-a-half-hour drive away. Panic was settling in and gasoline and water were running out quickly. It was time to go!

We left at noon but we weren't the only ones desperate to get out of town; the roads quickly became clogged with traffic. It was suggested on the radio to drive as long as we could with no air conditioning in order to conserve gas. Unfortunately, it was 107 degrees when we left. We talked about taking the chance and running the A/C. We began to pray.

We prayed for safety and protection, and for courage and strength. We even prayed for our tank of gas and we carefully monitored the needle on the gas gauge. Surprisingly, when it reached the point of being half empty it didn't move again for a very long time. In fact, our single tank of gas lasted twelve hours, during which we drove just under one hundred miles from Tomball to Giddings and watched in horror as numerous cars pulled off the road from being overheated or from running out of gasoline. There were hundreds of vehicles lined up on both sides of Highway 290. We passed gas station after gas station, all with no gas to purchase.

After finally fueling up in Giddings, we reached Kerrville some seventeen hours after our trip had begun. However, the adventure continued. The hotel where we had reservations sold our pre-paid rooms out from under us and we couldn't find a hotel within 200 miles that had any vacancy. With the increasing number of people evacuating Houston, all they could do was refer us to the Red Cross.

We weren't sure what to do, and so we decided to head home and try to make it back before Rita hit Houston. At a minimum, we could return to Brenham and stay at a shelter there for the night. After all, we saw nearly twenty National Guard trucks arrive as we were pulling out of town earlier that day. Surely, they were pitching tents and setting up shelter for those in need.

Well, God had other plans, and it didn't take long before we were referred to a friend of a friend who had a house in Kerrville. Once again, we weren't alone. There was a family that had traveled up from Baytown. Robert and Debi had with them their two grandsons and four dogs. They too had evacuated Houston because of the hurricane, and they too had no place to stay. Our "friends of friends" opened their home to me and my husband and to our new friends and their four dogs.

Not only were Jerri and Bill gracious hosts, they also ran a beautiful bed and breakfast out of their home and they gave us Victorian-decorated rooms with all the comforts of a grand hotel. We spent the next two days together in our place of refuge, enjoying the safety provided us, delighting in the plentiful food and drink, and learning about the lives of our new friends. Those were two very special days, and it was then we learned that even hurricanes have silver linings.

Sunday, my husband and I returned to Houston where we discovered that our home and belongings were intact. We hugged each other in tears and shared our thanksgiving.

~Kristen Clark

37

Bank-Owned Happiness

If you count all your assets, you always show a profit.
~Robert Quillen

The recession has had the oddest effect on me. It's made me happier. I know how strange that sounds, especially in light of the fact that we are losing our house, our earning power has dwindled and last week the IRS wiped out our checking and savings accounts. The bank charged us extra for the privilege of accommodating the government, so we were minus $100. After the initial shock, my husband and I started brainstorming ways to pull out of the quagmire.

Remember the show *Boston Legal*? At the end of each episode Denny Crane and Alan Shore would sit outside on the balcony with their scotch and cigars and talk to each other, eventually professing their love. One evening my husband, calling me by the name "Alan," asked me to meet him outside. He said something about having a Denny Crane moment. He led me to our little backyard. There he had a fire going in the outdoor pit, and on the patio table were two tablets with pens perched on top, next to two glasses of wine. At his suggestion, we began to write down all the possible resources to get money. And like David E. Kelley might have written, we also professed our love to each other. Then we talked about all the wealth we do have—wonderful kids, loving friends, a sense of humor, talents, dreams and goals. Do you know how easy it is to fall into depression without a dream or a goal? We even have great furniture that will look fabulous in a tiny apartment.

Last Valentine's Day he brought me a bouquet of rosemary for our front yard and told me to pretend they were flowers. I didn't have to. I was deeply touched—more so than if they had been a dozen American Beauties.

Before our financial downfall we were on autopilot. He was doing his thing and I was doing mine. Gary Neuman, on an *Oprah* segment, once said that the average couple talks to one another around twelve minutes a day. I think we were average. Now we are facing our challenge as a team and we talk several times a day and call each other when we make some money. We high-five each other and find ourselves cheering when one of us even earns so much as twenty dollars. We laugh often and hug even more.

We weren't indignant that the taxman came. We owed it. When the economy started slipping, so did our monthly income. We just couldn't find enough to pay it.

We didn't hide our financial loss, either. It is what it is. Our friends and family helped find us find work, our daughter decided it was time to pay her own rent and our son told me that he wanted to give us his whole paycheck. I was looking through my appointment book the other day and found five twenties secretly stuffed in there by a dear girlfriend. That was the perfect amount to give the bank for letting the IRS clean us out. Our blessings are abundant.

The day I was able to release both my fear of losing our house, and pending shame, came a year ago when I could not make the full mortgage payment. Months of torment had been affecting my psyche. I had been stressing, not sleeping well at night, needing instead to sleep away the empty day. One afternoon, as I was grinding my teeth, I confronted myself about the situation. I asked the all-time stress-releaser, "What's the worst thing that could happen if I can't pay the mortgage?" The only answer I could come up with was, "We would have to rent."

Rent? That's it? We have no equity now. Aren't we already renting in a way? Is it so horrible to rent? Perhaps being a homeowner for the last thirty years may have caused me to develop some kind of negative feeling about renting, but honestly, is it really that bad? Are my children happy and healthy? Yes. Do I love them dearly and do I also feel the love and appreciation bounce right back at me? You bet. Then, if I must rent, why not rent nearer to the people I love so deeply? Why is it I still live 400 miles south of where they are, anyway? I didn't have a salient answer.

At that moment I began to get excited. I went on craigslist to see what rentals were going for in their area. For what we would need, a little house with a yard near my kids came to one-third of our mortgage payment. I began imagining myself in my new lifestyle and then I started doing all the preparations to make it a reality. With each day that has gone by since I let go of my fear, I have grown more and more eager to start my new life. I wait with anticipation that we may receive our foreclosure notice, only to be disappointed day after day. The banks are so confused. There are already 764 bank-owned and foreclosed places in my small zip code. I must be patient. But it's hard. I may be the only American who's looking forward to foreclosure. That's only because I let go of the past and figured out a brighter future.

I do not feel a lick of shame from this turn of events. I am just one of millions struggling to get by. It's temporary. Our lives are changing whether or not we like it—so we might as well find a way to like it. I count my blessings regularly, including the fact that I am able to see the glass half full.

So, now, rather than looking at this huge financial loss as a disaster, we are using different language. We're talking about a fresh start, not starting over. I feel like we're moving toward something, rather than away from disaster. My husband and I are on a mission TOGETHER and we have been shown more love and appreciation than ever. And every night we sit outside and plan our future, profess our love and wait till the bank gets itself organized to take our house away.

~Marilyn Kentz

Carrying On

What seem to us bitter trials are often blessings in disguise.
~Oscar Wilde

Sometimes it can take years to be thankful for a gift when it arrives wrapped in such sorrow. It all began seven years ago on a Thursday in early November under a crisp Colorado blue sky. I remember it was warm enough to run in shorts. As I ran, I wondered why my breasts hurt—late period, hot ears, hot breasts. At forty-five, I was new to menopause. My neighbor said, "Perhaps a pregnancy test would be a good idea."

In the small bathroom next to my psychotherapy office I stared at the two blue lines of a positive pregnancy test. I shook like a teenager in trouble. As I greeted my 9:30 patient I knew I needed a session more than she. Afterwards I called my husband of nineteen years, the father of my three children. "It happened again, could you come down, the baby thing?" It was like a telegram without "Stop" every few words. That was how it all began and I'll always feel it was a ride I never asked to get on or off.

At our doctor's appointment my husband and I sheepishly faced my obstetrician. "At your age miscarriage is very common." The ultrasound showed a flicker, the small heart. "The flicker is good but you never know." Two weeks later we returned. The flicker flicked. It was my husband's forty-sixth birthday. "Happy Birthday Dad," she said, handing him a fuzzy black and white photo.

Telling the children was next. Getting the five of us together on a weekend was not an easy task. My fifteen-year-old had other priorities that didn't include a Saturday night family dinner. Our nine-year-old's mouth stayed open as our twelve-year-old ran crying from the table. "Ever heard of birth control?" I was pulled in many directions that night as ambivalence, excitement, fear, and uncertainty seasoned my chicken and broccoli.

The CVS (chorionic villus sampling) test drew near—a test we had decided on to determine if the baby was healthy. I could only remember the name because of the drugstore chain. I sat in a cold examining room watching the baby frolic on the ultra-sound screen. I was told a large needle would be inserted into my uterus to draw tissue from the placenta. Not to worry—the baby would be fine. The pain felt deep, felt wrong, it was over. They showed me the baby again still swimming softly. "You may have cramps, don't worry. Don't vacuum, fold laundry, or cook for twenty-four hours." They'd call us in two days to let us know if the baby was healthy. Later I wondered if bending over for thirty seconds to vacuum up Christmas tree needles killed my baby.

I was making the kids pancakes when the phone rang. We had a healthy boy! At ten weeks, I flipped the pancakes, exhaled and decided I could survive pre-school once again.

And then it was another Thursday, this time, melting snow marking the end of February. I proudly celebrated the three-month mark, feeling I'd made it to shore and could breathe a little easier. I sat in my doctor's waiting room surrounded by large stomachs. I placed my hands on my small stomach embracing my child, finally willing to do it all again. I carried my baby and freshly baked coffee cake into the doctor thanking her for a healthy child.

She rubbed the clear "gook" on my stomach, positioning the cold doppler so we could hear the heartbeat. Once again I lay peering at the ultrasound screen. I saw nothing but blackness and my doctor's shaking head. I cried and she apologized. He was gone. Tearful nausea filled my emptiness as I fumbled with my drawstring pants. Somehow I moved to a black leather chair in her office holding my knees to my chest, weeping like a lost child, late picking my daughter up from Brownies. My world was small snapshots after that. I drove home conscious of my breathing as if I were in the labor I would never have.

We were instructed to arrive two hours before the necessary D&C procedure. I lay and waited as my husband worked on his laptop. A nurse arrived and introduced herself as my "cocktail waitress" for the evening. She was kind and I cracked a smile as she patted my hand and called me "Dear." I kept talking, kept weeping, telling my "cocktail waitress" how sad I felt. It was over and they all kindly complimented my strength as I kindly thanked them. My husband held my hand as I sipped sweet grape juice. We drove home on a cold night and had to pull over. I threw up beside a stranger's driveway.

As tears welled from my empty womb, loving friends told us to plant a tree, which my husband painstakingly planted in our front yard. I bought a rock that read "Remember" and placed it in our garden. But my healing began only when I told my story on the page. Instead of the cries of a tiny newborn I was listening to my own creative voice. My writing burst forth like a baby's first breath. A tiny soul had delivered me this beautiful gift. I haven't stopped composing since I said goodbye. Our children, even those we never meet, truly are our best teachers. Our miscarriage was not a "miss" but a carriage from the stage of procreation into a new stage of creation. With much gratitude, at age fifty-two my writing blossoms like the beautiful tree planted a few years ago.

~Priscilla Dann-Courtney

The Strings that Pulled Me Through

Happiness is a thing to be practiced, like the violin.
~John Lubbock

The words rang in my ears for days. With her arms around me as I fell apart and my world drowned in black, my surgeon whispered to me, "Leah, thousands of women have been where you are and thought it was the end. They are still here." She was right. Those words didn't mean anything to me then. I only remember I never cried so hard. I couldn't stop.

I was like a zombie. My feet moved, I continued breathing, but I couldn't think. When I saw her face as I walked into her office, I knew immediately it was cancer.

My mother and sister had jumped on a plane to be with me. They tried to distract me with jokes, luncheons, and outings to the movies. Their lightheartedness would make me forget... for awhile, but a lengthy operation involving the removal and reconstruction of my left breast awaited me and I began to wonder what I had done wrong in my life to deserve such a sentence.

The night before my operation, I was quiet on the outside, but inside I was screaming, I was on my knees begging the sun to remain, the night to stay away and the clock to stop ticking the hours away, counting the minutes down to the second I would be wheeled into that operating room. It was then that I came to grips with the possibility of my death.

I had been on the operating table for nearly ten hours and I knew my body would never be the same.

The day came when we all went to the oncologist to talk about the plan for the dreaded chemotherapy. I was prepared to hear that I would have to endure six months, which was the standard treatment at that time. When my doctor informed us I was to have a year of chemotherapy, the nightmare seemed to begin all over again.

My sister, mother and I huddled with our arms around one another, praying for the strength to accept this new sentence. My tears had begun again and the world seemed to go silent.

It was at this time I finally began to see that I had a mental strength, a positive attitude my mother had ingrained in me. My sister reminded me of this. She calmly sat down at a table with a piece of paper and folded it down the middle.

In one column, she explained, were the difficulties I would have to endure. In the second column, all the things I was grateful for. This was a technique my mother (who, ironically, was outside pacing and smoking) had taught us. I always knew what the outcome would be. The column for things I needed to be grateful for: my grown son, my completed education, a supportive family, good insurance coverage, a good job and a difficult divorce behind me, would always outweigh the other. As the year of chemo and radiation jumped out at me, it became clear. I had so much to be thankful for.

If you have never experienced that cold poison introduced into your system, it's very difficult to explain the sensation. I would try to think of other things as I looked away and my doctor would put the needle in me. The feeling was chilling, like ice flowing through you instead of blood. Having been informed it was the strongest kind of chemo at the time, I had prepared myself for the vomiting, the nausea and the sleepless nights hovering over the toilet. I braced myself that day. I had my vomit bag beside me. I was ready. I waited and waited, but the nausea, the vomiting never came... not that day or any other.

Sitting quietly alone in my room one day, I thought about my year off from work and my year of treatment. The way I saw it, I had two ways to look at my situation. It all came down to this: Either I could tell myself that I was losing a year of my life, taken by cancer, or I could tell myself that since I would be at home and undergoing treatment without the reaction to chemo others had, I would actually be given a gift of a year. Then I saw it. Even though it had been leaning against the wall for the past three years gathering dust, there it was... my violin, one I had yet to learn to play. It seemed to scream at me, "Here I am! Look at me!"

It was a gift, given to me for my birthday one year by a good friend. The old violin, in a case nearly as worn, had been restrung and was waiting for me to fulfill a dream I never had time to pursue. For me, the sound of a violin was the closest sound to angels singing. I told myself I would finally be given the time to make mine sing.

I began to pursue this goal in earnest as I signed up for the beginning strings class at the local community college. But the rounded, smooth notes I planned to produce emerged in abrupt, stop and start screeching of unrecognizable "melody."

As I mastered each song, I would go on to other simple songs on my old but angelic instrument, always with the impending orchestra performance a few months away at the forefront of my mind. The role of our beginning strings class was to accompany the more advanced class in the playing of the "William Tell Overture." What a lofty undertaking I had set for myself!

In a few weeks, I knew my hair would begin to fall out. So, I had it shaved off before I could see long strands of hair lying on my pillow. Meanwhile, I would imagine the voice of the violin speaking to me to encourage me to keep practicing, to work to make my dream come true. Soon, those sharp, shrill screeches began to glide into smooth, buttery notes, responding to the touch of my fingers, propelling me forward to reach my goal.

Now, I had something meaningful to do with my fingers, with my mind, something that made my heart soar when I felt the strings vibrate under my fingertips. It was as if they were calling me. After years of silence, the strings awakened my spirit again, the way it had been awakened when I was a child and first learned to play piano and when I was an adolescent and learned to play guitar. The violin, however, was more intense. It was medicine for my soul and spirit, literally counteracting the dark liquid flowing through me. It lightened my fear, replacing it with hope.

A few months later, as I sat in the strings section of the college orchestra, my dream became a reality. Though I was bald under my scratchy wig, it didn't matter. Those angelic chords were being played by me, by my fingers, as I was surrounded by my musician friends. I knew deep inside me that there was a light and an end to this journey. The strings of my violin had pulled me through.

~Leah M. Cano

Hurricane Hummers

Birds sing after a storm; why shouldn't people feel as free to delight in whatever remains to them?
~Rose F. Kennedy

lthough many people envy the residents of sunny Florida, with our almost constant, summertime weather, the fall of 2004 brought nothing but sympathy from our northern friends and relatives.

During a period of two months, the east coast of Florida was hit by three major hurricanes!

But in the midst of boarding and un-boarding windows and living without electricity and hot water for weeks at a time, a tiny miracle arrived in our yard which seemed to make everything else bearable.

When we woke up on the morning of September 5th, after Hurricane Frances had hit our coast with winds of up to seventy-five miles per hour, my husband and I stood on the porch on the sheltered side of our home and watched the still-powerful winds topple and break huge, ancient, mighty oaks.

Suddenly, in the midst of these destructive winds, we spotted a flash of color in our garden. No more than ten feet from where we stood, a ruby-throated hummingbird emerged and hovered in front of our native firebush plant, jockeying back and forth with the gusts of wind to get nectar from the swaying plant. Unbelievably, this bird came back time and again to drink from this plant.

After years of trying to lure them, this was the first time we had ever seen a hummingbird in our yard — or in Florida!

Because of their scarcity, the sight of a hummingbird in Brevard County, Florida, is almost a miracle in itself. But to see the determination of this tiny three-inch bird, which weighs about a tenth of an ounce, in the face of a storm that put fear into the hearts of millions of Florida residents, was truly remarkable.

The next morning, most of the firebush plant was gone, victim of the winds that continued to batter our state for hours. But much to our pleasure and surprise, our new hummingbird visitor was still there, dining on the plants that remained.

Although we didn't have power and the boarded windows blocked out the light, my first action of the day was to dig out an old, previously un-visited hummingbird feeder, and boil up some hummingbird nectar on our propane stove.

The next day, when the stores opened again and most practical people were standing in line buying batteries and bottled water, I was at a local department store with an armload of new hummingbird feeders, which I quickly filled and hung outside. That was enough to get the hummingbirds to move right in!

I had lived in Florida for thirty-seven years and had never seen a hummingbird, one of my favorite forms of wildlife, in our state. Although I had been trying to plant all the right plants to attract them, it took a hurricane for me to finally lure them to my yard and to really observe them up close.

Almost every day since the hurricanes, I have had the joy of observing the visiting hummingbirds. With a feeder right outside my office window, I get a daily bird's eye view. I have watched as they chase each other through the yard and I have had them fly right between my arms as I refilled their feeders. And I have become very familiar with their buzzing and chittering sounds that let me know they are always around, even when I can't see them.

They remained through the next, more powerful hurricane (Hurricane Jeanne), and have stayed every since.

The hurricane season of 2004 affected everyone in Florida, some more than others. They affected me in a very positive way.

Every time I see the hummingbirds, I am reminded of the many blessings that nature holds for us: messages of beauty, strength, and determination. But perhaps the greatest message is that wonders are out there waiting to pay us a visit. We just need to keep planting seeds of beauty and faith, and we need to keep an eye out for the miracles!

~Betsy S. Franz

41

The Uninvited Guest

Attitude is a little thing that makes a big difference.
~Winston Churchill

No one was more surprised than I when the oncologist told me that I had stage IV lung cancer. At fifty-four, I was in excellent physical condition. I never smoked, have watched my weight and have exercised regularly for years. Tests revealed that because the cancer in my lung had already spread to my bones, surgery was no longer an option. My wife and I were stunned.

My first response was disbelief. Surely my tests must have been mixed up with someone else's. But the reality of the situation quickly sank in, and I realized that the course of my life was not in my hands, but in God's. We cried several times on the way home from the doctor's office, and had to stop the car to regain composure.

All I could think was, "What am I supposed to learn from this? What must I do with the time I have left? How much time do I have?" I wasn't thinking "why me?" or "this isn't fair," but that the sudden turn of events was a wakeup call for me. I never imagined that there would be many blessings to come as a result of my illness.

Needless to say, the news of my cancer was unexpected and would mean a total change in my life and lifestyle. When he shared the diagnosis, the doctor said matter-of-factly, "You have a one in ten chance of survival." I looked at him with a mix of fear as well as confidence and said, "Great, I'll be in the ten percent group."

I realized that the only thing I could control was my attitude toward the situation, and prayed for the strength to deal with it, knowing that God doesn't give us tests we cannot pass. Perhaps easier said than done. The thought of leaving my wife, of not seeing all my children married or knowing my grandchildren, was almost too daunting.

I kept thinking of the frightening statistics that the doctor rattled off in his office. As we collected our wits, we began to consider the bigger picture and looked for grains of hope. Prayer, meditation and reading inspirational books were as much in the prescription for recovery as the medications, treatments and tests that would soon become part of my regimen.

After the initial shock, my first test was to share the difficult news with my mother. We went to her home, and I said, "Mom, I have something unpleasant to tell you—I have cancer." Her reaction was as if the rug had been pulled from under her. I quickly spoke up and said, "We have the best medical team to help us and we know that with God's help, we're going to see this through."

The expression on my mother's face turned from sheer fright to calm, as she took her cue from us, that we were confident in our path and that we had complete faith. Likewise, our children were comforted to see that their parents were facing this head-on, and they in turn remained as upbeat as they could. Pain is a fact of life—how we deal with it is a matter of choice.

The news of my condition spread quickly among friends, family and neighbors, and the outpour of kindness was overwhelming as well as humbling. We received countless calls and e-mails from everywhere. My eyes filled with tears as so many expressed their wishes for my recovery.

One woman we know sends me a get-well card with an encouraging handwritten message every day. Several friends have volunteered to drive me to chemotherapy and radiation treatments. Our next-door neighbors have always been like family, and opened their home to our children and grandchildren when they came to visit from out of town, as ours is too small for all of them.

I have learned a great deal from this journey. One question that I've thought about—Is there anything worse than cancer in your body? Yes, it's cancer of the spirit. There are so many people who look like they are alive and healthy. But they are miserable with themselves and everything around them. No matter what happens, they are unhappy. Regardless of the positive in their lives, they look for the negative. And no matter who tries to love them or be kind to them, it's never good enough.

While I wouldn't have chosen this challenge, I continuously look for the blessings in it more than the curses. I remember asking my wife, "Can you imagine going through this without a solid spiritual foundation?" I shudder at the thought of how I would have dealt with my condition without it.

Anger, blame and bitterness are reactions to illness that are fruitless. I have seen the full range in my cancer support group. If these dear people have taught me anything, it's to accept a challenge for what it really is—and face it head-on. I have shared laughter, tears and many heart-to-heart talks that would never have taken place without my illness. And, while I certainly don't pretend there's nothing wrong, I don't dwell on what I cannot influence or control.

My uninvited guest arrived as a complete surprise, but it eventually and unexpectedly gave me the opportunity to do what few people are able to do—live life to its fullest—each and every day. No, I don't mean doing super cool stuff, traveling to exotic places, acquiring extravagant toys or "grabbing for all the gusto" I can as an old beer ad used to suggest. I mean living each moment with full appreciation that there might not be another.

When my wife was seriously ill a few years ago, one of our daughters prophetically said, "We will all grow from this." Sure enough, we did. And we will undoubtedly grow from our present situation. Of course, we don't know for certain what my fate will be. In the meantime, we have the power of prayer, faith and the kindness of others to guide us along the way. As one friend said, "Pray like it all depends on God, and work on getting better like it all depends on you." Amen.

~David Hyman

Chapter 5

Count Your Blessings

The Joy of Giving

*I have found that among its other benefits,
giving liberates the soul of the giver.*

~Maya Angelou

Charity Begins...

It is the thrifty people who are generous.
~Lord Rosebery

With three weeks before the end of the year, it's time to do the majority of my charity donations. I get my spreadsheet of charities where I track donations and income tax receipts, pull out the stack of pledge cards I've been saving throughout the year, and open my checkbook.

I pick up my pen, but instead of writing the checks, I hesitate. It's easy to give money to charity when you know you have money coming in. It's not so easy when most of the money is going out.

Over the last few weeks, I've been informed that two of the websites I write for have decided to "proceed cautiously because of the recession." An editor at a newspaper I've written for told me they're no longer using freelancers. And just yesterday I got an e-mail from a health magazine that I frequently contribute to. In response to my query, they told me they're not looking for any new ideas for the next six months.

In other words, I can't expect any more assignments from these places for at least that long, maybe longer.

Although I've been looking for other writing venues, so far I haven't done well. The marketing group that I belong to is mostly listing positions for bloggers and freelance writers that pay less than five cents a word, some as low as a penny. No one can survive on that.

While I actually had the best writing year of my career, it's becoming clear that next year is not going to come close to matching it. And I should add that "best" is relative. I read somewhere that the average writer makes less than $15,000 a year, and that's with factoring in the megastars who make hundreds of thousands of dollars. I'm still below average.

Although my substitute teaching helps pay the bills, I haven't been getting as many calls lately. To save money, the school board is closing schools, meaning fewer teachers are needed.

So, can I really afford to give to charity? Doesn't charity begin at home? My home. I'm tempted to close my checkbook, but I don't.

I look around my house. Yes, it's worth less now than it was before the housing market tanked, but I still have a small, nice house in a good area of town. Since I'm not looking to sell, I can wait out the market slump.

My fridge and cupboards aren't bursting with food, but that's because I haven't gone shopping this week. These days I don't buy a lot of meat or expensive prepared foods, but neither do I have to choose between food and paying for utilities. Unlike an increasing number of people, I've been able to donate food to food banks rather than having to use them.

A lot of the clothes I wear are secondhand, but that's partly because I'm inherently frugal and partly because I don't care about fashion. If I look carefully, I can usually find good quality clothes that have been "gently" used.

Then I think about some of my friends who aren't as lucky as I am. One lost six teeth over a couple of years because she couldn't afford regular dental care. I just had a filling replaced last week. Yes, the bill hurt almost as much as the procedure, but the pain wore off for both.

Another friend, with massive health and mobility problems, lives on a meager disability pension while her husband works two jobs to keep them afloat. My knees may creak more than they used to, and my kidneys aren't in the best shape, but I can still get around.

A third friend lost seven years of her life when a stroke wiped out large chunks of her memory. Unable to work, she lives on government assistance which, for her, means stale crackers and tuna fish—which she hates. Yet one month, when she had managed to save five dollars for a treat at McDonald's, she ended up giving that money away to someone she thought was needier. Me? I treat myself to breakfast out every Sunday and every couple of weeks my mother sends me twenty dollars to go out for dinner.

Suddenly, I feel very lucky and very rich. I grab my pen again and begin to write checks. I don't know what next year will bring, but for now I can share my good fortune with others.

Charity may begin at home but it doesn't have to stay there.

~Harriet Cooper

43

But for God's Grace

In about the same degree as you are helpful, you will be happy.
~Karl Reiland

I had been a blood donor for years, but never had I been an apheresis donor of platelets. I had lots of excuses for not doing so, including, "It takes too long," and "It looks uncomfortable."

But then I lost two good friends to cancer. They were both named Mary, they were both in their forties, and they both died within months of each other. It was heartrending for me.

While grieving my losses one day, it dawned on me that their lives had probably been prolonged by the generosity of total strangers; people who had willingly taken time to donate their platelets, and who had not caved in to any excuses.

As the days went by, I couldn't get my mind off apheresis. I finally realized that donating platelets was something I had to do.

When I called the Red Cross to make my appointment, the receptionist patiently answered my myriad questions, assuring me I'd be fine.

But when I arrived at the donor site I still had to fight the butterflies fluttering in my stomach. I really didn't want to do this, but I couldn't seem to make myself leave the building, either. So, during the screening process, in hopes of calming my fears, I asked even more questions.

Finally, after feeling somewhat at ease about the entire process, the assistant asked me some questions and then said, "Follow me."

When we got to the back of the room, I was impressed with the sophisticated apheresis machine and quickly became mesmerized by the way it so effortlessly separated blood.

Before long, it was my turn to be hooked up to it. Within minutes I was snuggled under a blanket in a comfortable recliner, a needle in each arm, and to my surprise, contentedly watching television. The rest of the prep work had gone without a hitch; I had almost forgotten where I was and what I was doing.

Then it happened. My nose began to itch.

Normally that wouldn't be a big deal, I'd simply scratch it. But when I remembered that I had to keep both arms straight and was unable to bend them, for some reason I began to panic. My eyes wildly searched the room for a nurse, but the only staff member present in the room at the time was busy with another patient.

The panic worsened and I began trembling uncontrollably. A paralyzing fear swept over me as I struggled to fight an overwhelming desire to yank the needles from my arms and dash out the door.

Not usually prone to panic attacks, this was a new experience for me, and I had no idea how to handle it. All I knew was that the more I thought about my situation, the worse it got.

Finally, I shot up an emergency prayer: *God, I'm scared. Please help me.*

As if on cue, a nurse appeared. Assuming she had seen my distress and would immediately unhook me, I was taken aback when she very calmly asked if I would like some information about the recipient.

What? But what about me?

I collected myself and managed to stammer, "I... I... I can know that information? I can know who my platelets are going to?"

"Well," the nurse quietly continued while monitoring the machine, "we don't usually have any information on the recipients, and we cannot give out any private information on anyone, but in this case I do have a little of his history."

"Oh," was all I could respond, still struggling to get my bearings.

"He is a man from this area, about forty years old," the nurse continued. "With a wife and two kids, and... he has leukemia."

If she said more, I didn't hear her.

I froze, unable to even breathe, as I struggled to comprehend what she had just told me: there was a man right here in town, about my age and, like me, married with two children; but he was waiting for my platelets... in hopes of staying alive?

Finally, I looked up at the plastic bag that was gradually filling with my cream-colored platelets—and swallowed hard.

God, please forgive me for whining about being a little uncomfortable.

As the nurse walked away, the plight of my situation suddenly seemed extremely trivial. For, unlike my recipient, in less than two hours I would be able to get up from this bed and leave. I would go home and cook dinner for my family as normal. I would feel good, think clearly, and have energy to clean, work in the garden, or just take a walk with my husband while watching a panoramic sunset.

Ever so slowly I came to grips with what had just happened, and realized that not only had my nose stopped itching, but compassion had replaced the panic I had experienced just moments ago. No longer uncomfortable, I was completely at peace.

When the whole process was finally finished and I was gathering my things to go home, I stopped by the receptionist's desk and humbly signed up for another appointment.

As I walked outside and felt the warmth of the sunshine on my face, and deeply inhaled the fresh air, I couldn't help but be consumed with the thought: but for the grace of God, go I.

~Connie Cameron

44

Never Too Poor to Give

No one has ever become poor by giving.
~Anne Frank

"**D**on't you have any toys you want to share?" I asked my son during our church's Christmas toy drive. "What about all those things in your closet you haven't used in years?"

"I don't have anything," he said. "We're so poor."

We're only "poor" because we refuse to buy him the texting phone he wants for Christmas, which would also require a monthly texting charge.

"You're never so poor you have nothing to give," I found myself saying to him, a phrase my mother often used on me.

How could I help him understand, when I myself still whined about things I wanted, like the *Fowler's Modern English Usage* book that cost nearly $40? I knew Santa Hubby wasn't going to pony up for that one. What about that Vera Wang coat I wanted from Kohl's, the one with the $150 price tag? No, that wasn't happening, either.

At work the next day, one of my students said, "I didn't spell your name right," as she handed me a Christmas gift—a beribboned box of chocolates. No wonder she hadn't spelled it right—I had only worked at the center for a couple of months, and my name is not easy to pronounce, even in English, which is this woman's second language.

The woman had been out of work for months!

"Thank you, Joanna," I said, trying to hold back the tears as I hugged her.

I hadn't expected a gift—I work at an adult education center, where we deal with people every day who struggle economically. The economic downturn is not new to those who come in our doors—those who are laid off, without work, and need an education to get ahead or for a sense of pride. When I was hired, my boss told me she tries to keep snacks around the center and cooks "stone soup" once a week, where whoever can bring something in does, because "You will hear growling bellies here. They give their food to the children before they themselves eat."

"Some of them get food stamps," my boss continued, "but by the end of the month, things are tight. We try not to plan field trips where they would have to pack a lunch because sometimes they just won't show up because they don't even have a sandwich to bring along."

And yet these people, so grateful for a second chance at getting an education, unable to sometimes even afford the gas money to come in, manage to do something for us nearly every week. Some bring in food; others do chores around the center. They help and encourage one another, and us. They give what they are able to give.

When I looked at my Christmas gift from my new friend, I wondered if it had been an offering out of a meager food budget, and I wanted to refuse it. Instead, I said "thank you."

When I brought the candies home to share with my family, I told them just how precious each chocolate was if you thought of how much the unemployed woman's family makes a year. Why, it was the equivalent of a *Fowler's Modern English Usage* book! I said it again, understanding so much better in my heart, "You're never so poor you have nothing to give."

Perhaps the way I could help my son understand best was for me to understand first.

Immediately, I went to my bookshelf and chose several of my favorite novels to share with the center. When I had them boxed, I turned to find my son nonchalantly lugging a white laundry basket of toys he had played with when younger. "I don't want these old things," he said.

I saw among them his beloved Buzz Lightyear and his favorite stuffed dog, Squishy. I set them aside for the toy drive and kissed him on his forehead. He had learned the way I had — by example. Now the students had not only impacted me, but my family as well. Here I had thought I was the teacher, but Joanna and the rest of the students at the center are the ones teaching me. Because you're never so poor you have nothing to give.

~Drema Sizemore Drudge

Unexpected
Blessings

Kindness, like a boomerang, always returns.
~Author Unknown

A few nights after Thanksgiving, my husband and I began planning the Christmas presents we would buy for our three boys. Money was tight, but thanks to careful budgeting we were in good shape. We couldn't wait for Christmas.

At 10:00 P.M., my husband answered a knock at the front door. There, standing in pajamas, were two neighborhood children, ten-year-old Andy and his seven-year-old sister, Beth. Tears streamed down their cheeks as they held a few wrapped Christmas gifts, an overstuffed pillowcase of dirty clothes resting on the cement beside them.

"M... Miss Kelley..." Andy said. "Can we stay with you?"

"What happened?"

"My dad and my aunt got into a fight and she kicked us out," Andy managed between sobs.

I looked into the darkness for their father. "Where's your dad?"

"He left. He told us to come here."

"Of course you can stay," I said, moving aside to let them in. It was late and they had school the next day. They could spend the night, go to school with my boys, and then I could figure out what was happening.

I woke my son and told him to go sleep in his brother's extra bunk bed. Then I put Andy and Beth into his bunk beds.

"Don't worry," I said. "Tomorrow I'll find out what's going on."

The next morning, after the kids left for the bus, a knock sounded at the front door. It was Mr. Brown.

"Miss Kelley, I hate to trouble you, but can I come in and talk?" he asked politely.

"Please do." I moved aside for him to enter.

"I appreciate you letting Andy and Beth spend the night," he began. "My sister-in-law kicked us out. I didn't know where else to send the kids."

"How did you know they spent the night?" I asked, remembering that I saw no one last night.

"I was hiding in the bushes. I need to ask you another favor," he continued. "Can Andy and Beth stay here until I get on my feet?"

"How long are we talking about?" I was dumbfounded.

"A couple of months at most."

So many thoughts raced through my head. Christmas was in a few weeks. Money was already tight. We could barely afford the food and bills now. More kids meant more food, more water, more laundry soap, more bathing soap, more shampoo and toothpaste.

"I know it's a lot to ask," he said. "I don't know anyone here. Please let them stay. I don't want them to suffer because of my mistakes."

"Okay," I finally said. "The kids can stay. But ONLY the kids. You will need to stay at a shelter or something. But you can visit them. And this is just until you get on your feet."

"Thank you," he said. "You don't know how much I appreciate this." He promised to find a job quickly and work hard to get them a place to stay. "They have more clothes, but they're dirty."

I opened my garage, where the washer and dryer were and let him bring in the loaded pillowcases.

After he was gone, I cleared a dresser for them and placed their presents under the tree.

I wondered about Christmas. Was this all they had? I assumed it was, especially since Mr. Brown had no job. How could Santa visit my kids and not these two? He couldn't. I silently prayed that we would be able to afford a nice Christmas for everyone this year.

The phone rang. It was the school. Andy and Beth had talked with the guidance counselor and she wanted to know what was happening with the children. I told her what Mr. Brown had told me, and that the kids would be staying with me for a few months.

When the kids arrived home, I sat them all down in the living room to talk. Then I told Andy and Beth about our daily routine. "Directly after school, we always grab a snack and sit at the kitchen table to do our homework."

The new kids easily settled into our routine. Somehow we managed with food and daily supplies. But the bills hadn't come in yet. I was worried about how much more we would be paying. And with the extra money we spent on snacks and supplies like toilet paper and laundry soap, I wasn't sure we'd be able to pay them without taking money from our Christmas fund.

Two weeks later, the school called again. The counselor asked what we were doing for Christmas.

"Good question," I said, laughing a little anxiously. "I'm not sure yet."

"Do Andy and Beth have Christmas presents?"

"They brought a few with them, but that's all they have," I said. "We don't have a lot of money, but Santa will come. I guess Christmas will just be smaller this year."

"We adopt families at Christmas," she said. "We would like to adopt Andy and Beth if that would be okay with you."

Silence.

"We already have people standing by to bring the gifts to your house. We have two bicycles and toys and clothes. You could put them away until Christmas."

"Okay." Inside I was silently thanking God. My boys wanted new bikes for Christmas too, but if we had to buy presents for Andy and Beth, we couldn't get them. We couldn't afford five bikes and we wanted everyone to have an equal Christmas.

Within a half hour, four cars pulled up and eight people began carrying in bags and boxes filled with gifts and food.

The phone rang again. It was another group that wanted to bring food. Just as the first group was leaving, the next group drove up with bags filled with food. My cupboards had never been so full.

After taking inventory, I hid the presents for Andy and Beth. That evening, my husband and I went shopping for our boys. We were able to get them everything they wanted and all the kids would be having a comparable Christmas. Our excitement returned.

But then the bills began arriving. I opened the water bill first. It was much lower than it had ever been. I stared at the paper thinking it must be some mistake, but silently thanked God for the blessing.

I opened the electric bill next. It was lower too. Even though we had used more, our bills reflected less. I knew that our holiday would be extra special this year.

It was. The kids awoke to a tree piled high with presents. We ate turkey and ham, potatoes and gravy, all sorts of vegetables, rolls, and deserts. Mr. Brown spent the day. And no one talked of anything sad. We played. We ate. And we thanked God for the blessings he bestowed on our two families.

Andy and Beth remained for two more months. And God continued to bless our home. We gave in our need and got more than we'd ever had before. We received love from a family that needed our help, we received joy from helping others, and we received faith that came from a shower of unexpected blessings.

~Kelley Hunsicker

46

For Richer, For Poorer

Nobody has ever measured, even poets, how much a heart can hold.
~Zelda Fitzgerald

I stood alone in the dairy section and stared at the price tags on gallons of milk. I blinked, swiped at the tear that trickled down my cheek, and snatched up a gallon marked "manager's special." I ducked my head as I pushed my cart away, not wanting other shoppers to read the distress on my face.

With both my husband and me out of work, our family was living entirely on the remains of our checking account. I knew that things would be infinitely worse without that bit of padding, but it was still hard to watch the numbers get smaller with each bank statement. Particularly with no job prospects on the horizon. So even the $1.59 for the gallon of nearly-expired milk felt like an enormous expense to me. I had no idea when, or if, we could replace that $1.59 with income.

Our fourteenth anniversary was a few days away, but I was having a hard time even thinking about that. I knew it would not be like any of our previous thirteen anniversaries.

The day after our wedding, we drove to a lovely bed and breakfast for our honeymoon. In the parlor that evening, over wine and cheese, we met three wonderful older couples. All three were celebrating anniversaries: twenty years, thirty-five years, and forty-eight years. When they asked us how long we'd been married, we giggled.

"One day," Pete answered. After congratulations had been shared all around, we were showered with advice. I don't recall most of it, but Pete and I took it to heart when the couples agreed that we ought to make our anniversary a real occasion every single year. They had all found that going away as a couple, for a week or for just one night, had made a difference in their marriages.

And for the past thirteen years, we had followed that advice. On anniversaries three and six, with tiny babies at home, we chose to go out for an especially nice meal instead. We took this promise seriously enough to work it into our budget every year, setting aside a bit of money each month to pay for our special anniversary celebration.

This year, I knew it would not happen. It could not happen. All of our money had to go toward food and housing. I was forgoing haircuts, eating my meals just shy of being satisfied—not to save on calories but on pennies. Surely I couldn't mourn an extravagance like a night at a hotel. But I did.

I desperately wanted to hide my sadness from Pete. He was discouraged enough by the mere fact of his unemployment. So I didn't even talk about our upcoming anniversary, because I didn't know how to bring it up without the conversation turning toward our traditional celebration.

But he knew. I could see it in the way that he looked at me, the tenderness in the way he kissed my forehead. As the days passed and we came closer and closer to our anniversary, his face seemed to grow darker. Not in anger, but in thought. Determination.

The morning of our anniversary, I awoke after Pete. I pushed myself out of our empty bed and shuffled into the bathroom to wash my face. And then I stopped. In the middle of the bathroom counter, there was a small scroll of sorts. White, narrow, tied with a shiny red satin ribbon that I recognized from our daughters' hair bow box. As I picked it up and pulled at the end of the bow, my fingers shook. As I unrolled the paper, what I saw brought tears to my eyes—tears totally unlike the ones I'd shed at the dairy case. Pete had typed out a love poem from a book he'd given me for my birthday the year before.

So many images came into my mind as I read and re-read those words. I saw Pete thumbing through the book, reading all those poems until he found the perfect one. I saw him sitting at the computer — when had he done that, since we were nearly always in the house at the same time? — clicking through to find a fancy, poem-worthy font. I saw him trimming the printed-out page, most likely with a ruler to keep the edges straight. I saw him going into our girls' bathroom and digging around for a ribbon in that messy, tangled box. And I saw his thick man-fingers struggling to roll the paper up tight and tie the shiny red bow. Had he kept the little scroll in his nightstand drawer until this morning? Had he smiled, scroll in hand, as he eased out of bed while I slept?

Described in plain terms, what I received for my anniversary was a rolled-up piece of paper tied with a used ribbon scrap, bearing a recycled poem from a one-year-old book. What I really received was a piece of my husband's heart and evidence of his continued commitment to me and to our marriage. I did not need a night at a bed and breakfast or even a fancy restaurant dinner to see that, and to feel its impact.

Pete spent no money on this anniversary gift, and I was glad. Because numbers in bank accounts, as I was learning the hard way, are anything but permanent. And often, so are the things that we spend those numbers on. But the time and the creativity and the thoughtfulness that came straight from Pete's heart will stay with me forever.

~Mandy Houk

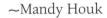

47

Third World Banquet

Poverty can teach lessons that privilege cannot.
~Jack Klugman

One of the greatest lessons I've ever learned, I learned in the sixth grade. My teacher was Mrs. Schmidt, and for years before I reached her class, I couldn't wait to have her. She was the cool, young teacher who really did make learning fun. She taught the same lessons every other teacher did, but her way of doing it was different. Like they say today, she thought "outside of the box."

One afternoon as we were settling into our desk chairs after recess, Mrs. Schmidt presented the outline for our upcoming project: The Third World Banquet. It was a luncheon we were going to put on for the sixth-, seventh- and eighth-grade classes where each student would eat a meal that symbolized food of a first-, second- or third-world country.

For the next month we planned the event, raising money, gathering parents to help, and brainstorming over the details. Before long we had a plan. To make it fair, every student participating would blindly draw a strip of paper from a bowl. If the paper was marked with a one, that lucky student would be eating a first-world style lunch. If it was marked with a two, they'd be eating a second-world style lunch. And if the paper was marked with three, you guessed it, they'd eat a third-world style lunch.

The day of the banquet finally arrived and just before the lunch bell rang, the bowl was making its way around each classroom for the students to choose their fate for the afternoon. Of course everyone hoped to pick a ticket marked with a one.

Moments later, we stood at the doors to the school gym (which served as the dining hall) waiting patiently to be directed to our seats inside. Soon the parents were escorting the first-world kids to rows of tables that were set with tablecloths, napkins, silverware and plates. The second-world kids were led to another group of tables. There were chairs, but no extra comforts like tablecloths or salt and pepper shakers. Lastly, the third-world kids were led to a roped-off area of the floor that was covered in brown paper on which they were to sit.

Very soon after the realities of our banquet were made known, the faces changed. The first-world students of course were beaming, walking around like little kings and queens, slapping high-fives at their good fortune. The third-world kids appeared suddenly forlorn, trying to find comfort on the hard floor beneath them, envious of the classmates who sat in chairs all around them, dreading the moment they would find out their lunch for the day. In the middle were the second-world kids who sat almost expressionless, a little disappointed they weren't quite as lucky as their first-world friends, but certainly glad they weren't on the floor either.

Before long, lunch was served. The first-world students got spaghetti and meatballs with garlic bread, salad and a choice of drink. They were taken care of first, waited on hand and foot, served seconds if they wanted, and given refills when their cups were empty. They even had cake and ice cream for dessert!

The second-world students were served peanut butter and jelly with half pint-size cartons of milk. At those tables, there were no seconds, no endless refills, no dessert at the end. But it wasn't nearly as bad as the third-world kids had had it. And for that, they were grateful.

Inside the roped-off area of floor in the "third world," it was crowded and uncomfortable. As the students situated themselves, nearly on top of one another, a few pitchers of water, cups and small bowls of rice were passed out. But of course there were no forks.

As much as the experience of the banquet on a whole stays with me today, it is a small detail that I remember most clearly, a detail that has a place in my story thanks to an old classmate, Tyler. He was one of the bigger boys in class. From his appearance, one would think he would be rough and tough and interested in causing trouble. He played along and fit in with the rest of the kids but underneath was really a gentle soul. So there we all were all dressed in the same red, white and navy uniforms, but divided by wealth (or lack thereof).

The first-world students sat with one another eating and drinking and laughing in their comfortable "first world," forgetting about the "poverty" that surrounded them—poverty that for some of their best friends had suddenly become a reality. The second-world kids, with whom I sat, had quickly forgotten all about the spaghetti they weren't eating, just thankful they hadn't chosen papers marked three. The third-world students sat on the hard floor, rationing the water and scooping sticky, flavorless rice into their mouths with their bare hands.

It was at the end of the lunch that Tyler, who sat in first world and who, in his everyday humble and kind-hearted shoes, seemed the least affected by his status, sat up in his seat. Something suddenly made him see the lesson Mrs. Schmidt was hoping we would all see. When offered seconds on his dessert he said, "Yes, please." But it wasn't for himself that he wanted that second piece of cake. It was for one of the less fortunate. Not a minute later, he was out of his chair with a string of fellow first-worlders behind him on their way to the second- and third-world sections of the gym. His gesture of kindness had a domino effect on everyone around him, and within minutes the plates of chocolate cake were sitting on the bare tables in second world and taking the place of the rice bowls in third.

Having been prepared for this, the parents were waiting with plates of cake for everyone and were soon passing them out to each of the students who'd not been so lucky earlier in the meal. Smiles were finding their way back to the once poverty-stricken faces.

By evening we'd all be filling our bellies once again with family dinners, going about our carefree lives as fortunate children, forgetting about the hunger in the world or the hunger some of us had experienced earlier that afternoon. But for that hour in the gym at our Third World Banquet, we understood, even though it was only for a brief time, what it felt like to be hungry, because we had eaten only rice or because we'd witnessed our friends with nothing. I still think about that humbling afternoon, and how Tyler's one small action made such a great difference.

~Andrea Fecik

48

Hungry in the Big Apple

*Sometimes it is better to give your apple away
than to eat it yourself.*
~Italian proverb

My first winter in New York City was something I had been anticipating for a long time. At twenty-three years old, I was working and playing in one of the most exciting cities in the world. I couldn't wait to experience the Macy's Thanksgiving Day Parade and attend the Rockettes' Christmas Spectacular at Radio City Music Hall. The streets were lined with enchanting window displays that lured passersby with their magical beauty, tempting children with treasures that lay waiting inside, while the scent of warm roasted chestnuts lingered in the chilly air, arousing your lethargic appetite. This holiday season was going to be one of the best, or so I thought.

I rushed towards Penn Station with the hordes of people just getting off work. It was the same race every day to get to the express train before it reached its capacity. Normally mild-mannered individuals morphed into ferocious beasts marking their territory and devouring anyone and anything in their path. Coming from the South, this ritual was alarming to me, but here in the Big Apple, it was a way of life I was going to have to get used to. It was rare that I made the express train and today was no exception. As the heavy steel doors closed, I turned in search of a bench to rest my weary body. Off in the distance, I saw something stirring in a dark corner of the station. It was too big to be an animal, though I had heard rumors of city rats being the size of small dogs. As I took a closer look, the object came into full view.

"My god, it's a child," I whispered.

I got up and slowly made my way towards the area. Huddled closely together were a young woman and little boy. Both were masked by layers of dirt and grime and what had once been their clothes were nothing but tattered rags draping their frail bodies. Neither was wearing shoes or a coat. The flow of traffic around me continued at a fast pace, never once ceasing to acknowledge this poor family. Did anyone care? Looking down at my watch, I noticed the time. My fiancé was going to worry if I didn't make it home soon. Reluctantly, I turned and ran for the approaching train. All I could think about on the ride home was the image of the young mother and child. I was flooded with guilt for not giving them my own coat to keep warm.

When I got home, I told my fiancé, who grew up in New York, about what I saw that afternoon. He explained, "Sweetheart, I know you're not accustomed to seeing the homeless and I understand you want to help, but there are an abundance of these families in the city and it's impossible to help them all. Don't worry; you'll get used to them."

The words he spoke stung my ears. I didn't want to get used to seeing those poor people suffering. But I was only one person, and there wasn't a lot I could do to help, was there? The next morning, we raced around the apartment trying to get ready for work. I hurried to the refrigerator and grabbed our lunches. We had decided to start taking our lunch since it was so expensive to eat in the city every day.

When we reached Penn Station, we went our separate ways. As I made my way up the stairs into the frigid air of the city, I shivered. The coat I was wearing wasn't much help and my feet were becoming numb. Just as I was beginning to feel sorry for myself, I saw an old man curled up under the awning of a deli. He was barely clothed and his cheeks were hollow. Glancing down at the paper bag pressed tightly against my chest, I knew what I must do. I shuffled over to the old man and offered the bag. His weather-beaten hand reached out and took my gift. He opened the top, and looked inquisitively inside.

"I thought you might want something to snack on later," I heard myself say.

The old man looked up and grinned, "Thank you child, God bless you. Now run along before you catch a cold."

"Yes sir," I whispered.

He nodded and pulled an apple from the bag. I watched him begin to consume the fruit before continuing towards my office. Meager as it was, I had found a way I could give to the homeless. From that day on, it was rare that I showed up to work with my lunch still in tow, but I never once felt a pang of hunger.

~Tasha Mitchell

49

Making Christmas Hope

*Christmas is the one day of the year
that carries real hope and promise for all mankind.*
~Edgar Guest

The holiday season was approaching, and our economy was still in a downward spiral. For several months, I had been attending a new church. Reverend Lori's messages were of everyday spirituality, and humanity to our fellow people, and hope, especially in these trying times. Her messages always inspired me and I wanted to follow up and make a difference in someone's life.

So many people this past year had lost faith and, more importantly, hope for a brighter future. People were feeling desperate. The streets were becoming more dangerous. I was thinking about the homeless, how they continued to find strength to go on, and how they would spend Christmas this year.

Across from my church was a park, and as fall came and went, I noticed a larger number of homeless people making their home there. I wanted to make their Christmas special this year, and hopefully remind them of Christmas pasts with their family and friends before hard times came their way. Yes, food and cash would help, but they could receive those any given day, and I wanted to make Christmas Day different.

I bought some Christmas gift bags in bright colors with Santa's face and "Ho-Ho-Ho" written across the front. Wanting to be practical yet capture the spirit of the holiday, I purchased Santa candy, peppermint candy canes, individual bags of nuts, cookies, and bright red tissue paper. Okay, this was a start, yet it wasn't special enough in my mind. Then I saw the fluffy little brown and white teddy bears with red bows around their necks.

Most of the homeless at this park were grown men. Would they like my gifts? My friends Marlene, Jerry, Ken and I assembled the bags. Christmas music playing loudly in the background, our hearts felt open and right about our mission. Placing the sparkly red tissue paper inside each bag first, followed by the candy and snacks, the cuddly bear, and a couple of dollars as a gift, we twisted the tissue paper sealing all the treats inside. Early Christmas morning, we set out to the park, stopping at a local Dunkin' Donuts to pick up coffee and doughnuts for the men too.

Never having done this kind of community outreach before, we were not sure how we would be received. The next hour was beyond our wildest expectations. As we approached the park, we saw a few more people than we anticipated, and we said to each other, "I hope we have enough bags." We were then spotted, and twenty or more people approached our car slowly, some walking, some limping, some jogging, still not knowing what to expect as we opened the door. They looked so tired as their eyes scanned the huge bag carrying all our goodies.

We had expected to hand out bags to everyone right there by the car and leave, but the men walked us over to a pavilion where most of them gathered to eat, sleep and just hang out for the day. Once there, we started to pour hot coffee and pass out doughnuts.

No one asked what was inside the bags. Everyone was patient as they took a cup of coffee and a doughnut, sitting down, savoring every sip and bite. As we said "Merry Christmas" to each, their responses of "Merry Christmas" back to us began to strengthen. They started to smile and their eyes brightened. We started to hand out the bags. Some got two bags by mistake and they turned and gave their extra to someone else, saying "Merry Christmas," happy to share their treats. One younger man, seeing the teddy bear, looked up and said,

"I have myself a teddy now." He put it inside his shirt pocket and patted it gently, his eyes gleaming.

Their resilience inspired me that morning—how they put aside their hardship for a couple of hours, opening their hearts, forgetting their troubles as they shared what they had. As we drove away, our own hearts were filled with gratitude and hope for brighter days ahead, and as we looked back, the group gathered under the pavilion waved until we were out of sight.

~Paula Maugiri Tindall, R.N.

Her Make-a-Difference Life

Act as if what you do makes a difference. It does.
~William James

"I've something to show you," my girlfriend, Sue, said the minute I opened my front door. Shivering, she stepped inside, accompanied by a blast of cold air that would make any polar bear happy. It was the day before Thanksgiving, and Sue and I were about to embark upon one of our heartfelt gabfests. I get together with Sue, a single mom and teacher, several times a year, and her laughter stays with me long after she's gone.

We did our typical hug, how are you, you look great routine before settling into my living room, where Sue took a gallon-sized Ziploc bag out of her purse. "Rae made these," she said with pride for her tough-minded, tender-hearted, twenty-seven-year-old daughter. "She's selling them for extra money, doing all she can to supplement her job. Want to buy some?"

The "some" she was referring to were homemade holiday greeting cards, hand-stitched and adorable. I fell in love with a card featuring a plump embroidered snowman, its blue on black background and silky white thread already putting me in a Christmas frame of mind. Wanting to support Rae, I bought ten dollars worth of cards, but there was only the one snowman, and I told Sue I'd have trouble parting with it. She confessed to feeling the same way—she had one snowman left for herself—so we agreed to mail them to each other for Christmas, thus ensuring we'd each get to keep one. Now I know that sounds crazy, but my friendship with Sue is all about crazy.

After she went home, I smiled when I glanced at the snowman I would eventually send her. But the card didn't make me think of Sue as much as Rae, so impassioned about her job at AmeriCorps, the humanitarian aid organization. I knew Rae earned less than $10,000 a year and had a mountain of school loans and bills to pay, but I also knew that she would sacrifice whatever was needed to continue her work. It inspired me to see someone so young making such a difference, despite financial struggles of her own, and it put a bit of perspective on our country's current dire economy.

It all started for Rae when she traveled over a college spring break to Albuquerque, New Mexico, to build homes for Habitat for Humanity. During that time she discovered that she loved working outside, elbow to elbow with fellow students and faculty. She was first up on the roof each morning, last to put her tools away at night. Volunteering for Habitat confirmed what she was just beginning to understand about herself—she wanted to help others for a living.

This confirmation was further reinforced by a missionary trip to Africa that summer. Rae had heard about the trip at school, and in a matter of months, had raised the necessary funds to go. If Albuquerque had whispered in Rae's ear, Africa truly opened her eyes. She'd seen how Africa was portrayed on TV, but the sheer poverty there didn't hit her until she experienced it in person. She was unprepared for the magnitude of human suffering and felt instantly ashamed of all she had back home in the states. She and her mom had certainly never been rich in the "land of plenty," getting by as they did on Sue's teaching salary, but they had a full life, and they had never gone hungry.

As Rae's group traveled through the slums of Nairobi to the orphanages of rural Kenya, she realized just how much she'd been blessed. Her heart went out to the children most. Curiosity clear in their wide, dark eyes, they poked at her freckles and stroked her blond hair. They delighted in the cookies and soccer balls the volunteers brought—things that Rae acknowledged she'd taken for granted all her life—and more than anything, they just wanted to be hugged. That was the paradox of it all, she marveled. These kids were truly happy, grateful for simple things. She met one little boy in a place called the "Blue Estates," so dubbed for the "houses" made of corrugated blue tin, with potato sacks serving as beds and water the color of mud. At journey's end, Rae couldn't stop crying. This little boy had become her friend, and chances were she'd never see him again. What would his future be?

With Africa forever in her heart, Rae knew she could never go back to an office job, although some people said it was time to get "real" work. She ignored their advice and joined AmeriCorps, where she's now employed with a program called "America Reads—Mississippi." In a Jackson inner-city school, she helps kids from kindergarten to fifth grade with reading and life skills, and she knows these kids don't have it easy. Most don't sleep well or have enough to eat; some come ready to fight. So Rae does what she can. And if she ever feels a twinge of envy over someone else's designer jeans or cool car, all she needs to do is remember "her kids."

She's comfortable with her life because she lives within her means. She and her fiancé Eliot, a Habitat staffer, have shopping down to a science, frequenting discount stores and donating to Goodwill. They laugh a lot too, which contributes to one of Rae's main goals: to show her kids, with their sad eyes and fragile smiles, how to laugh. She probably gets that laughing thing from her mom.

It's spitting snow when I run out to get my mail a week after Sue's visit. Back inside, I open a familiar-looking envelope, and there it is: my snowman, the one that Rae made. Inside, Sue had written: "Here's mine, as promised!"

I laugh, despite the grim economic reports and the concern that some in my family may lose their jobs. Overwhelmed by Christmas, I finish my cards several days before the big event. I know Sue must be wondering, so inside hers, I jot: "Finally yours—bet you were worried!"

I can almost hear her laughing across the miles, and somehow just the thought of that makes me laugh too. It occurs to me that maybe that's how we're all going to get through this, with a little laughter, a little craziness to keep us sane. Maybe we should try viewing our dire American economy not purely in materialistic terms, but as a chance to get back to the heart of things. Maybe this is our opportunity to rebuild our "land of plenty" in a different way, a kinder way, to join together and be grateful for our blessings, or as my friend Lisa says, to rejoice in the fact that we are here and alive.

Maybe we must remember, as another friend Ellen once told me, that God's timing is always perfect, and that our human connectedness is part of a larger divinity that's as powerful as reaching out to a small boy in Africa, or as simple as... exchanging little snowman cards.

~Theresa Sanders

51

Sister

What wisdom can you find that is greater than kindness?
~Jean-Jacques Rousseau

I don't remember her name and would not recognize her if I were to pass her on the street. I don't know if she is still living, as she was already elderly when I was a ten-year-old child some thirty years ago. But I do remember the kindness bestowed upon a group of underprivileged children by a stranger and the difference it has made in the life of one of those children. Me.

I remember the first time I saw her standing in the doorway of our small apartment. She was a petite, elderly woman who wore a long skirt, long wool coat and what I thought at the time was a hat reminiscent of the Roaring Twenties with its circular brim that lay flat against the head.

I could not hear what was being said as my stepfather, a man who liked no one, listened to her plead her case with such determination that I knew it had to be something she found of great importance. I was not told what was to happen that following Sunday.

A half hour before she arrived that Sunday, I was told to dress in my best clothes for I was going to church. She smiled brightly as I got into her car, the car of a complete stranger. I did not even know her name, but here I was, along with four others I recognized from our low-income neighborhood, on our way to church.

As we pulled into the parking lot, I remember how beautiful the old stone building was with its tall steeple and stained glass windows. The service seemed long, and not accustomed to the rituals of the

Catholic Church, I felt out of place. But even as a child, I held a strong belief in God and felt at peace within those walls.

Once the service had ended, I expected to be taken home, but instead we headed in the opposite direction. We were taken to a small apartment with meager furnishings that portrayed a simple, unspoiled lifestyle. Two tables were set up with large boxes containing puzzles. As she made us hot chocolate, we were instructed to begin working the puzzles. It was a quiet time, free from the turmoil and constant criticism we would encounter when we returned home. And the soft words spoken by the woman we came to know only as "Sister" (I think she may have been a nun at one time) were a welcome comfort.

I came to look forward to Sundays. To hot chocolate, to puzzles that remained where we had left off the week before, and to the love I felt whenever Sister smiled at me.

Once our 1,000-piece puzzles had been completed, Sister no longer came to pick us up on Sundays. I was told she was ill and no longer able to travel. However, I wondered if perhaps it was time for her to "rescue" the next group of children. To give them hope that kindness still exists and can be found within those we call strangers.

I am forty-four years old now and have made a point to show kindness to strangers when given the chance. I am told I am crazy and too trusting, but I know God will watch over me. I know Sister may not move amongst us now, but I hope she smiles when she sees that her efforts to reach out to those less fortunate continue in those whose lives she touched in that special way.

~Tammy L. Justice

Chapter 6

Count Your Blessings

Attitude Is Everything

Happiness is an attitude.
We either make ourselves miserable, or happy and strong.
The amount of work is the same.

~Francesca Reigler

Our Bad Day...
Week... Month...Year

You want an elixir for life's drama? Laugh!
~Robert W. Merriweather

O n Tuesday, my husband of ten years told me—over the phone, mind you—that he was no longer in love with me and he wanted out of our marriage. A marriage that had produced two children, who were just three and six at that time.

On Wednesday, I watched silently as he told our children that he would be moving out, that he would not be living with us anymore. He promised them that things would be different from then on, but still great. After my husband left the house to go to work, I held my children as they cried. And I cried too.

On Thursday, I took the children to McDonald's for lunch while my husband packed his clothes and other belongings. I managed to choke down seven French fries before running to the restroom to be sick. Oh, and I also explained to my six-year-old son why Daddy's side of the closet was now empty.

On Friday, I called my husband at the co-worker's house where he had told me he would be staying. The co-worker knew nothing of our break-up and hadn't seen my husband outside of the office all week long. He even commented that my husband had seemed rather chipper that week, and wasn't that odd given the circumstances.

On Saturday, I attended my son's hockey game, cheering in the stands as though my entire life hadn't fallen apart four days ago. My husband arrived late to the game and sat with me in the bleachers, you know, to keep up appearances to the other parents.

After the game, my husband and children and I walked toward the parking lot. Jordan's team had won the game and he was in high spirits. "Dad, we're going to go for pancakes now, right? Just like we always do?" The hopeful look on his face was heartbreaking.

My husband glanced my way and said, "I don't think that's a good idea. Don't you think it would be... awkward?"

"We were married for ten years and we've been separated for four days. I think we can handle eating breakfast together," I said.

He looked down at Jordan and patted his head. "I'm sorry, Buddy, but I can't this time. I really need to get home."

Home. Wherever that was for him these days.

"But you have to go," Jordan insisted. "We always go out for pancakes if my team wins. It's a family tradition."

Then light dawned in his eyes. Of course his father wouldn't go with us for pancakes. That was a family tradition, and he no longer wanted to be part of our family.

"Sorry, bud," my husband repeated before walking off toward his truck. Jordan began to follow him.

"Jordan, honey, our car is this way," I called, pointing in the opposite direction.

He turned around and gave me a what-was-I-thinking look. "Sorry, Mom," he said. "I'm just so used to following Dad."

The words hit me like a sucker punch in the gut: "I'm so used to following Dad." I realized that I was too. I had been following this man around for more than a decade, since I'd been a teenager. I'd been working so hard to please him, to make him happy, to do whatever he said was the right thing. I'd been doing that for so long that I no longer trusted my own instincts. And why should I, when I'd been so terribly wrong about the person I'd chosen to follow? And even more importantly, what on earth was I supposed to do now?

I looked at Jordan and whispered, "I know how you feel, baby. I really do."

We got to the car and I told the kids that we, just the three of us, were going to go stuff ourselves with pancakes. Both kids cheered.

Jordan, his eyes bright, said, "Does that mean we're still a family, Mom?"

"You bet it does, sweetheart," I answered, choking back tears. I buckled my daughter into her car seat, started the engine, and turned the radio up loud. I wasn't sure how much longer I could stave off my tears, and I didn't want the kids to hear me crying. Again.

The song "Bad Day" by Daniel Powter was playing. I heard Jordan in the back seat singing, "You had a bad day, you're taking one down, you sing a sad song..."

He stopped singing suddenly and said, "Hey, Mom, this song reminds me of us right now. But we're not having a bad day. We're having a bad week." I looked in the rear view mirror, expecting to see tears in his eyes, but instead, he had the sweetest smile on his face.

"You're right, honey. It definitely hasn't been the greatest week for any of us."

He shook his head, and the smile grew into a goofy grin. "We might even have a bad month."

I smiled back at him in the mirror, incredibly grateful for this kindness, however unintentional it was on his part.

"Heck, maybe it will even be a bad year," he said and began singing the song with his new lyrics. "We had a bad year..." Both he and my daughter laughed as though everything in our world hadn't turned upside down.

And I couldn't help it. It was crazy, but I laughed too. The three of us drove toward the pancake house yelling insanely about the rotten year we were about to have. And it was the happiest I'd felt since my Tuesday morning phone call.

Twenty minutes later, we were seated at a booth at IHOP with stacks of sticky, sweet pancakes in front of us. Jordan lifted a bite of the gooey mess toward his mouth and said, "Hey, Mom? I think our bad week just got a little bit better."

I blinked the tears from my eyes and smiled at him. "I do believe you're right, honey."

And in that moment, I learned that sometimes in life, we are put in situations when we have to laugh to keep from crying. And that, crazy or not, laughter is almost always infinitely better than tears.

~Diane Stark

53

Chicken Soup for the Soul

Where's Your Focus?

What we see depends mainly on what we look for.
~Sir John Lubbock

Middle of August. Washington State. Twelve-year-old Boy Scout with a forty-pound pack. Six days of fun-filled hiking with the Scout troop for fifty miles through the middle of the Cascade Range. Sounds like a great adventure right? Well, that's at least what a younger, more naïve version of myself was led to believe.

We said goodbye to our moms who dropped us off at the trailhead. Eagerly, we turned away from the highway, said goodbye civilization, and headed into the mountains. It didn't take me long to feel that maybe this fifty-mile hike thing wasn't going to be everything our Scout Leader had said it was going to be. It seemed the trail only went in one direction, uphill. And when we wanted to stop for a much needed break, we couldn't. The mosquitoes were just so bad! They were in our ears, eyes, even our noses! It was better to just keep moving to try and stay ahead of them.

When we reached camp after an exhausting first day I wanted nothing more than to eat a warm meal and then go to sleep. I got everything ready. I got out my mess kit, fired up my stove, and cooked some delicious pasta. Boy did it smell good! Now there was only one thing left to do — grab my fork. As I leaned over to grab my fork, the handle on my mess kit broke. I watched as my meal plummeted to the ground. I had knocked my dinner over and it lay on the ground, covered in dirt and pine needles, mocking my hunger. I ended up nibbling on some granola bars and beef jerky and spent the first night longing for my bed at home.

By day two of the hike, I was convinced that nature was out to get me. The endless hills, the hordes of mosquitoes, and with every step, I seemed to get a new blister. But I trudged on. By the late afternoon my scoutmaster and I reached camp first and were glad to be rid of our heavy packs. Finally some relief, right? Well, the catch was that my buddy who was carrying our tent was still a couple of hours behind.

So in the meantime, I tried to cook some dinner, again. I'm happy to say that my mess kit worked well this time. I'm not happy to say however, that the heat of my stove attracted all kinds of bugs. Now they must have thought that my food looked delicious because they kept landing in it and getting stuck. It got so bad that at one point, my pasta looked like it had fresh ground pepper on it! I gave up on yet another dinner.

At this point, all sorts of thoughts raced through my head. My muscles and feet ached with pain. My stomach groaned with hunger. I looked to the sky, wishing there was some way a helicopter could come and take me away from the madness.

I looked over to see my scoutmaster seemingly oblivious to everything going on. Who was this guy? Didn't he see my predicament? Now this was the kind of guy that just belonged in the woods. He was a big, strong, manly man. I think he even wore a flannel shirt with suspenders.

I was feeling pretty sorry for myself now and in my moment of self-pity, I didn't want him to see me. So I wondered off and found a small thicket of trees where I could hide. Can you guess what I did next? I sat down and I cried. That's right. I cried. A tired, little, sore, hungry, pitiful Sean sat alone in the wilderness crying. I didn't know what else to do! After my moments of self-pity, I realized that I was awfully close to where the rest of the older guys would be coming up the trail. I pulled myself together and wiped away the tears. Well, the evening finally came, along with my tent, and I tried to sleep away my troubles.

What happened the next morning was incredible. Looking back, I really consider it a blessing—a key learning point in my life. The morning of the third day found us hiking along a beautiful ridge. The views were amazing! It hit me in that moment that I had been focusing on all of the wrong things! How could I possibly feel sorry for myself when there was so much beauty and majesty all around me? I made up my mind right at that very moment that I would focus purely on what I did want and not anything that I did not want.

As if like magic, the mosquitoes seemed to disappear. The trail flattened out. My muscles stopped aching. I soaked in every ounce of beauty I could. The rest of the trip was incredible. It was late Saturday afternoon when we finished our trip. And I came home a bit less of a boy and a bit more of a man.

Often times, I feel, we go through life with our focus only on ourselves, on our problems. There are bills to pay, traffic to deal with, quotas to meet, businesses to run, etc. But there is so much good in the world and so much beauty all around us! All we need to do is simply change our focus. When our focus is shifted from the inside and changed to the outside, I know, from personal experience, that life truly becomes abundant.

So the key to managing that emotional stress is to change your focus. My question is: where's *your* focus?

~M. Sean Marshall

54

Chicken Soup for the Soul

A Change in Lifestyle

Our only security is our ability to change.
~John Lilly

My parents lived through the Great Depression of the 1930s and I heard stories from both of them about how their lives changed because of it. The same was true of my in-laws whose lives were also impacted negatively. For example, my husband's grandfather owned a factory. Owing to the stock market crash, he lost the factory and went back to work in the very factory he'd once owned. He could no longer afford to send my father-in-law to college. My father-in-law worked full time as a pipe fitter and went to school part-time to earn his degree, which took seven years.

My own mother graduated high school in 1929, took a job as a bookkeeper and promptly lost it after the stock market crash. She hardly worked after that for years and lived at home with her parents. My grandfather owned a six-family house but didn't bother trying to collect rent from the tenants as no one could afford to pay. It was fortunate that he had a steady job.

Somehow, my husband and I never dreamed that we would live through anything similar. However, as they say, history often repeats itself. In 1929, the stock market crashed in the month of October. The same thing happened in 2008. My husband, who believed in being fully invested in the market, was in a state of shock. Each day the news was more dire.

"We've lost more than half of our assets," he told me.

I just stared at him. "How can that be?"

"I thought we had good, solid investments, but it seems I was wrong."

"Well, we do have pensions," I said. "Hopefully, they won't be affected. Since we have never lived a high lifestyle to begin with, I don't think we have to worry."

"I did hope to leave our children and grandchildren a generous inheritance," my husband said. He shook his head in disbelief.

"We'll still be able to give gifts. Love is the most important gift anyway." Our children are grown and we always try to be generous to them and our grandchildren.

"It just won't be the same."

"The world is always changing," I said. "You never know what will happen. The main thing is not to get discouraged. As long as we have our health and can afford the necessities of life, there's no reason to be upset. When you have your health, you can always earn more money."

I hugged my husband and he kissed me in return.

"I guess you're right," he agreed. "We love each other. We have our health and enough money to live on comfortably. That's all that matters."

We have downsized from a house to a co-op apartment. It was a major change in lifestyle, and there are definite benefits. Unfortunately, our house was on the market at a time when the real estate market was seriously in trouble. We decided to offer our house for considerably less than it would normally be worth. Even so, our first buyer changed his mind days before closing. Our second buyer had trouble with the mortgage company. But finally, our home was sold.

As we shook hands with the new owners, I told them how fortunate they were.

"Not only are you getting a bargain in the price, but this house has good karma. We bought the house from a family who lived in it for nine years. They were a happy family, a husband, wife and five children. It was a cheerful house and we had a good feeling about it. We raised our children here as well."

"That's good to hear," the young woman said with a smile. "We have two young children ourselves. And I believe in karma too."

We nodded our heads in agreement, understanding each other.

"You'll live only six houses from the best elementary school in the township and your children won't even have to cross a street," I said. I wasn't trying to sell them the house because they'd already bought it, but I figured the real estate broker probably hadn't told them any of this.

"Our children used to come home each day and have lunch with me," I told them.

"We like the woods in the back," the young man told us. "We're going to plant a large garden in the backyard."

They seemed so young and happy and full of plans. My husband and I had to smile. At least some good was coming out of the economic crunch. We no longer needed a house. It was good to know that another young family would now be living in what had been a happy, loving home for us. Also, the house needed work that we no longer had the energy to perform.

These may be tough times economically, but as for me, I intend to look forward, not back. As Shakespeare said in *Macbeth*, "what's done is done and cannot be undone." It's the present and future that matter. We can learn from our mistakes and make our lives better.

~Jacqueline Seewald

Nathalie's Lessons

Physical strength is measured by what we can carry;
spiritual by what we can bear.
~Author Unknown

We learn valuable lessons throughout our lives. Schools teach academics, churches teach religion, workplaces teach business skills and technology, but there are other sources. Sometimes, "people" teach us lessons about life. What we learn from them can enrich our inner being and change our outlook on life. Nathalie was one such person.

Nathalie appeared in my life at a time when my whole world had been turned upside down. Pain, suffering, disappointment, and isolation kept me in a depressed state and I had turned my back on God. I felt sad, alone, and hopeless.

One morning in the early fall of 1960 I sat in my wheelchair waiting to be taken for therapy. Following therapy, I would be returned to my hospital bed. This was my daily routine and I hated it. I hated therapy, the hospital, nurses, doctors, but most of all, my life. While staring at the floor and dwelling on my misery, I became aware that someone had been wheeled in directly across from me. I didn't look up. She spoke, "Hi! How are you this morning?" I still didn't raise my head as I wasn't sure she was talking to me. A little louder, "Hello! My name is Nathalie. How are you this morning?"

Nathalie was thirty-four years old but already had a few grey hairs. She was seated in an old, wooden wheelchair with a high back, angled backward to support her upper back and head while the front supports were raised to accommodate her legs. She wasn't particularly pretty but there was an aura of warmth and brightness about her that made her seem somewhat attractive. She went on about the beautiful fall weather, cheerfully remarking, "Isn't it beautiful outside?"

I scowled, "I wouldn't know. I have been in here so long I don't know if there still is an 'outside.'" Returning my scowl with the biggest smile I have ever seen, she said, "I promise you that 'outside' is still there. In fact, 'outside' is beautiful this morning. I saw 'outside' from the window of my room." With her head, she gestured toward the window at the end of the hall, "See, there's 'outside.'" I couldn't help but smile at her quick-witted response. She had broken through the invisible wall I had built around me.

Nathalie had been diagnosed with rheumatoid arthritis two years earlier. The disease had progressed rapidly, leaving all of her joints fused into one large bone. The only parts of her body she could move were her head (moderately from side to side), and her arms (up and down slightly at the shoulder joint). Those two movements were all she had. Her feet were angled downward. Her elbows were frozen at a right angle positioning her arms across her chest. Her fingers were gnarled and arched. She could neither sit nor stand. Her only options were lying in bed or reclining in the wheelchair.

Nathalie and I quickly bonded. We saw each other every day for the following month until I was allowed a furlough—though scheduled to return. Her therapy treatments were brutal, as the therapists attempted to break all her joints loose by sheer force. The beads of sweat would form on her reddened face and tears would well up in her eyes but she didn't make a sound though the pain was almost unbearable. When therapy ended she would smile and remark, "Whew! I'm glad I don't have to do that again until tomorrow. I pray every morning that God will help me through just one more therapy, and He does, doesn't He?" I thought, "How could she be so cheerful after suffering such agony?"

Each day, sitting in the therapy room, we'd chat and even sing hymns together. At Christmas, we had a wonderful time singing carols. Nathalie sang in church choir and had a rich alto voice. She made those long hospital stays (months on end) almost fun with her witty remarks, her good nature, her spirituality, and perpetual smile. Everyone loved her.

She told me she had been married when she became confined to bed. She soon needed perpetual care. At that point, her husband left her for another woman. I responded angrily, "How could that rotten..." Fiercely, she started wagging her head, "No! No! Don't say that. You don't understand. He couldn't spend the rest of his life waiting on me hand and foot. He had a right to a life. I wanted that for him and I certainly couldn't offer him a wonderful life. I forgave him." I said no more.

The more I knew about Nathalie and her life, the more amazed I was at her absolute, deep faith, and trust in God, her love of people, and her zest for life. She looked forward to every day with enthusiasm and hope. Her painful therapy did very little to help, although she was able to stand, with help, in the years to come. Extensive therapy on her hands allowed her to brush her own teeth and develop primitive writing skills. Therapy continued but she still could not walk or sit. Every time I even thought about complaining or feeling sorry for myself, I would think of Nathalie. Once home, we kept in touch for the next forty years.

Since we lived more than one hundred miles apart, writing letters was the easiest way to communicate. She couldn't write often since writing took such a tremendous amount of effort. I will never forget the letter she wrote to me thirty years or more after our hospital stays. She started by telling me that she had gotten the best Christmas present she "had ever had in her whole life." Immediately, I thought of something material, like a new TV. She wrote, "You know how I love singing in choir. Well, you are never going to believe this one."

Eagerly, I read on to see what she was so excited about. "I have been sitting in the church aisle outside the choir section all these years and guess what? I sat in the pew at Christmas. Truly the best gift God has ever given me. I finally sat in the pew!" My eyes filled with tears thinking of this humble servant of God so filled with gratitude over something I had taken for granted my whole life.

Nathalie lived more than forty of her seventy-six years within her "arthritic prison," uncomplaining, while her faith in God remained ever strong. Only through death was she finally free from pain and suffering.

Though we spent less than one year together in a forty-year friendship, Nathalie is someone I will always remember. As a spiritual role model, she taught me priceless lessons about humility, hope, and acceptance of life.

~Joyce E. Sudbeck

56

If I Didn't Laugh, I'd Cry

Every survival kit should include a sense of humor.
~Author Unknown

The phone rang just as I finished my morning coffee. I cringed at the insistent intrusion into my day so early in the morning, but I also knew it meant bad news.

"Want me to get that?" I yelled to my husband John.

"No, I will," he said with resignation in his voice.

We both knew what the call was about before he even picked up the receiver. His sales client for the morning was canceling, again. This was becoming a daily ritual.

With the downturn of the economy John had fewer and fewer sales calls. Designing and selling kitchens wasn't exactly a lucrative business right now. Add to the mix the fact I had retired early last year due to health challenges, that John is well into retirement age, and, well, "Houston, we have a problem."

My husband had turned from a loving, carefree guy to being what I called "a grouchapotamus." We used to laugh and kid about all sorts of things but lately there wasn't much laughter in our home. I was becoming increasingly tense and John was keeping to himself. I knew something had to give or we were going to explode or implode—I wasn't sure which.

I called my friend Gerry to chat about my problems.

"Anna, don't worry. His bad moods are his way of handling what he can't say. He can't tell you he's scared and worried."

"But, I would tell him if I was," I argued back.

"Guys aren't like that," she counseled. "They just don't talk like we do."

"You can bet on that," I said. "I'm going to try to get him to open up if it kills me."

"Well, good luck with that," Gerry replied.

We went on to talk about other happier things, our kids, and the latest television shows.

John had worked in the yard all day and fell asleep right after dinner. So much for our chat.

The next morning I waited until he had finished his coffee and broached the subject of feelings.

"So, how are you feeling about the loss of your clients and sales?" I asked.

"How do you think I feel?" John replied in a testy tone of voice.

Well, suffice it to say, it went downhill from there. Before long we were screaming at each other, hurts were hurled back and forth, and before I knew it I blurted out "I want a divorce."

"Fine, but you'll have to leave," my husband yelled back.

I left the house in tears and jumped in my car. I trembled as I drove in circles for a half hour and finally pulled over and parked in a neighborhood near our house. I hated to call our grown daughter, but she was wise beyond her years and I needed to hear a friendly voice.

"Hi Karen," I blubbered through my tears.

"Mom, what's wrong?"

"I think Dad and I are getting a divorce after forty-four years," I said.

"You're not serious."

"Yeah, I just can't live with him like this. We're bickering all the time and he won't talk to me," I sobbed.

"You two can't break up. You've always worked through the hard times," she counseled.

"Yeah, but this time is different. He won't let me in. It's his damn ego; you know it's all tied into his performance as a salesman."

"Go home, talk to him in a loving way. Scott and I had a really bad fight one time and I told him I wanted a divorce. I didn't know what to say after that. I knew I had to mend things so I prayed, 'God, you have to help me, I'm lost here, I don't know where to turn or what to say,' and when I talked to Scott, the right words just came out. Try it."

"Ok, I'll give it a shot. It can't get any worse," I said.

I went home but John had left for his weekly sales meeting. I started some laundry and then I made my lunch with a heavy heart. Just as I was putting a pot of tea on the stove, John walked in. My heart flipped when I saw him. What was I going to say?

Before I had a chance to speak, he came over and put his arms around me in a big bear hug.

I was surprised but I hugged him back.

"I love you," he whispered. "I hate it when we fight."

"I love you too, so much."

"So, are you going to divorce me?" he asked with a sheepish grin on his face.

"No, I figured in this economy I can't afford it," I replied.

And he let out a big belly laugh, something I hadn't heard in a long time. I won't lie and say everything is great all the time, but we started a dialog that night that continues to grow. Maybe it's the couple that laughs together that stays together.

~Anne Dunne

57

Through a Glass Darkly

Love looks not with the eyes, but with the mind...
~William Shakespeare

"Y ou have the eyes of a seventy-year-old. Have any of your relatives been diagnosed with macular degeneration?"

Surely the top retinal specialist in Oklahoma had misdiagnosed my wife's condition. She couldn't have macular degeneration at forty-seven years old.

"No," Pam said. Her voice resounded with confidence, hiding the shock I knew she felt. "I haven't noticed anything abnormal. What should I prepare for?"

I could see the doctor's face from my chair off in the corner. Even with the only lights in the examining room being his medical computer and the reflective glow of the eye chart, the furrow in his brow and frown on his face clearly showed the seriousness of the matter.

"There is no cure for dry macular." The doctor pulled a packet of patient care instructions from a folder on his desktop. "Mrs. Wetterman, you need to check your vision chart at least once a week. If you see any distortion, call my office immediately." He wrote something down on a notepad, tore off a sheet, and handed it to her. "You need to get on a regimen of vitamins, specifically those listed here. The best science says they help to slow the progression of this disease, but they don't provide a cure."

My wife scuffed the floor with her shoe. "I need glasses. I'll grant you that. But I can read, and I can see to drive. This is so bizarre."

The doctor shrugged. "Only God knows why you can see as clearly as you do. When I look at your retina, the scarring is severe. Possibly, there's a small unscarred area that's positioned just in the right spot to allow you the vision you have. How long this will last is a guess."

• • •

Sixteen years fraught with obstacles and challenges have gone by since that day. For me, being unable to fix her vision has been the hardest part. It's not like staining a cabinet or making a bookcase. That's what men do. We fix things.

My wife is strong, loving, and the most intelligent person I know. From the first day I met her, I knew God had set her aside just for me, and that's what made this so hard. She gave up college when we married to raise our kids and support my career. When our boys were old enough, I encouraged her to pursue a career of her own.

My wife's a beautiful woman, deer-brown eyes and hair, tall, and graceful. But she's also dynamic and capable. When our youngest boy turned eleven, Pam started working. She went back to college, obtained her degree, and received promotion after promotion. She advanced within her company to Manager of Credit and Collections, supervising more than two hundred employees in eleven states for one of the largest utilities in the nation, and I supported her every step of the way. But now I feared this disability would steal future opportunities away from her.

She stood up to her physical challenge with the same confidence and determination that made her a success in business. But over time, her condition worsened.

"I can't see my computer screen as well as I used to," she said to me one evening in 2003, eleven years after her initial diagnosis. "I'm making stupid mistakes."

A perfectionist, she demanded excellence from herself, so I went on a mission. I found a product that not only magnified her screen, but also read text and e-mails to her. She could even select the voice she wanted to read to her from a menu of male and female voices. She selected a man's voice and called him Peter. For the first time in my life, a tiny smidge of jealousy popped up in me.

Regardless, her condition continued to worsen. We'd just returned from a Caribbean cruise in 2004, and the evening after we got back she came to me with tears running down her cheeks. "I need to go back to the doctor. Things aren't right with my eyes."

That appointment was life-altering. "I'm sorry," the doctor said, "but your vision is now such that you're not going to be able to drive."

Her lips quivered, and her smile faded. A cloud of gloom settled over my heart. My eyes moistened, knowing she was in pain. I couldn't tell her I understood that pain. I doubt anyone could understand unless it was happening to them.

"God, this isn't fair," I mumbled.

As we drove home, I mulled over her situation. Independent and self-confident all her life, she'd suddenly lost her freedom. Cutbacks at work had already taken her administrative help away. Key reports and correspondence had become harder and harder to read and respond to, even with Peter's help. Errors cropped up more often. And now on top of it all, she had to depend on someone else for simple things like a ride to work or a trip to the grocery store.

"I'll always be here, sweetheart," I said. "Life will be as normal as I can make it."

Sobbing and a gentle pat on my hand was her response.

By 2006, Pam could no longer see well enough to do her job. She applied for and received Social Security Disability. She could have spiraled into an unending pity party, but she didn't. Last year when my office had a bowling gala, Pam went. She couldn't see the pins. She barely could see the arrows on the lanes. She didn't astound anyone with her score, but she did.well enough that a stranger watching her couldn't have guessed her condition. That's the strong-willed fiber of the woman I married.

Pam recognizes people by their voices. She doesn't make out facial features unless you're right in front of her. I tell her I look like Robert Redford, and she humors me, affectionately saying she loved me in *Barefoot in the Park*.

I retired this year to pursue my writing full time. Guess who edits my work? My wife. Peter reads my writing to her, and she listens. When something sounds amiss, she reads the large-print text out of the little peripheral vision she has left. She catches things a full-sighted person might miss.

Pam works as a volunteer for Lab Rescue. She's active with the Sunday school class I teach. Together we can overcome any obstacle life throws our way. At the end of next month, we'll celebrate our forty-fourth wedding anniversary. We'll drive to Eureka Springs, Arkansas, and spend the weekend. Maybe, if the road allows, I'll pull over at a scenic outlook and describe the view while she experiences the wind and the sunshine.

I have my share of physical problems, and she helps me with them as I help her with her vision. Do I have questions for God about all the trials we've had to go through? I do. But I have all the more awe in the wonder of His plans when I hold my wife's hand. Does she cry sometimes because of things she can't do? Yes. But it's momentary. Then, she and I count our blessings and enjoy our life together.

~Bill Wetterman

58

Playing the Game

Necessity may be the mother of invention, but play is certainly the father.
~Roger von Oech

Church clothing drives. The same dinner every day for a week, maybe two. Generic toys instead of the ones everyone else had.

When I was a child, my mother went on food stamps after her second divorce. There was no alimony from her first marriage, and it didn't seem like there was any from her second one either. Every Saturday, my mom would rush me and my brother to the local church, not for mass, but for their Saturday morning bag sale. A grocery bag full of used clothes would only cost a dollar, and the early bird would, indeed, get the worm, or first dibs on the better clothes. When I'd complain that all the other kids were wearing OshKosh B'Gosh — how could I possibly wear these generic overalls, and two sizes too big, at that — she would say, "You should be so lucky to have clothes to wear at all."

My mom would always stuff as much clothing into each bag as she could; I don't know how she did it. When she caught me watching her cramming our future wardrobe into a bag, she said, "We have to play the game."

"What game?" I wondered. I learned she wasn't talking about board games, like my favorites, *Candy Land* and *Clue*. "The less you spend, the more you win, literally," she said. "And the more money you will save. It's a game to spend as little as you can. Someday you'll see."

When the cool kids would laugh at my mismatched, unlabeled clothes, I would run home crying. My mom would simply say, "Remember, we're playing the game. You should be so lucky to have clothes to wear at all." But, at nine, I didn't understand. I'd rather be naked.

That was how I grew up, but as a working adult I have not had to live that way. Until now. At thirty-two.

As a kid, if my family and I ever had one food staple, it was a ten-pound bag of potatoes, for my mother said that you can always do something with potatoes. Peel, grate, sauté, boil, broil... the options were endless. So I may have had a diet high in starch, but, as my mom liked to say, "We're playing the game. At least you have food to eat." She would couple the potatoes with canned corn—dented cans, of course, for they were cheaper. Sometimes, my brother and I would even help dent the cans, throwing them all over the store floor, probably over repressed anger for having to wear oversized overalls to school and eat potatoes for every meal.

When my brother asked if we could start having pizza for dinner like his friends, my mother said sure. She found a cookbook for twenty-five cents at the library's used book sale and made a pizza—on an English muffin. I did a double-take. It almost looked like a pizza, but it definitely didn't taste like a pizza. English muffins weren't meant to be topped with generic tomato sauce, and an even more generic fake mozzarella cheese (which resembled rubber more than anything else). But, as usual, my mom had a quick quip and justification for this dinner, "We're playing the game. You should be so lucky to have any food to eat at all." She'd also point out that at least she had made something from scratch; she didn't just open a can of Chef Boyardee (although I would have much preferred the latter).

At the time, I hated her. And English muffins. My friends got to order Domino's pizza, and I had to eat these mini "pizzas" that tasted nothing remotely like pizza. Pizza crust and English muffins had nothing in common. Life was unfair.

When I had wanted the latest Barbie doll, my mom bought me the generic one (you know, those ones with the oversized heads that don't resemble Barbie dolls at all) for ninety-nine cents instead. "No girls will want my fake Barbie to play with their real ones," I said. "You should be so lucky to have a doll to play with at all," she said. Yeah, yeah, yeah.... Did my mom realize how lonely this generic "Barbie" would be? "We have to keep playing the game," she added. Yeah, a kid really wants to hear that; I was sick of playing the game. When would it be over? I just wanted a Barbie. A real one. "No one's going to know the difference," my mom said. "A doll is a doll." But not to me. I knew the difference.

My mom kept saying, "This too shall pass," and how we just had to have faith that this was an ebb, not a flow, and that we would be okay someday. But when? At nine, I barely knew what "faith" meant, let alone "ebbs" and "flows."

Years later, I learned that my mom only allowed herself to spend ten dollars a week back then. Ten dollars to support me, my brother, and herself. Who knew that what I learned growing up would help me so much now? Now, more than twenty years later, I have been laid off and my bank balance is unbalanced (negative). How did this happen? They say "history repeats itself," but this is ridiculous.

Funny how, as a child, I barely took to heart what my mother had said, all her "you should be so lucky..." comments. And, of course, that favorite phrase—"We're playing the game." But, now, over the last few months, I have recalled more of what my mother taught me than ever before.

Suddenly, I find myself "playing the game." I go to thrift stores, trading and selling my old clothes. (Little did I know what an "in" thing thrift stores would be with my generation, all these years later. Now, I could care less about brand-name labels; in fact, I'd much prefer no label at all.) I watch as the store owner reviews my old clothes, and the way onlookers stand by excitedly, waiting to buy them, just like my nine-year-old self had once done.

With the few dollars I make from the thrift store, I buy a ten-pound bag of potatoes to peel, grate, and mash up. But I always avoid the English muffins... unless they don't have tomato sauce and cheese on them.

My mom was right: As a child, I was lucky to have clothes, food, and generic "Barbies." And, as an adult, I am lucky to have them, too (that generic Barbie is on my bookshelf now). I'm happy to still be "playing the game"... and winning.

~Natalia K. Lusinski

59

Why Me?

Gratitude is the memory of the heart.
~Jean Baptiste Massieu, translated from French

What have I done to deserve this?

Things look bad. People are in despair. Even the fog outside my window is symbolic of a world shrouded in mourning.

And yet, I sit alone in my chair... relaxed, content, and at peace. Why should this be?

Every news story, every bill, and every bank statement looks worse than the one before. I'm not able to get a job. Sixty-year-old widows just can't compete. For three decades I worked as a caregiver to my paralyzed husband, John. But that's not good enough for a résumé.

Now John's elderly parents require my help. Their minds are failing. It's a sad process to watch and a heavy responsibility.

So... why should I be at peace?

As I sit, I study the faces in a smattering of pictures on my wall. Their smiles serve as visible reminders of personal victories over life's battles.

One photo is of my mother when she was my age. She's stylishly dressed in a black suit and a crisp, white blouse—attire reflecting her position as a hotel executive. But it's her schoolgirl grin that reveals the woman inside.

My mother possessed a boundless love of life. I got such a kick out of her spunk. In her day, business executives were almost exclusively male. But Mom elbowed her way to the top... because she had to. There was no one else to support her family.

Thirty years earlier, Dad died in a car accident. He left no savings or life insurance. At age twenty-nine, Mom faced the responsibility of providing for three small children. Immediately after Dad's death, she retreated to her bedroom for a week of weeping. But when she came out, she never looked back. Her elderly mother moved in to serve as our 24/7 babysitter. Then Mom charged headlong into the working world.

She started as a banquet waitress in a luxury hotel, working long hours—even around the clock, if she could. Determined to succeed, she became the most resourceful, insightful person in her department. The rich and famous regularly called on her to serve their sumptuous feasts.

But at home, Mom cut corners wherever she could. Our clothes were secondhand, but adequate. We ate well, due to the kindness of neighbors and friends. We learned to never turn on a lamp or an appliance unless there was no alternative. Believe it or not, Mom and Granny used to ration "luxury" items such as Kleenex.

Sometimes Mom struggled to pay the mortgage, but we had a roomy home, heated by a lone fireplace. Granny got up before dawn to start the fire. Then, we'd all dash out of bed to bask in its warmth.

Mom didn't own a car until I was in my teens. We were told, "You have two good feet to get around." Public transportation was available for longer trips.

Every summer we tended a large garden, yielding bountiful crops of vegetables and berries. What couldn't be used fresh was canned or frozen.

In her "spare" time, Mom made ballet costumes, and attended recitals, little league games, and parent-teacher conferences. When she should have been sleeping, she'd take us to the beach or the zoo. On rare occasions, we'd go to the theater or the symphony. She did everything possible to enrich our time together.

Mom was a living encyclopedia on how to survive in hard times.

Best of all, she came through it all victoriously—grinning from ear to ear.

Another face smiling at me is John. What a husband! He was a funny guy, a brilliant scholar and a high achiever. But, at age twenty-seven, multiple sclerosis took him down.

At the time of his diagnosis, we'd been married only six years and were expecting our son at any moment. We were just starting our lives! John already limped from the onset of paralysis in his legs. The doctor told him to quit his physically demanding job or his health would decline rapidly. How would we survive?

The initial shock sent John reeling into depression. But, after a few months, he rallied and returned to college to obtain his Master's degree in Business Administration. He fought his way through school. He fought the deterioration of his body. He fought for the sake of his family. And, through it all... he kept us laughing.

Although John's paralysis eventually forced him to depend on an electric wheelchair, he refused to let it hold him back. Instead of languishing in self pity, he concentrated on being the best possible husband and father.

John used his financial skills to manage our household. Since we had to live on a small disability pension, he set strict budgetary guidelines. He taught me how to handle money responsibly, adding to Mom's lessons on penny-pinching.

Yes... I started rationing Kleenex.

John also insisted I learn how to care for the car, do minor repairs around our home, work on a computer, and handle family finances. He trained me in the skills I'd need after he was gone.

When I'd moan about being too busy, John would say, "Sit down, shut up, and learn this stuff!"

I wish I could kiss him for his patient insistence. The skills he taught me now serve both my needs and those of his parents.

The last photo to catch my eye is one of Granny, taken in 1898. She's a tender, young woman wearing a long, white dress and a serene glow.

Even when Granny was eighty, she retained that serene look. I remember her sitting in a worn, upholstered rocker gazing wistfully into the fireplace. Her hands would be neatly folded over the "Good Book," as she called it. Granny seemed lost in absolute contentment, worlds away from our childish antics — oblivious to the chaos around her.

However, this was a woman who'd faced many trials. As the youngest child of a Civil War amputee, she spent her young adult years caring for her widowed father. She married late in life and had three children. Her husband died just before the Great Depression. The family nearly starved. But Granny fought on... getting little jobs here and there working as a nurse.

She loved children and taught us much through play. With Granny's help, we learned to create great adventures just by using a little imagination. Blankets became tents, magazines became alphabet games, and closets became spaceships.

Life didn't leave Granny bitter. She lived in a place of peace.

I gaze with gratitude at my gallery of good examples. Their lives have taught me how to: work hard, be frugal, fix leaking faucets, manage a small income, nurse the ailing, play with children, and feast on life's little joys.

Outside my window, the fog is lifting. Birds fill the neighborhood with joyful songs. Squirrels bounce playfully from tree to tree. They're not worried. Neither am I.

I sit peacefully, staring into the fireplace. My hands are neatly folded over the "Good Book." Although, the world reels in chaos, my heart and home are filled with peace.

Having done nothing to deserve this... I bow my head in thanks.

~Laura L. Bradford

The Unlikely Cheering Section

Always look on the bright side of life.
~Monty Python

I was twenty-one and in a Toronto hospital after knee surgery. Back then, nearly thirty years ago, the procedures were more invasive and took a longer time to heal. I was in a room across from a young man whose story was shared with me by the nurses. His name was Ross, and it was obvious he had been in a serious trauma. He was in a full body cast, and had been in the hospital for at least nine months. According to the staff accounts, he had been in a car that was struck by a drunk driver, and suffered massive injuries.

His head injury reduced him to a very young level and he was learning to read again in the hospital. My mother, who visited me frequently, enquired about his situation. Evidently his family had accepted a settlement and had essentially "left town" with the funds, leaving Ross as a ward of the province, and with no additional funds for anything beyond the hospital basics. I recall that the staff members were trying to help Social Services locate his family and take some action on his behalf.

Ross and I were unlikely roommates. He was bright, cheerful and totally delighted by visitors of any type. He borrowed books from the hospital trolley and tried, loudly, to read them. Across the room from Ross was me — a bitter twenty-one-year-old who was both in pain and angry at having an injury that kept me from all the things I enjoyed.

My mother visited several times, and always found herself sitting with Ross, reading with him, and spending time enjoying him. Others who visited me didn't know how to take him. Ross never had any visitors for himself. My mother considered him a joy, and she was deeply concerned over his situation. We could see that the staff loved him deeply, but there was little they could do. He had no money, and I remember him straining his head to see the TV I had at my bed. He couldn't afford the TV rental, so mine (and I suppose other patients in that room) provided him with a bit of distraction—even if he couldn't hear it through the headphones.

Several days after my surgery, the therapy staff arrived to get me moving. The first step was to raise my leg from the bed under my own power. It was extremely painful, and through tears and frustration I said "I can't." It was a surreal experience, just like in a film where you watch something and the sounds are spacey and detached. One voice was very clear, rising above the therapist who was sternly telling me I could do this, and that voice was Ross. All through this situation, he cheered for me, encouraged me, kept saying "Come on Peter, you can do it!" I raised my leg, and once the session was over I fell back onto my pillow, sweating from the stress. The pain was intense. Ross was there, telling the nurse and the therapist how great I was for doing it!

That was an amazing moment in my life. I had a revelation that both humbled me, and encouraged me for years to come. This young man had been robbed of his life, then of his entitlement that was intended to rebuild his life. He had nothing; he had lost physical, mental and worldly things and was simply a young man on a bed. Yet here he was, cheering for me. He didn't utter words of encouragement; he shouted them because he was with me going through that. Looking back, mine was a relatively easy situation. Others have gone through great pain and suffering far beyond mine. I began wondering, what compelled this man to cheer for me and not bemoan his own situation? It was a reflection of the very foundations of my faith, and of his heart that could not be crushed by the accident that crushed his body.

After leaving the hospital, I never saw Ross again. Yet, Ross was always with me. My life was filled with ongoing knee problems—more than twenty operations, including total replacements of both knees. That was a lot of surgery, a lot of therapy, a lot of struggle. For me it seemed relatively easy. Each time I had to come back from a procedure, I had Ross in my heart. When it hurt, Ross could be heard cheering. When I was discouraged, Ross was with me, reminding me that I could get through it.

I often had surgeons, therapists and others commenting on how quickly I recovered, how soon I was walking normally. That has never been a great achievement on my part. Ross reminded me that there are always people who are worse off, and that we can always heal. We are made that way. Ross, in his battered state, was healing too. I find myself thinking of, and praying for, Ross frequently. He taught me hope when I was most hopeless.

As something of a postscript, I learned after I left that a gracious angel had arranged for Ross to have a month of TV in the hospital. It was a small act of love, but I always knew my mom to be such an angel. I know she thought of Ross often.

Thank you, Ross, wherever you are today. I still hear you cheering when the going gets tough. If I ever feel discouraged, I'll remember those heroes who deal with disease and disability daily, and I'll push forward to live each day to its fullest.

~Peter J. Green

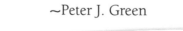

The Ten Best Things

The best things in life aren't things.
~Art Buchwald

"You know what I really can't stand?" Wendy asks rhetorically. "It's when people say cancer is a gift. I mean is that really something you'd like to receive? Would a friend give a friend cancer?"

"Yeah," chimes in Alice. "Some gift. Can I give it back? Say I don't want it? Maybe exchange it for something different?"

We are all getting in the spirit of it now. "Can we rewrap it and give it to someone else?"

"Or donate it to a white elephant sale?"

"Say politely, thanks but no thanks?"

As we all erupt into laughter, I sneak a glance around the room at the eight or so women assembled in a loose circle. The only prerequisite to joining this writing group was having received a cancer diagnosis at some previous point in our lives. A positive (in the clinical sense, that is) pathology report was our ticket for admission. A perk of getting cancer, if you will.

It's kind of funny to group cancer and the idea of perks in the same thought, but for all that we are chortling about it, there has been a silver lining to being diagnosed with cancer, even if it wasn't immediately apparent. *Pollyanna* wasn't one of my favorite childhood books for nothing, and almost as soon as the initial shock of my diagnosis began to subside, I tried playing the "glad game," like Pollyanna.

In the first place, I had to be grateful for all the technology and the vigilance of my doctor that enabled my cancer to be caught early, when it was, as they tell me, the most treatable. I held this thought close as I endured the treatment, reminding myself continually to focus on the future, and that this was merely the means to an end.

Time passed, and as my family and friends pulled around me, I slowly, almost imperceptibly at first, began to heal. The physical recovery, surprisingly enough, proceeded more rapidly than the emotional recovery. It took much longer to accustom myself to the uncertainty of life post-cancer. I was to discover that cancer challenges all of your basic assumptions and beliefs and causes you to reassess your priorities. Given that the average life expectancy for women in this country is somewhere around eighty years of age, I'd always figured I had plenty of time before I had to give serious thought to my own mortality. Cancer changed that all that.

The voice of Sharon, our group facilitator cuts through our laughter. "Let's get started now," she says. "While we're all thinking about cancer, I want you to write about something that is different about your life as a result of being diagnosed with cancer. Take about fifteen minutes."

Heads bend to the page, and pens move as everyone else begins writing. I alone stare vacantly out the picture window, tapping my pen, and thinking. What should I write about? How I stopped stressing so much about every little thing because suddenly everyday petty concerns didn't seem as important? About all the compassionate people I met along the way as I embarked on my cancer journey? About how I became more open to taking risks, like walking into this writing group with absolutely no writing experience whatsoever, because after cancer nothing else looks really scary?

Slowly, I begin to write "The Ten Best Things about Cancer." I stop and underline it several times before I continue.

There has to be a bright side. Every cloud has a silver lining after all.

Ten: I can never repeat the shock of the initial diagnosis.

Now that's something. Isn't that a bit like lightning never strikes twice? (Although sometimes it does.)

Nine: I appreciate each and every day now.
Even more than I did before.

Eight: I have something to talk about with people, if conversation ever lags.

Seven: I can almost guarantee that anyone I talk to has a cancer story of their own — themselves or a family member or a friend of a friend.

Six: I belong to an exclusive club of fighters and survivors.

Five: People tend to cut you some slack when they find out you've had cancer.

Four: I've met some truly amazing and inspiring people that I cannot conceive of having become acquainted with under any other circumstances, and for this, I'm truly grateful.

Three: I've learned that looking out for myself is not a luxury anymore, but a necessity.

Two: I've learned to stop and smell the proverbial roses (and tulips and crocuses and daffodils).

Finally, One: I am a survivor, as my pink shirt at next year's Race for the Cure will surely attest to. I have battled my arch-nemesis , Cancer, and for now, I have prevailed.

The gong gently calls us to attention. "Come to a stopping place," Sharon tells us, and there is a sudden furious scribbling of pens as everyone scrambles to wrap up their piece. As we go around the room sharing our writings, I am struck once again by the determination, courage and cautious optimism shown in the face of adversity by all the women in this room.

Over and over, I hear common themes echoed in the writings.

"I've learned not to take anything for granted," Amy reads.

"I stopped putting things off for the future. Besides attending this writing group, I've signed up for a watercolor class, something I always wanted to do." This is from Kristy.

And Donna: "I take the time now to explore life's highways and byways, and enjoy the ride."

And it gets me to thinking. Knowing what we know now, would any of us actually have chosen to have been diagnosed with cancer? The answer has to be emphatically no. I'm sure that I am speaking for all of us when I say we would have been glad to avoid the nerve-wracking wait for pathology results, the life-altering shock of diagnosis, being poked and prodded endlessly with needles, the surgeries, chemo and radiation treatments that tried the very limits of our endurance, and the relentless scans and blood tests to ensure that we remain, for the moment, cancer-free.

Yet for all that, one thing becomes patently clear to me. I doubt very much that any of us would give back what we have learned along the cancer journey: to be kinder, more compassionate, more life-affirming people and never to forget how much we still have to be grateful for. Cancer may not have been a gift, but it was certainly a wake-up call.

~Cara Holman

62

Never a Bad Day

If you don't think every day is a good day, just try missing one.
~Cavett Robert

There are few places more unpleasant than a Florida post office with broken air conditioning. Throw in the rush of the holiday season and you have a pretty good picture of where I was last year during my lunch break, two weeks before Christmas.

People crowded around me in the line, balancing boxes on hips and shoulders, all watching the three postal workers behind the counter. Red and green stars hung from the ceiling overhead and brightly colored posters advertised the latest stamps.

The wait stretched on and on.

The folks behind the counter moved as fast as they could, doling out postage, handling packages, tracking down lost mail, but they were way over their heads. As time slipped past, the mood of the line grew uglier and uglier. You know the drill: loud sighs, sarcastic comments, people tapping their feet.

In short, it was all the social unpleasantness you can imagine concentrated into one overly warm room.

The one bright spot in this whole situation was the silver-haired gentleman in front of me. Looking completely unaffected by the extended wait, he asked if I was ready for Christmas. That started a conversation and we spent the rest of our time in line chatting. He was mailing a package to some grandchildren that he hadn't seen in several months, and was nervous that he might not have picked out gifts they would like.

That led us to a discussion of gifts and gift-giving in general. As the people around us grumbled and complained, we talked about presents we'd received and given, both the hits and the dismal failures.

When his turn came, the man stepped quickly to the counter. The postal worker immediately apologized for the wait, but the man told him not to worry and they settled down to the business of mailing his package.

As he was walking away, the postal worker called out "Have a good day!"

Someone in the crowd heard and let out a cynical "ha!"

The older man turned back, smiled gently at the haggard man behind the counter, and said, "Son, I've never had a bad day in my life. And this," he gestured vaguely at the crowd of unhappy people, "certainly is not enough to make me start."

He caught my eye, gave me a wink, and walked out.

~Patrick Matthews

Count Your Blessings

I've Got What I Need

He who knows that enough is enough
will always have enough.

~Lao Tzu

63

Homeward Bound

Peace — that was the other name for home.
~Kathleen Norris

The movers pulled out of our driveway. I glanced for the last time at our home of twenty-two years. We'd planned to spend the rest of our lives there, but health issues and financial issues forced us to sell. As we pulled away from the curb, I burst into tears.

Startled, my husband slammed on the brakes. "Karen, what's wrong?"

"I'll be fine. Reality just hit home."

"I know, honey, but you've been so strong. Your sudden outburst scared me."

"I'm okay," I said, smiling, trying, to look convincing.

As we drove through heavy traffic, I closed my eyes, and my mind flashed back a few months. John had been on disability. He'd been fighting an ear infection that had resulted in severe hearing loss.

Sitting in our doctor's office, we anxiously waited while he looked at John's latest audiologist report.

"Good, looks like you've gained back some hearing. I think we are finally getting that infection under control."

"That's good news. My disability is coming to a close, and I'm retiring for the last time," John replied.

"You and Karen have worked long and hard for that retirement," Dr. William said reassuringly.

Later that afternoon, John and I sat in our front yard sipping iced tea. I glanced at the "For Sale" sign, and sighed.

John seemed to read my mind and said, "Karen, I think we should back out of selling our home. We don't really want to live anywhere else."

"John, we really need to stick to our decision. We've sat down with our financial advisor, and he agrees we are doing the right thing. Do you remember what we learned six years ago?"

"Yeah, I remember, the bluebird."

"Yes, you'd been retired for four years and because I'd been forced to retire early we were struggling. We were talking, and praying, when we noticed the bluebird. We watched as he dug up a peanut, and we marveled at his ingenuity. He'd stored up food for when he needed it."

"That's right, and then the phone rang. It was my former employer asking if I wanted to come out of retirement. They needed qualified, experienced supervisors to work on a special project. It was supposed to last nine months, and it lasted five years."

"John, we need to count our blessings. Because, you went back to work we were able to stay here longer."

Later, that afternoon, our real estate lady, Trudy, called and said, "I have a beautiful home to show you. It's a three-bedroom, manufactured home in a beautiful park. The price is right."

The next day, John and I drove out to the desert community. The clear blue sky against the rolling hills seemed to welcome us. Soon, we pulled into the park. As we parked in front of the home a bluebird landed in a nearby tree. I smiled, and said, "I wonder if that's the same bluebird?"

John laughed. As we entered the living room, it was love at first sight. I walked through a dream kitchen, and knew I never wanted to leave. John loved the spacious master bedroom, and the family room.

That afternoon, we made an offer. The next day, Trudy called and said, "They've accepted your offer."

"Look at that sunset," John said, bringing me back to the present.

The movers were waiting for us. Two hours later, we sat in our family room staring at boxes. The next day our family showed up and the unpacking began. We were grateful to have the help. As it was, it took a couple of months to settle in.

We started walking every afternoon. Soon we began meeting our neighbors and using the clubhouse and the other facilities. It didn't take long to fall in love with the beauty that surrounded our park, the peacefulness, and the marvelous sunsets every evening.

Then one Saturday, we went up to Orange County to visit family. Later that evening when John pulled into our driveway, he said, "It's good to be home."

I smiled. "Home is where the heart is."

"That's right, Karen, as long as we're together—we are home."

~Karen Kosman

Mango
Mud Blessings

If there is magic on this planet, it is contained in water.
~Loran Eisley

Sometimes the simple pleasures of life are so simple that I take them for granted. Things that I've come to consider as my right, instead of a blessing. I realized this after my first trip to Honduras. My dear friend, who serves there as a humanitarian and missionary, had invited me to speak at a women's conference she was putting together.

The night before I was to fly out, I finished packing and decided a warm bath would help calm my excited nerves and help me sleep. I twisted the hot water handle on the tub and waited... and waited... and waited. I drummed my fingers against the faux marble and grumbled, "For crying out loud, already. Let's have some warm water!"

It took forever for the hot water to work its way through the pipes to the back of the house. Well, maybe not forever, but it sure seemed that way. Besides, I didn't have any time to spare. My alarm was set to four o'clock. I had to get some sleep. Needless to say, the bath wasn't relaxing. I got in, bathed, and got right out.

The next afternoon I arrived in San Pedro Sula, Honduras. It was so good to see my friend and her husband. On the five-hour drive to their home in Yamaranguila, I took in the beautiful countryside. So lush and green. A lot like the hills of my northwest Arkansas home, except for the occasional banana trees and pineapple groves.

After the conference, my friend took me to meet some of the families she and her husband had come to know and love. Thankfully, she acted as my interpreter while we visited. The people I met lived in abject poverty. They lived in ten by ten stick-and-mud houses and slept on dirt floors. The women cooked outside on stoves fashioned from stacked concrete blocks topped with old steel barrel lids that served as the cooking surface. Still, even in these awful conditions, everyone I met had a smile on their face. They were so gracious and almost always insisted we stay for coffee.

On our way to one home we passed the mother and daughter-in-law who lived there. They were kneeling beside a pond that was covered with green slime. One woman pushed the scum back with a stick while the other dipped the water into a bucket. I shot a prayer toward the heavens, "Dear Lord, Please don't let them offer coffee."

They followed us to their house and invited us inside. While we chatted, chickens walked in, cocked their heads as if to check out the two pale strangers, then sauntered out. A cat sat in the window opening watching. However, he was so emaciated that none of the birds had anything to worry about.

Children played outside in the dust. They sounded just like my children when they were small. One little girl ran inside. She held a mango in each hand. The one in her left hand was half eaten. Juice had mingled with the dirt on her skin and small rivulets of mango-mud ran down her wrist.

This little brown-eyed beauty held out her right hand and offered me the other mango, which I gladly accepted. Her eyes danced and joy spread into a smile. As she scratched her lice-filled hair, I remember thinking, "She has no idea she is poor."

When it was time to leave we walked outside and I noticed a muddy stream that ran beside their home. My friend pointed at it and said in English, "That is where they bathe. It is also where the animals drink and defecate." I have to say that was the most sobering time in my life.

The evening I returned home I went into my pristine bathroom and twisted the hot water handle on the tub. Only this time instead of drumming my fingers against the faux marble, I thought of that precious little girl covered in mango-mud. Her bath would consist of splashing in the cold, dirty, water in the creek. No soap, no bubbles.

I eased into my tub filled with warm, drinking-quality water and perfumed with lavender oil. While soaking, I mused on this simple pleasure. Clean water wasn't my right, it was a blessing. A blessing I was now determined to share with others.

~Linda Apple

65

The Best Gift

Love is, above all, the gift of oneself.
~Jean Anouilh

With two teenagers on the verge of college there wasn't much money left over for holiday shopping. Although I had never conveyed my concern to my daughters, somehow they knew. They had seen me glued to the news reports following the nation's economic crises. They had watched their dad grimace over the checkbook and credit card bills. They had seen me remove items from the grocery cart that we didn't absolutely need. They had witnessed me scrimp like never before. They're smart kids who are also exceptionally thoughtful.

I was on my way to the mall to do a little Christmas shopping. With a short list in one hand and car keys in the other, I asked what they wanted for Christmas. I braced myself for their reply. They looked up as if praying to God for enlightenment on what to say. If I were their age I'd ask for a curling iron, a cell phone, an iPod, gift cards, movie tickets, and new clothes. They looked me square in the eye and said, "We're good."

I stared back in disbelief. They were teenagers with final exams and SATs only one week away. The college application deadline was dangerously close. They had choir practice, volunteer obligations, and parties. They had concerts to prepare for and school projects to complete. How in the world could they be "good?"

"What are you really thinking?" I waited nervously for a reply. "There must be something you want."

They quietly deliberated and Juliana, older and wiser, swallowed hard before answering. "We don't need a thing." They nodded. "Seriously," she reaffirmed.

I stared at her in disbelief, waiting for her to smile or crack a joke, but she was adamant.

"We're really good, Mom," Andrea said. "We have everything a girl could want. You and Dad have given us everything. We're happy," she said motioning to Juliana, "just to have you."

I felt my heart skip a beat as time stood still. Her words reverberated in my head as my eyes welled with tears of joy. Both girls wrapped their arms around me and hugged me long and hard. The truth was that we didn't have much money left over for unnecessary gifts. We could barely afford the things we really needed with sky-rocketing college costs looming on the horizon.

That moment was the sweetest and most tender I had ever experienced. Their words were all I needed. I didn't need a present under the tree and neither did they. I had something much better. Words spoken from the heart of the children I have built my life around for the last eighteen years lifted me to a much higher place. They couldn't have given me a better gift. I cherished their warmth and reaffirmed my love for them.

"I insist you let me get you something. We can afford it," I lied.

Juliana pulled back and her solemn voice took over. "Then get us something we can share."

"We're really good at sharing," Andrea chimed.

They were killing me with kindness. I looked at my daughters in awe and silently thanked God for blessing me with two great kids. How could I be so lucky?

I put my car keys away and assembled the Christmas tree in the family room in its usual spot. It was the one job I detested and I usually pawned it off on Patrick, my easygoing husband. This year I cherished the time together. Next year they would be on a college campus and the thought of not having them around me all of the time scared me. I appreciated each strand of twinkle lights that we wrapped around the prickly branches. I loved every second of it.

Andrea opened the box of ornaments and dangled one on a branch near me. I remembered it fondly—a heart-shaped ornament I bought for Patrick the first year we were dating.

Andrea gave me an endearing smile. "This ornament sums up the way I feel."

Juliana peered over her shoulder and read the inscription. "Love really is the best gift of all."

~Barbara Canale

66

Staircase of Faith

*In actual life, every great enterprise begins with
and takes its first forward step in faith.*
~August Wilhelm von Schlegel

When my son Andrew was born three years ago, my husband and I decided to live beneath our financial means—way, way, beneath our means. I wanted to stay at home to care for Andrew, and that would mean cutting our already average income in half. It was a vast commitment, and our family's well-being hung in the balance.

The cost of our ever-rising health insurance, home mortgage, and monthly expenses loomed before us; but our desire to raise our son without the use of day care outweighed any other costs.

Needless to say, we were a little intimidated by what the future held. But I was consoled and filled with courage by something Martin Luther King, Jr. once said: "Faith is taking the first step, even when you don't see the whole staircase."

It felt like we were taking a running leap onto a one-step staircase when I quit my teaching job.

I already had experience living meagerly—as a single woman on a teacher's income. I always knew I wanted to stay at home to take care of a family if I were blessed with one, and gave up expensive clothes and shoes to save for the future. I bought an eight-year-old Honda, ate out and went to the movies less, and moonlighted. I lived in a safe but no frills, low-rent apartment less than two miles from school, and went on vacation twice (including my honeymoon) during eight years of teaching.

I think it was during those single years of tightening the purse strings I first learned about humility, gratitude, and living on less. My thinking began to change about what it really meant to do "without."

I would catch myself feeling irritated that I had to walk down a flight of steps tugging and toting my overflowing laundry basket, detergent, and armored truck's worth of quarters to another building to wash my clothes. I would even chide myself—if you weren't such a tightwad, you could just spend your savings and move to a bigger apartment with your own washer and dryer.

Then one day my barrage of complaining thoughts was interrupted with this thought: what would someone in a wheelchair feel like if she were in your shoes? Wouldn't she be rejoicing that she could walk to the laundry room?

I would silently resent it when I ate macaroni and cheese for dinner, and then I would hear about someone in Haiti who would have to drag a cup through the mud to catch enough water for a drink.

I began to realize that wealth is relative. If my basic needs were met and I was loved, I was rich.

The flip side was that as my savings increased; I slept better at night knowing I could afford to take care of emergencies as they arose.

I began to appreciate the small things, like a warm cup of cocoa on a snowy day all snuggled up in my warm apartment, or the toothless grins and pudgy-armed hugs of my primary students. I was giving up things, and yet I felt wealthier than I ever had. When I gave up my desire for lofty possessions, the simple things in my life became loftier.

While I came to my stay-at-home stint with some knowledge of thriftiness, I realized it was one thing to live frugally when I was single. It was quite another to do it while my husband and I were responsible for supporting our son.

Nonetheless, we were up for the challenge.

I nursed my son for eleven months, alleviating the cost of

formula, and we washed cloth diapers, something I wanted to do for the environment anyway. I began comparing prices, buying store brands or using coupons, and rebating. Cashing in on franchise drug store rebates was like finding a gold mine—I got almost all our toiletries and some household items free.

My husband learned how to fix our cars and do repairs around the house, and I continued driving my still-ticking sixteen-year-old Honda. I gladly gave up my cell phone, and began to freelance write and babysit to supplement. We ate out only on special occasions and stopped buying expensive gifts for one another, opting for beautifully written cards and time together as a family. Most importantly, I prayed without ceasing.

When my son happily opened his gifts Christmas morning, my husband and I didn't need anything under the tree to be content. We already had everything we wanted (and even some clutter that we didn't), and it was a relief to enjoy the season without the stressful scramble to purchase all the material trimmings. I told my husband, "Staying at home with Andrew is my gift. It's like my birthday, wedding anniversary, and Christmas all rolled into one."

We have been living on less for more than three years now. Before we took that leap of faith, I didn't know the blessings that would pour down on us, and what I have witnessed has been amazing. At this date, we are less than two years away from owning our home and being completely debt-free. We have ample insurance, save for Andrew's college education, and give to our church, individuals, and donation centers as much as we can.

The quality of my life has not changed; the wealth in my spirit has become an overflowing river. Andrew and I walk to the creek bordering our backyard, his dimpled hand in mine. He throws in a twig to watch it drift away, and I am marvelously aware of how that tiny bundle has grown since that first day when we could only see the first step in the staircase.

With the ever-changing economic climate, there are days when I still feel a little uneasy. But then I realize that my hope and security do not lie in the stock market, the deed to our house, our savings account, or anything material that can rust or fade away. How many people who have lost a loved one to disease or tragedy would give all their material possessions just to embrace that loved one again? My faith and contentment cannot depend on what our bankroll looks like. As for my husband and I, we are glad to climb an ever-lengthening staircase of faith and are savoring the priceless time we have with our newborn.

No, we don't own an expensive house or drive vehicles manufactured in this decade. We don't wear the latest fashions or dine out regularly. We don't buy our son expensive toys or baby gear. And do you know what? He doesn't notice because he doesn't know what OshKosh B'Gosh is or what "make and model" means. He just wants time with us. We give him as much time as possible and shower him with learning and love. We read, play, and sing, and the quality of our lives continues to get better every day.

It was when we loosened our hold on material possessions that we realized we were rich. If you are approaching a staircase and you can only see the first step, I challenge you to take a deep breath, have some faith, and leap. You may be surprised where you will land.

~Janeen A. Lewis

67

Offbeat Jobs and E's Story

There are no menial jobs, only menial attitudes.
~William J. Brennan

As I sat in my English as a second language class with my two students, I turned to the conversation part of the lesson. I was prepared to resume the topic of "offbeat jobs" that we had started in the previous class. First though, I asked M how he was doing in his new job as a car salesman at a large car dealership in the area. He told me that he was no longer working there but was looking for another job. Then I turned to my other student, an elderly man from Africa, and asked him about his job. "What is your job, E?" I asked.

He explained that he was on the cleaning staff at a nursing home. Then he went on to say that in his country, he had been the owner of an air conditioning business with several employees working for him, including engineers and technicians, whom he had personally trained, being an air conditioning expert himself. Unfortunately, due to political conditions in his country, the economy suffered greatly and it became more and more difficult for him to carry on his business, even though it had been successful for more than thirty years. Consequently, he retired, and decided to devote himself, as he put it, to preparation to meet God. And as is the custom in his country, he would depend on his children to support him in his old age.

However, there came a day when he wanted a change and he

came to America. Some of his family already lived here. When he arrived, he realized that here in America everyone was expected to take care of him or herself and therefore, he needed to get a job. His wife had found a job as a cleaning person in a movie theater and he was able to get a job in the same place as an usher. He said that it was very humiliating at first, because his supervisors were young people, the same age as his own grandchildren, and they treated him very rudely and disrespectfully. But he told his wife that this was probably good for his soul. It was very humbling to be sure, but he, after all, had been an employer himself for so many years, directing those under him and now he had been given the opportunity to experience what it felt like to be the person at the bottom.

Eventually, he and his wife were able to find work in the nursing home facility, and he said that they are very thankful because they are able to work together. Also, he told us that he loves his work because he has the opportunity to show love and kindness to the residents of the nursing home, even if it is simply through his smile and kind words.

As he spoke, I felt my heart warmed by his story. I never imagined that this quiet stooped old man had had such a life and could share so much to encourage both the other student and myself. I told him that I believed that when he gets to heaven, God will put His arms around him and say, "Well done, good and faithful servant."

Many people would consider this man's job to be one of the lowliest in our society and would wonder how a man who had been an educated business owner could find peace and fulfillment in his present job. When he first came to this country, he was told that with a year of study, he could find a good job in his field of expertise, but he decided to choose a different path and he is very happy with the choice he made. He no longer carries on his shoulders the heavy burden of owning a business, and is able to spend his non-working hours in prayer and quiet contemplation or in spending time with his family.

I was deeply impressed by E's quiet faith and positive outlook. His words touched a chord in my own heart, because as a small business owner faced with the present economic instability, I suddenly felt a tremendous sense of peace. Even if we were to lose our business and our so-called security, there would always be a place for us somewhere where we could carry on loving God and people, in spite of circumstances.

Who would have guessed that the subject of "offbeat" jobs, designed to be an interesting, entertaining and humorous topic of discussion for the improvement of English conversation skills, would lead to the story of this precious man's experiences and open our eyes and hearts to a new perspective?

~Laraine Paquette

Note to Myself

*If she never takes off her high-heeled shoes,
how will she ever know how far she could walk...?*
~Germaine Greer

I had just snagged a sharp pencil to jot down some tips the newscaster was listing as ways to "recession proof" my budget. When I started writing, I realized that most of the tips were things I was already doing. The remainder were bad habits that, thankfully, I had never started. And just who were these people anyway who she claimed were splurging every day on those rip-off double mocha lattes?

I had already learned my hard lessons about frugality when Hurricane Katrina careened through east New Orleans claiming everything in its path. At that moment, my world collapsed along with the ailing levees, and unlike the current financial slump, it wasn't a slow downward spiral—it was an implosion. Katrina struck with ferocity overnight, literally. And for some of her victims, the economic disaster just serves as a double whammy—chapter two in an already painful trek towards recovery.

Prior to Katrina, rebounding from a hurricane was a science most New Orleanians had become quite adept at. It was simple really. We'd just skip town, lay low, and then return in a day or so to continue life as we'd always known it. Pull up some wet carpet, replace a few essentials and keep on trucking. It's a New Orleans thing. We'd done it countless times before. Not so this time.

Sometimes we'd even make a mini-vacation of it, nestle in a cozy cottage out of harm's way and joke about scoring a few days off from work. This go-round, we had hunkered down in a Houston hotel sipping margaritas, lazing like tourists. As we watched the news coverage, it became increasingly clear that the situation was more threatening than we had thought. Instead of the usual go-signal to return home, we heard a panicked reporter announce the jaw-dropping news that water was surging up to twelve feet in some places, and we couldn't re-enter New Orleans for another few months! Can't go home? Can't return to our jobs? Well, where will we go?

The day before the storm hit, I had been caught off guard with no time to rush home and pack before evacuating. I had just gone to the drycleaners earlier that day and, thankfully, had several changes of clothes in my car when I realized my options were scant: either head for the hills now or get trapped like a rat in town!

Like the overindulgent latte crowd, I had a few budget busters of my own, chief of which was an unquenchable shoe fetish I had developed long before Katrina. Like most of my girlfriends, I owned a busload of fashionable footwear. When I realized that I wouldn't be returning home soon, and the only pair I now owned was the one on my feet, I went into a tailspin. In New Orleans, I had grown accustomed to collecting compliments on how stylishly my feet were decked out. I mean I was really working the shoes. In some circles, I had been hailed as the diva of shoes. For me to now possess only one pair surely had to be some cruel joke—one quirky twist of irony I was too shell-shocked to handle.

I rushed to a dollar store to stockpile some bare necessities, my mind reeling. For the moment I hadn't fully comprehended the scope of all the things I'd need to purchase to stay afloat. All I knew was that I just had to have some new shoes! I spied a little shop right next door, dashed in, and plucked a pair from the shelf. These were quickie shoes—wham-bam-thank-you-ma'am shoes—shoes I would never have given a second glance, let alone permitted near my feet in my pre-Katrina days. In New Orleans, I'd scour the Web for hours in pursuit of the sleekest, most elegant boots. I only frequented the finer, upscale boutiques. I'd linger in the salon, enjoying the indulgence of snagging the latest trends to add to my already burgeoning cache. I loved the attention from the salesmen, laying box after beautiful box of the best the store had to offer at my feet. For me, purchasing shoes had become a drug. I didn't care about negotiating a sale. I just wanted to look good.

The ones I now held in my hand were "sensible," non-descript—a strange purchase in a strange store. I shoved them on my feet like a junkie copping a fix. At that moment, a sudden sadness seized me. I realized how my priorities had become displaced, how much stock I had put into getting approval from others. I thought about the countless possessions I had amassed over the years, room after room of excess—stuff I didn't need or didn't even remember I'd bought—a garage chock full of eye-candy likely buoyed up now by the river's swift overflow.

Before Katrina, I'd occasionally sort through my shoe collection deciding which ones to give to charity. I'd rank them and concede only the well-worn ones—not the chic Italian slingbacks—those were keepers. Giving little thought to who might receive them, I just wanted them out of my way to make room for newer, more expensive styles. I even patted myself on the back for being so "generous" to the less fortunate.

That was four years ago. Now my "storm shoes" hold a special place of honor in my new home, mounted on a frame on my nightstand. They are the first thing I see when I open my eyes in the morning. They serve as a stark reminder of where my feet have trod. Those shoes carried me through a difficult time, kept me centered, somehow providing me enough breathing room to figure out what my next steps would be. But more than that, they remind me that I don't need material things to affirm who I am in the world. On that fateful day, I had written myself this mental note with one indelible stroke: Girlfriend, be thankful for what you have—because it can all be gone in a flash. Cherish everything and everyone in your life. Share all you have with others. That simple advice is emblazoned on my heart. To it, I'll scribble one additional caveat: Don't wait for another hurricane or economic crisis to remind you of that. Now, there's a note worth taking.

~Elaine K. Green

69

The Skid Row Float

Yet they are thy people and thine inheritance,
which thou broughtest out by thy mighty power
and by thy stretched out arm.
~Deuteronomy

When I was a kid, accepting cast-offs from well-intentioned friends and relatives was a recurring event for my family of seven. Used sofas came and went with regular frequency. Not so surprisingly, the acquisition of a new couch usually coincided with the passing of one of my lovely old great-aunts. In fact, the really old aunts avoided us completely if word got around that our sofa was truly on its last legs. I think these grand old ladies had a secret pact to remain ignorant of our current couch crisis, and that was the key to their longevity. As a child I believed whole-heartedly in Santa Claus, the Easter Bunny, and that receiving the sofa of a deceased relative was actually part of the funeral rite.

I remember vividly back in the summer of 1964, the good Lord called Aunt Alice home at the ripe age of eighty-seven, and somehow our dear old camelback, larger-than-life sofa knew it. Secure in the knowledge that a replacement sofa waited in the wings for us, the "Cranberry Queen of Velveteen" as we fondly referred to it, slipped from the two brick makeshift legs that supported her rear, breathed her last soft sigh and thumped to the floor right on schedule.

A few days later, as we all gathered to pay our last respects to

Aunt Alice, a somber cloud of silence hung heavily over the congregation. Until my annoyingly squeaky yet perfectly audible voice punched a big fat hole in it. "Mom," I said. "Is Daddy going right to Aunt Alice's house now to pick up the couch or do we have to wait until the cemetery part is over?"

In one fell swoop my mother stretched one arm clear across my four older siblings, clamped my lips shut with one hand, airlifted me back past the four siblings with the other, and plunked me down at her side. Time elapsed: three-tenths of a nanosecond. While in flight I caught my dad clamping his own mouth shut and I wondered what that was about. After all he hadn't uttered a word. I knew something was up though because a series of muffled giggles rippled through the crowd at the precise moment I became airborne.

Personally, I saw no humor in the situation at all, let alone any reason for my mother to physically button my lips and pluck me from my seat. Obviously not having anywhere to sit when it was time to watch The Flintstones panicked no one but me.

After the funeral service was over (including the cemetery part) Dad headed out to collect Aunt Alice's sofa and Mom's task was to dispose of the wreck in our living room. Because of its deplorable condition, her goal was to haul it to the Goodwill donation station at the end of our block. Frankly, all the good will on Earth couldn't have resurrected this hunk of junk, but the anonymous donor option trumped leaving it for the trash pickup. If she was going to do that, she might as well hang a neon sign on it with a blinking arrow pointing to our front door.

The problem: four daughters and one son all under the age of sixteen make a mighty sorry-looking moving and hauling team. Especially when pursuing an incognito operation.

The solution: With limited options and dripping with anxiety, Mom summoned the courage to recruit my brother Bobby and three of his teenage friends. A decision so immediately followed by regret a NASCAR stopwatch couldn't have clocked the time in between.

To Bobby and his band of merry men, carrying an oversized, threadbare, broken down, ugly (from its moment of birth) sofa the length of one city block spelled, P-A-R-T-Y. Wise to the antics of teenage boys, Mom suggested they wait until dark. They laughed. She insisted. They picked Mom up and moved her out of the way.

I can still picture those boys lumbering down the alley in single file with that clumsy old couch carcass raised high over their heads, chanting some quirky made-up rhyming verse throughout the whole ordeal. When they finally reached the end of the block, Bobby looked back at Mom and shouted, "Hey, look, Mom. It's a parade and we own the Skid Row Float!" Even the long arm of Marie Tait, mother extraordinaire, couldn't reach clear down to the end of the block to lock his lips shut.

The echo of his remark floated down the alley, rustling the curtains of every open kitchen window it passed. By the time his words reached Mom's ears, she couldn't resist laughing out loud as all hope of our anonymity disappeared.

An antique mahogany-trimmed Georgian style sofa stands in all its regal splendor in my living room today. Mom passed it down to me, but it belonged first to my grandmother who was the last surviving sister in the circle of delightful ladies known to me as my great-aunts. This sofa is not a modern assembly line version. It is a grand tribute to an age when crafting a sofa took several months of a man's life.

"They just don't make them like that anymore." That's what Mom said when she inherited it, threadbare and faded. She decided to have it reupholstered, though by then she could have easily afforded a new sofa.

It's a beauty all right and I am comforted by the vintage grace it lends to my living room. But truthfully I own something even better. Mine is the treasure of the "Skid Row Float" and the wealth of heartwarming family memories it rekindles in me. Often material possessions were in short supply at our house. As for memories, we made those by the dozen.

~Annmarie B. Tait

70

Lunch with a Facebook Friend

*The Internet is the most important single development
in the history of human communication
since the invention of call waiting.*
~Dave Barry

It was a typical Tuesday morning. The alarm didn't go off and everyone overslept. We ran out of milk, the coffeemaker overflowed and my husband stepped in the water that had cascaded onto the floor and soaked his last pair of clean socks. The printer cartridge ran out of ink while my son was assembling a history project that should have been done the night before, and the cat hacked up a hairball under the dining room table. Frankly, the day wasn't looking very promising.

My husband squished out of the house without kissing me goodbye and, as I shooed Lewis off to school, he grabbed his iPod, but forgot to grab his lunch and his history project. I unfurled a wad of toilet paper and cleaned up the cat puke (the last of the paper towels went to mop up the coffeemaker disaster), then collected Lew's lunch and homework and trudged to the car in my slippers. "What a stupid life," I thought.

My daughter had left the gas tank empty and the front seat littered with Frisbees, parking tickets, and paper cups. I coasted downhill to the school and rolled into the closest gas station, where the attendant pointed out that the inspection sticker had expired.

Back at home, I walked the dog, fed the damn cat, ran the dish-washer, threw in a load of laundry and took a tepid shower because all of the hot water was gone. I looked in my closet for something to wear and pulled on a white T-shirt. Then I pulled it off because it made me look fat. I tried to button up a blue button-down. Ugh. Four shirts later, I settled on a black turtleneck, paired it with my favorite black pants and searched the house for a roll of Scotch tape or a lint brush.

Normally, I don't agonize over what to wear. But today, I was meeting a friend for lunch.

Actually, she's not a real friend. She is a Facebook friend — someone who popped up on my laptop some twenty-odd years after we had attended college together in upstate New York. I signed up for Facebook a few months ago, although I realize it should probably remain the domain of the young (to quote my daughter: "Mom, old people are ruining Facebook!"). Kids have the time and technological know-how to take online quizzes, post pictures of their parties and keep the world abreast of their status — "Just ate a pint of Ben & Jerry's!" I have stuff to do — like hunt for my car keys and try to get the cat hair off my black pants.

As I drove to the restaurant, I checked my reflection in the rear view mirror. Never do this — especially if you're meeting someone for the first time in twenty years. Nothing will deflate your self-esteem more completely than the slightly green-tinged view of the top third of your head in direct sunlight. Ugh. As I walked into the restaurant, I hoped that my old friend looked worse. She didn't. I saw her sitting in a corner booth and she looked terrific. Her hair was coiffed, her clothes were designer. Frankly, she looked better than she did in college. I sucked in my stomach as I walked across the dining room.

"Sorry I'm late," I apologized. "It's been a horrible morning." I slid into the booth, grateful that my cat-hairy pants and the twenty pounds I had gained since 1983 were hidden.

"You look fabulous," she lied.

"No, you do... really," I said.

I wanted to order the turkey Reuben because I was craving

comfort food, but my friend ordered a salad and I said, "Make that two." We started to awkwardly outline the past two decades.

"What about you?" she asked, and I heard myself talking... Three kids—all doing great, a husband who can still make me laugh, occasional vacations, a house in a neighborhood that I love, and some interesting freelance work. I didn't want to brag, so I told her about the cat puke and the coffeemaker and how I almost ran out of gas. And then I realized—it might have been a bad morning, but it's still a pretty good life.

~Carol Band

71

Her Real Mother

Biology is the least of what makes someone a mother.
~Oprah Winfrey

We got the call in early July. The agency had told us in February that we should expect to wait six months to a year before a baby would be available for adoption, and so we had driven from New York City back to Kansas to visit family and tell them that maybe by Christmas there would be a grandchild. But here we were, getting lucky in only five months, speeding back to the city taking turns reading aloud from Dr. Spock.

Our daughter was two months old when we brought her home. The first morning—a Sunday—I awoke at 6:30 to soft grumbly noises from the other bedroom and realized there would be no sleeping in for a long, long time.

We named her Genevieve, after my mother. She had pale blond hair and blue eyes; I'm half Italian, with dark eyes and hair, so people who saw the three of us usually remarked, "Oh, she looks like her daddy." The social worker told us that if we had any questions about our daughter's birth parents, she would give us the information, but in our dazed, new-parent state, we couldn't think of a single question. This was our daughter; what was there to ask? The paperwork took six months, and then it was final. Genevieve Marie Peters, our little girl.

She was a quick study, good in school and at any kind of physical activity: gymnastics, dance, ice skating. We had this model child until the age of fifteen, when our lovely daughter vanished and was replaced by a smart-mouthed, big-haired, blue-eyeshadowed hussy (my mother's word) who knew the names of every rock band member but couldn't remember to turn her homework in. This new model was alternately sulky and highly verbal, specializing in screaming hysterics when she didn't get her own way, often stomping up to her room while spitting out that accusation most feared by adoptive parents:

"You're not my REAL mother!"

Thankfully, the drama of the teen years passed. When she was twenty-one, my daughter had a daughter of her own, and I had to smile whenever I would get a call: "Mom, can you take Cheyenne for a couple of hours? She's driving me crazy! You can't tell me I was ever this bad!" No, I thought, not at age two. Just wait a dozen years.

One day Gen called me with the question I'd been expecting for a long time. "Mom," she said, "would you be upset if I tried to find my birth mother?"

I told her no, that I'd give her all the information I had. But I was apprehensive. What if the birth mother wanted nothing to do with her? Beneath her tough exterior, my daughter was a marshmallow. I couldn't bear the thought of my daughter getting hurt. Even scarier: what if the birth mother was rich, and famous, and overwhelmed Gen with gifts? But I got out the paperwork, and the little dress she'd worn that day, pale blue with "Sweet Girl" hand-embroidered on the tiny pocket, and gave everything to her, hoping for a happy outcome.

Genevieve's birth mother had registered several years before with an agency that matched adoptees with birth parents. A few days later, my daughter called again, her voice shaking. She'd talked to her birth mother (I'll call her Joanne); there were no siblings, and Joanne, who lived in upstate New York, was eager for a meeting.

Gen made the trip. My fears, it appeared, were unfounded; Joanne had never had other children, which meant she was overjoyed to find her daughter and granddaughter. Over the next few months, there were more phone calls and visits. Joanne lived in the country, and had horses and dogs (Gen loves animals), while I, now divorced with a job that required considerable travel, had a tiny apartment. I reminded myself that my daughter was an adult now, and could make her own choices, and wasn't it great that she was getting to know her birth mother? But I felt my hold slipping, and when I was assigned to a six-month project in Europe, I was torn. I almost refused the assignment, thinking that a "real mother" would not choose to go thousands of miles away at this point. In the end, I went, hating the economic necessity of the situation but knowing there was no choice.

My assignment ended in mid-December, and I had made plans to spend Christmas with my family in Colorado. It was the first time my brother and three sisters and I had managed to coordinate our vacations, and even our mother, who hated flying, had made reservations. So when Genevieve called me, I thought she was going to say that she'd gotten reservations as well, but she had a different request.

"Mom, I need you to come to New York with me, to Joanne's."

I groaned. "Gen, that's going to be awkward, don't you think? Especially at Christmas." The last thing I wanted to do was spend the holiday at the home of a stranger, this stranger in particular. But Gen was determined.

"Mom, you have to come. Joanne keeps trying to mother me, and I need her to see I already HAVE a mother."

At that moment, a huge weight dropped from my heart. This was my kid, always would be, and I knew that I'd be changing my plane reservations and telling my siblings that no, I couldn't come out to Colorado this year — Gen wanted to spend Christmas with me. Me... her real mother.

~Susan Peters

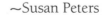

72

Three Months to Work

As a cure for worrying, work is better than whiskey.
~Thomas A. Edison

Only in Switzerland is it possible to get hired in one language and fired in another.

I should know.

As my recently appointed German boss shut his office door behind me, gesturing me to sit on his couch, and pulling his chair closer to me than any American-sized personal space would ever allow, I didn't even have to understand his German or even really listen. I knew what was coming. After my three-year stint as the Zurich advertising agency's English Copywriter, I was becoming the next victim in a long line of worldwide economic tragedy.

I was losing my job. And the only word I could say was *danke*.

"*Danke*?" my boss laughed, after he told me it was money problems but also language issues that contributed to the advertising agency's decision to let me go. But I wasn't sure whether the language problems included my lack of German or his lack of English. But either way, since he arrived, there was no mistaking that our communication had become a series of linguistic nightmares that only seemed bearable due to my constant smile-and-nod technique.

While my former boss had hired me to work on clients for whom he needed English copy, he also didn't care if I worked on other non-English projects since he could understand and translate my ideas and headlines later if necessary. But my new boss didn't hide the fact that he disliked that I even dared to think in English, not to mention that I tried to explain things to him in it.

Attempting to do everything I could to appease my new boss, with my two years of German lessons, I stopped speaking English entirely and tried to communicate in German fragments and gestures, sometimes even spitting out entire sentences while making sure that every possible *der*, *die*, *das*, *den*, *dem*, *denen*, or *des* article was properly disguised as a "duh."

During the last few months since my new boss arrived, I'd also spent many hours with one of my linguistically talented Swiss co-workers, who would help me painstakingly translate every headline and idea I wrote into some sort of passable German before I showed it to my boss, so that at least some of my ideas wouldn't be lost in translation. But the problem was, even properly translated, some things, like humor and sarcasm, just didn't come through.

As my boss relayed his layoff speech, his German passed through me in two categories—what I understood, and what I didn't. I heard that he thought I did everything well—just in the wrong language. I heard that he'd try to help me find another job—albeit with people who understood English better than he. And I heard he'd write me a *Zeugnis*—whatever the heck that was. And then he hugged me—something, after watching too many *Apprentice* episodes, I didn't know a firing involved.

The next part was even stranger. I had to go back to my desk.

Staring at my official layoff letter, which I had to sign myself to officially be fired (there are no pink slips in Switzerland but plenty of paperwork), I read the German paragraphs before me. May 31, said the letter. My last day at the agency. I stared out the window at the snow. Today was February 26. And I wasn't sure how I should act from now on, let alone how I would find the motivation to create ideas. Luckily the co-worker I shared an office with was out to lunch. So I had at least an hour to figure it out.

Three months to work. Three months to unemployment. Three months to pretend everything was still normal.

Trying to continue like nothing out of the ordinary had happened after being officially *entlassen werden* is a new experience for me. In the U.S., people I witnessed being fired were kicked out the moment the words were uttered. Frantic colleagues, fellow writers, and art directors, would ask those of us still with jobs to save their files and print their work before their computers and last few years of their life were snatched away. Sometimes they'd sneak in at night to print a résumé or some portfolio pieces to help them get their next job. And here I was, back at my desk, with full access to a color printer and company e-mail, trying to figure out how the heck I could possibly write another witty headline at a time like this.

So maybe my *danke*, for lack of anything better to say, was appropriate after all. I am thankful. Not to lose my job, but for the fact that I have more than three months to collect my work, print my portfolio, and look for a job—all while still being employed. After all, it is not in an American's upbringing to think being fired means anything other than a sneering Donald Trump shoving you, ashamed and humiliated, immediately out the door.

In Switzerland, I'm going to need these three months. Because before I can comfortably head to the Swiss unemployment office with my official firing letter bearing my signature, I'll have to learn an entire new German vocabulary. One that includes words like "laid off" and "job seeker." But luckily I already know the one word that should get me through it all—*mut*—courage.

~Chantal Panozzo

Chapter 8

Count Your Blessings

Thank My Lucky Stars

*Be glad of life because it gives you the chance
to love and to work and to play and to look up at the stars.*

~Henry van Dyke

A Blessing in the Storm

I am not a has-been. I am a will be.
~Lauren Bacall

For weeks, I have dreaded Fridays at *The Chicago Tribune*. Friday was the day that folks got tapped on the shoulder or called at home to tell them that they had been laid off. The company is going through a "reduction in force" to help keep the lights on. So far, nearly eighty in the newsroom have been put on the block.

The fear of working with an axe over one's head is enough to drive anyone mad. I tried my best to be a reassuring voice in the midst of it all. We all had our own logic about how it would go down. There were talks of employees being taken to off-site locations to hear that it was curtains. Others feared that they would take an elevator ride to the 22nd floor balcony, be given the news and then forced to jump.

Then it happened. I got tapped. It was Friday. August 15. One of the managing editors caught me while I was in the middle of editing a story for the Web. He said, "Emeri, do you have a minute?"

I knew. In one quick flash, my whole journalistic life passed before my eyes.

I thought about my days as a cub reporter at a small paper in Louisiana. I thought about how I spent my first day as a copy editor editing stories on 9/11 at *Newsday*. My mind drifted to the five years I spent at *The Baltimore Sun*. Then, I thought about how proud I was every time I walked into the Gothic Tribune Tower and how finally I was happy with my job. I loved my co-workers and the paper. I wasn't stressed. Now, eleven months after reaching euphoria, it would all be gone.

I walked slowly to his office and took a seat. With no compassion or a hint of emotion, he looked at me and said, "Your position has been eliminated."

He didn't care that I came to work nearly an hour early each day to get ahead. He didn't know that I was the person who made that big catch in a story about a little girl's death that made him so proud. Nor, was he concerned with the fact that I worked my way up the ladder to get to the mother ship.

At the end of the day, I was just "Editor, Subject Asst. Age 30." I was handed an envelope with my name on it. And, after a brief talk, I placed my badge on his desk and walked out of his office. I could take being fired. At least when you are fired, you know that you have done something wrong. However, when you are laid off without any rhyme or reason, it is much harder to swallow.

Maybe he thought I would finish my shift. I didn't. I said good-bye quickly to the metro editor, logged off my computer, placed my name plate in my bag and left. Mama always taught me to never let them see you cry. I chatted briefly with a co-worker outside the building and hailed a cab. Once inside, I became human again and cried.

I informed my mother that the nightmare I had the night before about losing my job was now a reality. She reassured me that God didn't bring me this far to leave me and that everything happens for a reason.

I got home at 10:50.

I slowly pulled out the blue folder and arranged each bundle neatly on the floor.

There was a ton of mind-numbing paperwork to sort through, and I couldn't even wrap my mind around it. I took a deep breath, said a quick prayer and realized that while my position had been eliminated, I wasn't. I had two degrees and was an adjunct professor at Columbia College. My ultimate goal was to make the transition from newspapers to academia. I just didn't know my path would shift so abruptly.

A simple e-mail to my supervisor at the college turned into a blessing in the storm on that dark Friday. I wrote not asking for a job, but to just inform her of my situation. She gave me more classes to teach. I guess it's true that when God closes a door, he opens a window. At 10:15 Friday morning, "my position was eliminated." By 5:30 Friday evening, my other position had expanded.

On Saturday morning, I wrote about my experiences for a journalism blog. On Sunday, I was contacted by Microsoft regarding an editing position that was opening at MSN.com. I flew to Redmond on faith, and I got the job. God was putting me back on track to making my goal a reality. I cried again. This time not because I was broken, but because I was made anew.

~Emeri B. O'Brien

Bus Stop Blessing

A bus is a vehicle that runs twice as fast
when you are after it as when you are in it.
~Author Unknown

She ran for the bus with all of the strength and determination of an Olympic sprinter, but the bus pulled away from the curb without her—the driver not seeing her or just not caring. She collapsed on the bus bench in a heap of failure, disbelief and sobs.

I could have just kept on driving. It was the first day of my vacation and I was off to wander the local mall, and, besides, it wasn't my problem, I didn't know her. Another bus would be along soon. But there was just something about her. There was an intensity in her need that I could not ignore so I stopped my car and went up to her.

I sat down on the bench next to her and gently mentioned that another bus would be along in half an hour or so. I introduced myself and asked, "What's your name?"

"My name is Sarah. I'm sorry to make such of a scene but I need to get to the hospital to be with my sick baby," she responded through lessening sobs.

Sarah explained to me that she was a struggling single mother and her one-year-old son was in the hospital. She had gone home late the night before to get some sleep and when she started back to the hospital in the morning, her car battery was dead. I could tell from Sarah's face that she was exhausted and that she felt overwhelmed.

"What's wrong with your son?" I gently prodded.

"My baby has pneumonia and he has been very sick," Sarah

replied. "I don't want him to be alone and afraid, I need to get back to him."

My heart melted and my plans for the day took a detour. "Please," I said, "let me give you a ride to the hospital." Seeing a little hesitation in her eyes, I continued, "Please, it would be my pleasure." Sarah's face softened and I saw the first hint of a smile as she nodded her head yes, and we began walking toward my car.

On the drive to the hospital I learned that Sarah's boyfriend had left her when he found out that she was pregnant and that she did not have any other family in the area. She has been struggling to work and raise her baby in a loving home. Though rough at times, things were going fairly well until little Daniel got sick. Daniel's illness set Sarah back financially and emotionally.

As I listened to Sarah's story I decided to do everything I could to help her out. I dropped her off at the hospital, gave her my phone number and asked her to call me when she got home. I assured her that my brother would come over and help her with her car battery. Though reluctant, Sarah took my number and promised to call me.

I shared the day's event with my Bible study group that night and asked the group to pray for Sarah and Daniel. The group did much more than that. One person had baby clothes left over she wanted to donate, another friend wanted to donate food and we even took up a collection of money to help Sarah out.

Sarah was very grateful and humbled by the help my group was able to give to her during the illness and recovery of her son. My brother went to help Sarah that night with her car battery and, not only did he get that battery to "spark" once again, sparks began flying between my brother and Sarah as well and now Sarah is my sister-in-law!

You never know what blessings God has waiting for you if you just take the time to stop and try to meet someone's need. Sarah and Daniel are a precious addition to our family, and that would never have happened if Sarah had not missed her bus on that fateful day.

~LaVerne Otis

75

The Poop that Saved Christmas

Diaper backward spells repaid. Think about it.
~Marshall McLuhan

After I was laid off in mid-October, I faced the loathsome task of informing our seven-year-old. I tried to put it in as positive a light as I could — when the company merged with another company, they had twice as many people without having twice as much work to do. I stressed that I hadn't done anything wrong and that it was nothing personal, but that they no longer had enough work for me, so I was basically finished with my job.

I said nothing about us having been treated more like an acquisition in spite of the fact that our company owned a controlling share of the new stock. I never cast aspersions on how our CEO cut us loose during the worst economic crisis since the Great Depression, nor did I point out that the company's profits had been up by more than eighty percent, which negated any claim that the layoffs were a necessary cost-cutting maneuver.

I figured that was too much for a seven-year-old to swallow, which is why I put on a smile and simply told him I'd be looking for a new job, ignoring the urge to warn him that he might hear weeping sounds coming from Mommy and Daddy's room.

Later came the talk of cutting our own expenses. We knew we'd be able to pay all of our bills through the end of the year, with little extra. Unfortunately, that time span included a period when tradition dictates that a family needs that little extra—Christmas. It's one of the two most important holidays on the Christian liturgical calendar, as well as the season to essentially stick a vacuum cleaner hose in my wallet.

Nevertheless, we switched the vacuum cleaner off, and Christmas was suddenly about religion again. That's also difficult for a seven-year-old to accept, but we figured it might be easier if he had advance notice. Hence came Part Two of The Talk, in which I explained that fortunately we'd bought a few small gifts for him and his brother before I'd lost my job, my money and my self-worth. This meant they'd get something for Christmas, but not nearly as much as in past years.

He took the news remarkably well; in fact, he even put a positive spin on it: "That's okay, Dad—at least Santa Claus will still bring us the big gifts."

After removing that dagger from my heart, I slunk to my computer to see if there was any possible excess in the budget I'd worked up. That Santa! He's always upstaging me. The budget review indicated that even Santa had no chance of scoring with the big gifts.

There's another aspect of the holidays that was affected by the layoff—travel. We needed to visit my parents, especially since my mom had a stroke in October. By the way, the news of Mom's stroke was the third bad thing to happen in that October week that included my layoff and the death of a long-time pet.

So we knew we should go visit my parents in Virginia for Thanksgiving, but for us to get there would have cost more than we had between the cost of the gas and the hotel room we needed because I was allergic to their dog.

Not so with my in-laws. Which is how we found ourselves driving to their home the weekend before Thanksgiving. They live a little closer, so the gas cost is better, but the big difference is in being able to sleep in their house instead of a hotel.

Halfway there, I started feeling guilty about my own parents. But my thoughts were interrupted by a more urgent problem.

"I needa go poo-poo," our toddler said.

"Okay, hold on. We need to find an exit. Will you sit on the potty at a gas station?"

"No."

Sigh. We've been fifty percent successful with his potty training. He mostly wears "big boy unnerwear" and is able to keep them dry, but when it comes to Number Two, he's been defiantly resistant. He warns us when it's on its way, but refuses to sit on a potty. Instead, we have to take off his pants and underwear, put on a Pull-Up, and let him do his business as if he's still in diapers.

So we pulled up behind the closest gas station/convenience store, and made ready for the deed. My wife was willing to do the hard part while I stood in the 20-degree night air, waiting for her to roll down the window and hand me a sealed freezer bag containing a soiled Pull-Up and wipes. My job was to throw it away while she changed him back into his big boy underwear.

When I finally took possession of the freezer bag, I had to walk around to the front of the store to find a trashcan for it. I had a hard time finding one, and briefly considered keeping the bag, so I could later mail it to my former CEO.

But I was resolute, and my search eventually took me inside the convenience store. I forgot all about the freezer bag once I noticed the glitzy display of lottery scratchers at the cash register. When I remembered my own lottery rules—including the increased likelihood of winning when a ticket is purchased in a nasty store in the middle of nowhere—I knew I had to buy one.

So I sidled up to the counter and asked for one of the scratchers, fishing in my pocket for money with one hand while I clutched the dirty freezer bag behind my back with the other. I glanced at the cashier's nametag: "Virginia." Ouch. Let the parent-related guilt continue.

We arrived at my in-laws in our usual flurry of chaos, the boys hyped on chocolate and excited about seeing their grandparents, me unloading our luggage as quickly as possible in order to minimize my risk of hypothermia. It wasn't until the next morning that I remembered the scratcher. I found a penny, and began the anticipatory scratching ritual. I won $200 on the first space, and was ecstatic. I figured no more prizes would be revealed, but continued scratching. Nothing. Nothing. Then another $100 — the holidays were suddenly looking up!

Next space, nothing. Then $100 again. Then a third $100. Was this really a $500 winner, or was I reading the numbers wrong? Next two spaces, nothing. Then another $200. Whoa. They don't make $700 winners, do they? Nope — next space, another $200! Nothing, nothing, then $100 in the last space.

When I told my wife we'd just won $1,000, she asked, "How is that possible?" That's when I had to admit I'd been frivolous and bought a lottery ticket. She asked where I'd bought the ticket, and that's when it hit me — I had no idea. Neither one of us could remember the exit number, the town, the highway, the gas station, or the store name. It was supposed to have been nothing but a poop stop, but suddenly my son had presented us with the richest poop in town. Courtesy of a cashier named... Virginia.

"Sweetie, I think we should go to my parents' place during the holidays, after all. We can stay in a hotel for one night. And maybe we should buy a couple more Christmas presents for the boys. And what the heck? Why not make a mortgage payment, while we're at it?"

Most importantly, while I was full of holiday spirit, I finally threw away that freezer bag before I could find my ex-CEO's address.

~Dan Bain

76

Exactly
What We Needed

All God's children need traveling shoes.
~Maya Angelou

I gasped and blinked back tears, hardly believing what I saw. For the second time in four months, the sight ahead of me stopped me in my tracks.

First had been the sight of my husband walking down the sidewalk to meet me, briefcase in hand, in the middle of the day: a picture forever etched in my memory. It was the day the Gulf War began, and the day the life we'd known ended. A friend had come up to my husband at work that morning and told him to clear out his desk. Small comfort that my husband was one of the last laid off as his company downsized from 2,500 to just 500 employees. His job loss at this date meant hundreds of engineers had already filled any openings local companies had. We both shrugged that thought aside, certain that my husband's abilities and God's guidance would connect him with another job in a short time.

And that's exactly what happened—almost—when four weeks later, another aerospace firm offered my husband a job on exactly the kind of project he'd been working on. We rejoiced because this company was closer to our church, and we envisioned a new house in a new neighborhood and our long Sunday commute whittled down to a few minutes.

That was Friday. On Monday, my husband was scheduled to

settle on a salary and sign all the paperwork. The new boss called instead to say, "The government pushed the contract back six months. Could you wait six months to start work?" Six months for what might never materialize at all? Our elation evaporated, leaving a vacuum quickly filled with confusion and questions without answers, not the least of which was my wounded cry, "God, why? Why put something so perfect in our reach, and then take it away? Don't you care about us?"

"Between unemployment and our savings, we can make it through the summer," my husband quietly advised me, "but we'll have to cut everything non-essential from our budget." We gritted our teeth, retrenched our hearts, and set our minds to eliminating as many expenses as we could. That meant I sewed shorts for our rapidly growing teenage son. If it embarrassed him to wear homemade clothing, he graciously never said so. It also meant our entertainment now consisted of borrowing videos from the public library, rather than even going to the dollar movie theater.

We tried to make a game of finding free or inexpensive new options to replace our old activities, intentionally putting a positive spin on our circumstances and conversations for the sake of our two children. My husband and I were both concerned as we watched our savings dwindle week by week, but the last thing we wanted was to pass our anxiety along to the boys.

Weeks turned into months as my husband networked, searched, and mailed résumés, diligently looking for work, with not even one interview to show for all his perseverance. I substitute taught as often as I could, but that meant many days when my husband had to stay home with our four-year-old son—days he couldn't devote to job-hunting.

Any vacation was out of the question, so when my sister called to ask if we'd like to go boating with them at the lake for the weekend, I joyfully and thankfully shot back, "Sure thing!" Excitedly I began checking off things we'd need: "Sleeping bags, check; fishing poles, check; bathing suits, check..." A sudden realization sank my anticipation like an anchor tossed overboard. Most lakes here in Arizona are formed by damming rivers and filling canyons with water. Our lakes don't have sandy beaches; instead the shallows are covered with sharp rocks, so you have to wear shoes to go swimming. Our younger son only had two pair of shoes: one dress pair and one good pair of tennis shoes. We couldn't afford for him to ruin either pair, but we also couldn't afford to buy another pair of even cheap shoes for him.

The last thing I wanted to do was cancel the trip and sink our sons' happiness at finally doing something resembling our old "normal" life, so I asked my husband, "Could we stop by the thrift store on our way to the lake on Saturday?" I had exactly one dollar to spend, but I felt cautiously optimistic that I could find an old pair of children's tennis shoes that might come close to fitting our son, so we piled our gear into the car that Saturday morning, relishing the eager "on our way" chatter from the back seat.

At the thrift store I leaped out of the car, praying, and dashed into the shop. That's when I stopped short, gasping and blinking at what sat on a display rack directly in front of me. Almost afraid to look, I turned over the brand new pair of blue "water socks," still sporting their original price tag, to look for a size. They were exactly the size our son wore, and they were exactly one dollar.

Many people would consider this a minor coincidence. To me, it was a major miracle. As we drove on, one elated four-year-old in the back seat happily trying on his glorious new shoes, I pondered all the "coincidences" that had to come together to create this small piece of providence:

- Someone had to buy the shoes in exactly our son's size.
- Those shoes had to be unsuitable for some reason.
- The purchaser had to choose to donate rather than return the shoes to the store.
- The purchaser had to donate the shoes to that particular organization.
- The shoes had to make their way to that organization's particular small thrift store in our neighborhood.

- They had to come in at exactly the time we needed to find a pair of shoes.
- They had to be marked for exactly what I could afford to spend.
- No one else could have spotted and bought them before me.
- I had to decide to stop at that particular thrift store, on just the right day, at exactly the right time.

At least nine coincidences had to converge to create this "ordinary" yet exactly perfect provision for us. What we found was more than just a pair of shoes! Though the shoes were exactly what—and even better than—we needed, what we needed most of all was hope: tangible, clear evidence to me that "someone" knew and cared about our needs. My wounded faith was healed at that moment, my heart dared to hope again, and I knew somehow our family would be okay.

It was two more months until my husband found a job, the week his unemployment benefits ran out. In yet another "ordinary" miracle, he applied for an assembly line position, but was hired as an engineer for an opening the company hadn't even advertised.

That was almost two decades ago, but those blue water socks have served as a ramp to launch my hope and confidence in many turbulent waters since then. I remember them and their miraculous message of hope now as my husband and I face retirement in another season of financial distress with our assets reduced by forty percent just a few years before we need them. Those two blue shoes still reassure me that God knows, God cares, and God will still fashion coincidence upon coincidence to create "ordinary" miracles that exactly meet our needs and stop me in my tracks with thanks and wonder.

~Rose M. Jackson

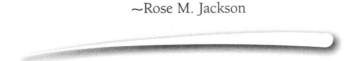

Tsunami Survivor

The purpose of life is a life of purpose.
~Robert Byrne

When I was in third grade, my school principal allowed me to start my Winter Break early with the condition that I kept a journal on what happened each day of my vacation. Well, here's my journal entry.

It seemed like an ordinary morning on vacation. My family and I were vacationing in Sri Lanka (our country of origin) for the holidays; it was the day after Christmas. My parents and I were very tired in the morning, delaying our plans to head for the beach by two hours. Two hours that seemed meaningless, but ended up meaning the world to us.

My father and I washed and went downstairs for breakfast at the busy hotel restaurant while my mother decided to sleep in a bit longer. We tried to eat slowly so that my mother wouldn't have to eat alone, but in the end it was no use. We waited even longer; still no sign of her. And then we spotted my aunt and uncle, who were to drive with us to the Hikkaduwa Beach. We chatted for a while and then my mother finally joined us.

I was nearly as eager to go as my dad, who had spent his life by the sea and had so wanted to take me to the beach... but unfortunately (well fortunately, actually) my mother needed to take her asthma medication, which required her to eat first. Then once more we waited as my mother dashed upstairs to get her water bottle. She apologized for her tardiness and we all packed into my uncle's van, delayed by yet another half hour.

It was a two-hour drive down to Hikkaduwa Beach; we were shocked at what we found. People were running and screaming as the police blocked traffic. My mother told me to duck (she feared it was a shooting or a bombing) and I hid my head in her lap as the police officer explained to my uncle (who thankfully was driving) that there had been a tidal wave and that we should turn back immediately. My uncle was reluctant, but decided that since I was there (being only a mere child) we were to turn back.

I am thankful to this day that it was not my father driving, for he was in denial over the fact that his ocean was taking lives with the push and pull of its waves and he would have continued driving us straight to our deaths. I was nearly in tears as we turned around. People banging on the van and screaming, "Let us in! Let us in!" and wailing in agony. We had neither room, nor time, to spare.

So we drove back and my father stopped at a good friend's house to see if everyone was okay. After a few minutes he ran back and said that his friend was at work, and the wife was in hysterics because she couldn't find her mother (who had been praying at a temple), and that he'd tried to bring her to safety but couldn't get in a word between the shrieks. The danger seemed to be gone, but he didn't like the looks of the water crawling towards them. Besides, we were all still in the van that could easily be swept away by the water.

And so we drove for a while upwards, to the Holy Cross Church, where we could still see the ocean but were too high up for it to reach us. We weren't the only ones there. Many people crowded together on the point, some of them wet. I saw a young man carrying an elderly lady on the steps, another elderly lady holding nothing but a few saved belongings and a picture of Jesus Christ who couldn't find her son or grandson, a few young girls wailing for their families, and of course those who were by themselves,; and would remain so. I tried comforting the lady with the picture and some of the wailing girls... I was in a trance-like state of mind. We handed out crackers and tried to make sense of what would happen next. I gazed out at the ocean; it was a murky brown, filled with debris.

Once we deemed it safe, we returned to the van. I was so exhausted; I couldn't take much more... and so I fell asleep. When I woke up we were going out to lunch as if nothing had happened. Had it been a dream? No, it had been a nightmare. My parents later told me that once we had turned around and headed for Holy Cross, the second wave had hit. It was that wave that had taken thousands of lives, and left many homeless. I have never looked at the sea the same way again. Also, about 200 cars that had not turned around as we did were swept away; some license plates were found in the Maldives, 767 kilometers away. It all came down to a minute or two that had saved our lives.

There must be a purpose I have to serve, a reason why I lived through that tragedy. I was witness to something that has affected the world.

~Sheoli V. Gunaratne, age 13

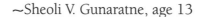

Beginning
at the End

This weary ol' workhorse is a unicorn, my friend.
~Jareb Teague

My writing career had been going well. No, I hadn't landed that elusive publishing deal, and literary agents weren't knocking down the door. Instead, I was writing a weekly personal column for a small community paper and another column about several local communities for the major paper in the city. A couple of magazines had used some pieces I'd submitted as well. Sometimes I even had the chance to write a feature. The small amount of income that I received helped pay a bill or two.

Most important were the contacts I made. Both columns had developed a healthy readership. I met wonderful people who indicated that they looked forward to my columns each week, and I learned many new things about the area where I'd lived for all my life except for a four-year hiatus away at college.

For more than three years, I was blessed with those opportunities. However, a new editor with the large newspaper cut my column for what she claimed were budgetary concerns. I protested that folks in my area would no longer have coverage of their events, but the editor assured me that one of the other freelance columnists would take up the slack. She also offered me another position covering new businesses in the area. I agreed even though the loss of my original column smarted.

For the next few months, I sought out business to highlight each week. Finding them became increasingly tougher as the economy slipped further in the tank. Added to that was my inability to please this editor with my writing. From the outset, she picked my work apart and asked endless questions, many that were answered in the piece I'd written.

Writing had become a chore. I submitted stories and waited for the snide comments, questions, and chastising to begin. No lead or angle for a story ever met her approval. The new assignment began in January, and in March, the editor killed the column. She ended my column and affiliation with her small kingdom in a curt e-mail that told me I could submit pieces to other sections of the paper.

Bam! Suddenly something that I'd enjoyed so was taken from me. I was cast aside and my work replaced with question and answer pieces about pets. Self-doubt set in as I wondered if my gift for writing had disappeared. The question popped into my head as to whether I'd taken writing for granted. The support and encouragement of my wife Amy sustained me, and she prodded me to continue to write. She ended by saying, "Don't look at this as a loss. God has given you a talent, and this is the end of one road that will lead to another."

I kept that in mind and spent much of my time in front of the computer. A collection of personal columns came to life, and a new book was begun. I'd recently retired from a thirty-year career as a high school English teacher, and any extra time was devoted to playing golf and completing a "honey-do list." In no time the sting of being let go by the editor and the ensuing bitterness over it disappeared.

In June Amy met with her two cousins for lunch. Both were working for another small paper in the area. Carol asked what I was doing since leaving the other paper, and when Amy told her nothing, she asked if I'd be interested in working with her employer. I agreed to meet with the publisher of the paper, and Sandra hired me. My job was to cover the same areas about which I'd written for the last three years. In addition, I would be named the community editor. Ironically, this small paper was distributed as an insert in the very publication for which I'd previously worked.

I was ecstatic with the opportunity. Not only could old relationships with the communities and the people who lived in them be renewed but the prospect of producing a section that would outshine the one of my old boss was also possible.

Some might call it karma, that idea that what goes around comes around. I prefer to believe that Amy was right. The good Lord had decided to use me in a new way. I was blessed again.

The work hours are longer now, but I don't mind. Sure, I lost a job, one that I enjoyed tremendously. What I gained was a new and broader chance to write. Most of all, I awakened to the fact that endings always lead to beginnings. That fact means that a loss is never more than a change in direction. Faith and patience help make that clear.

~Joe Rector

Everything Makes Sense in Reverse

Hindsight is always twenty-twenty.
~Billy Wilder

Sometimes life makes more sense when you look at it in reverse. That's certainly been true for me this year. Last Christmas, at the age of thirty-nine, I came down with an autoimmune disease which viciously attacked my knees and eyes. At its worst I could barely walk or see. For months I'd have to crawl across the floor of our apartment to use the bathroom or get a drink of water when my husband wasn't home to help me walk. For a while I could only see shapes and colors so I couldn't drive.

My parents kept begging me to let them come out to stay with me in Los Angeles but our apartment is small (and L.A. hotels are expensive) and I knew that there was nothing they could really do to help me — because of the excellent health insurance my husband had through his job at the Getty Museum I was receiving the best medical care possible.

My only problem was that I couldn't drive to my doctors' appointments because of my poor vision and I didn't want my husband to keep missing work to drive me. Three days after I explained this dilemma to my parents, a check showed up from them with a note saying that this was "taxi money" to get me to my doctors' appointments. Several months later another check showed up from my brother to help supplement our income since I was not able to work. It probably goes without saying that I was extremely grateful for the excellent medical coverage I had through my husband's work and I was also extremely grateful to have family members who could and would support me both emotionally and financially during this challenging time.

In terms of my day-to-day existence, I live in a village within Los Angeles called Brentwood so I was able to walk to the local post office, market, bank, and library. Because I was already familiar with the area, I could still walk to these places but then, once there, I had to rely on the kindness of strangers to help me address packages, shop for food, make bank deposits, and pick up "books on tape," which were a lifesaver. Again, I knew I was blessed. Los Angeles is a big city, but I lived in a village with a wonderful community of people who were kind and patient and helped me as I struggled to maintain some semblance of a normal life.

Despite my gratitude, I was often frustrated, frightened, and sad. I didn't know if or when my vision would return and I kept wondering why this was happening to me? My doctors had run dozens of tests and none of them could find the root problem that caused this illness. The doctors theorized that maybe it was my poor diet or the stress I was under at work that had triggered my body to attack itself—but they didn't know for sure and said that we would simply have to categorize this as a "strange episode."

As with most difficult situations, several blessings began to emerge. The first was that I radically improved my diet and began walking several times a week. Though I had lost forty pounds through Weight Watchers several years earlier, I was still averse to water, fruits and vegetables, and daily exercise until this illness emerged. I noticed that as I began exercising, drinking more water, and eating foods such as fruits, vegetables, nuts, and skim milk my body began to heal. I developed such an interest in this phenomenon that I decided I was going to leave the entertainment industry once and for all and instead try to work in a health-oriented environment.

With all of the downtime that this illness gave me I also began to contemplate my life and what was important to me. I decided that I wanted to do some volunteer work to thank God and the universe for providing me with such a loving family, a wonderful husband, and a compassionate community. I wasn't sure what kind of volunteer work I wanted to do so I just kept my eyes open hoping an opportunity would present itself.

Each week as I went to my rheumatologist I noticed several senior citizens walking around in front of what looked like a very nice hotel. They would always say "hi" to me and when my illness was at its worst and I was having trouble walking, several of them stopped to ask if I was okay as they zoomed past me with their walkers. I learned that the "nice hotel" they lived in was actually an assisted living community called Sunrise. I looked it up on the Internet and saw that there was a Sunrise community very close to my apartment so I vowed that when I was well I would ask if I could volunteer there.

Despite my assurance that I was healing, my parents eventually put their foot down and insisted on coming out to L.A. to see me. I had a wonderful time with them. We went to see the beautiful flowers at one of my dad's favorite places, Huntington Garden, and we spent endless hours chatting as we walked around my neighborhood and watched my husband, Tom, play tennis. I loved getting to see my mom and dad!

Slowly my vision began to return and the swelling in my knees went down. Four months after my illness I could see well enough to drive and I could walk with ease! Though I was still on medication, I was excited to feel well again so I began applying for jobs and I called Sunrise to inquire about volunteer opportunities. Within a month I had a fantastic part-time job at Curves and I was accepted as a volunteer at Sunrise!

Life was good again and I thought I had a clear understanding of the blessings this illness had provided—it had given me the downtime I needed to revamp my diet, assess my priorities, and contemplate a career change. And then something happened that simultaneously broke my heart and gave me blinding clarity as to the main reason why this illness had to happen.

My dad died unexpectedly. He passed away in his sleep. There was no pain. There was no struggle and there was no fear. I know my dad's peaceful passing was exactly as he would have wanted it but I am left in shock and with a gaping hole in my heart. My only solace, and it is a great one, is that because I got so sick, my mom and dad came out to visit me in L.A. The silver lining in this grey thunderstorm of despair is that I got to spend one last fantastic weekend with my dad, and for that I am eternally grateful.

~Rebecca Hill

Additional Views

There is much in the world to make us afraid.
There is much more in our faith to make us unafraid.
~Frederick W. Cropp

"The radiologist reviewed your mammogram and has recommended additional pictures."

With one telephone call, "what ifs" rose to swamp my thoughts. Was it... the "C" word? I pushed the thoughts away and reminded myself of a favorite Bible verse, "Don't be anxious for anything." But my thoughts weren't easily reined in.

My annual mammogram had followed a physical exam a few weeks earlier. Everything had been normal. Was a possible time bomb now ticking inside me?

The earliest appointment I could make was the following Friday, exactly one week later. My sleep was fitful for the next three nights. I alternated between trust in the loving sovereignty of God, and the recurring flood of "what ifs" that invaded my thoughts when I let down my guard. My husband, Russ, tried to be reassuring, but I saw worry in his eyes. How much of it was a reflection of my own fears?

Monday morning, I called to see if they had any cancellations. The appointment was moved up to Wednesday. In the meantime, I prepared to teach a Bible study. One of the questions caught my attention. "What attitude is required to see God at work in your life?" The answer was faith. Now I needed to act on my faith. That meant shutting out the "what ifs"—not allowing them even the tiniest toehold in my thoughts. I would trust my heavenly Father for whatever might come, "C" word or not.

On Wednesday, I recognized the receptionist at the diagnostic center. The familiarity bothered me. It shouldn't have been this way. She should have been a stranger to me, someone I saw once a year, not once a week.

She handed me a form. Before I could object, she said she knew I completed the same form last week, but they needed another one for this visit. I looked at the questions. "Reason for mammography?" Last week the answer had been easy. "Annual." Now I wondered what to write.

She sensed my hesitation. "Just write 'additional views.'"

Additional views? It sounded so... clinical. So objective. As if to obscure the fact that these "additional views" would determine if my body had turned against me. I completed the form, returned it to her, and waited.

A perky woman called my name. I recognized her as the technician from my prior visit. This time the familiarity was comforting, and I wondered at my inconsistency.

I pleaded for information about the first mammogram as she positioned me for the X-rays. "Tiny calcifications," she said, but hastened to add that calcifications are common and frequently not cancerous. The doctor would make a diagnosis based on the size, shape, and distribution in the "additional views." I struggled to process her words.

She reassured me with her warm eyes and bright smile. She was not permitted to give me any more information, other than to say that my doctor would have the results in a day or two. As I exited, she gave me another broad smile. Could I take that as a sign that everything was fine? I needed more than a smile.

I logged on to the Internet at home. A quick search provided definitions of macrocalcifications and microcalcifications. Relief over my "tiny" calcifications was short-lived. Macrocalcifications are almost always non-cancerous. Microcalcifications—the tiny ones—are a different matter. They can be a sign of cancer, though not always. I was reminded of the adage, "A little knowledge is a dangerous thing."

A phone call brought the test results. My calcifications were the micro kind, and they had appeared since my last mammography a year earlier. The doctor recommended a biopsy and gave me the name and number of a surgeon. I asked him if the surgeon was one he would trust with his own wife. "I already have," he said.

The surgeon could see me the next Tuesday at 8:15 A.M. I was grateful for the early appointment, but it meant still more waiting.

Wait. I had never liked that word. It always struck me as a waste — precious minutes passing unproductively, never to be reclaimed. I had heard it said that God is less concerned with the destination than He is with the journey, and I was beginning to understand what that meant. The issue wasn't whether I had cancer. The issue was how I would respond to these circumstances — with trust and faith, or doubt and fear. I chose to trust the One who had shown Himself faithful time and time again.

I arrived at the surgeon's office at 8 A.M. on Tuesday, the first time I'd been early for anything in months. The doctor examined me and explained the biopsy procedure. Computer positioning would direct the biopsy needle for removal of tissue samples. My facial expression must have changed, because the nurse handed me tissues, and the doctor hastened to assure me that eighty percent of calcifications are benign. I composed myself enough to ask how many of these procedures he had done. Both he and the nurse responded together, "A thousand." I felt a little better.

The biopsy was scheduled for the next Monday, with a follow-up appointment with the surgeon three days later for the results. More waiting.

My natural inclination was to keep busy, to fill the minutes and hours with enough activity to distract me from the circumstances threatening my world. But another Bible verse came to mind. "Be still and know that I am God." Again I had to make a conscious choice to release control that I didn't really have in the first place.

Russ and I arrived early the day of the biopsy. The procedure was uncomfortable, but not as painful as I had imagined. The doctor explained what he was doing at each step. Halfway through the procedure, I broke into a sweat as fear washed over me. I reminded myself that I was not alone. God would carry me through. An hour later we were home. I was sore, but the worst part was waiting until Thursday afternoon for the results.

I prayed for the biopsy results to be benign. But I remembered a question I had once asked a Bible study class. "If God chooses not to give you another thing in answer to your prayers, will you love Him any less?" I knew that no matter what happened, God still loved me and would work it out.

Thursday found us once again waiting for my name to be called. As the nurse led us to an examining room, she asked how I was feeling.

"That's what I'm here to find out," I said.

She held up my chart, pointed to the word "benign" and said, "You're good. Real good."

The doctor confirmed the diagnosis with a broad smile. He ordered a follow-up mammography in six months. I breathed a prayer of thanks to God for His undeserved mercy.

I thought back to the first telephone call. Had it only been three weeks? My life appeared no different from that day to now, but I am different. One thing remains constant, however—the loving care of my heavenly Father in whatever may come, "C" word or not.

~Ava Pennington

Little Blond Blessing

Grandchildren are the dots that connect the lines
from generation to generation.
~Lois Wyse

Every one of my eleven grandchildren is very special to me! The other day, ten-year-old Hunter was here, and I told him I had to hurry and write some stories for *Chicken Soup for the Soul* books about counting my blessings. He said, "Grandma, why don't you write about your grandson?" I knew by his big grin that he was referring to himself, and I just couldn't keep from hugging him!

Actually, this blond little boy and I have a very special bond. I was his caregiver just after he was born and his mother's maternity leave ended. When my stepdaughter Sharon went back to work, baby Hunter stayed with me every day, starting in June of 1999.

In July of 1999, we got the terrible news that our twenty-eight-year-old son was killed in an auto accident. My world was turned upside down as funeral arrangements unfolded and I could only see sorrow ahead of me. I had to make the decision whether or not to continue giving Hunter childcare, when I was still deep in the throes of grieving.

Just holding this little blond baby in my arms brought me so much comfort and love that I decided I'd continue keeping him while his parents worked. I think it was the best therapy for me that I could have discovered at the time. I remember rocking him and smelling his sweet baby head in my arms, and thinking of a long-ago little blond boy who brought the same happiness to my life! He reminded me so much of my own son!

There were days I could not stop the tears, but holding Hunter and crying onto his soft head just seemed to help me. I could feel his unconditional love when he smiled up at me, and often I observed him looking off into the air smiling, gurgling and seemingly talking to angels! I felt as if he had a new guardian angel looking after him that he'd never met... his Uncle Donnie whom he resembled so much as a baby! Donnie lived in North Carolina and had not yet made the trip to Tennessee to meet his new nephew before his time came to leave us.

This little blond blessing came into my life just when God knew I'd need it most — two months before the loss of my own son. They say things happen for a reason, and in this case, I do believe it's true!

Okay, Hunter... your Grandma DID write that story about you!

~Beverly F. Walker

Chapter 9

Count Your Blessings

A New Perspective

It's amazing the life that I'm living today,
and I count my blessings every day
for the gifts that God has given me.

~Sasha Azevedo

I Found My Son Again

*Every day is an opportunity
to make a new happy ending.*
~Author Unknown

Let me share with you a story to illustrate the power of gratitude and mutual understanding that emerged through empathic listening.

I have a dear friend who once shared with me his deep concern over a son he described as being "rebellious," "disturbing," and "an ingrate."

"Stephen, I don't know what to do," he said. "It's gotten to the point where if I come into the room to watch television with my son, he turns it off and walks out. I've tried my best to reach him, but it's just beyond me."

At the time I was teaching some university classes around the 7 Habits. I said, "Why don't you come with me to my class right now? We're going to be talking about Habit 5 — how to listen empathically to another person before you attempt to explain yourself. My guess is that your son may not feel understood."

"I already understand him," he replied. "And I can see problems he's going to have if he doesn't listen to me."

"Let me suggest that you assume you know nothing about your son. Just start with a clean slate. Listen to him without any moral evaluation or judgment. Come to class and learn how to do this and how to listen within his frame of reference."

So he came. Thinking he understood after just one class, he went to his son and said, "I need to listen to you. I probably don't understand you, and I want to."

His son replied, "You have never understood me—ever!" And with that, he walked out.

The following day my friend said, "Stephen, it didn't work. I made such an effort, and this is how he treated me! I felt like saying, 'You idiot! Aren't you grateful for what I've done and what I'm trying to do now?' I really don't know if there's any hope."

I said, "He's testing your sincerity. And what did he find out? He found out you don't really want to understand him. You want him to shape up."

"He should, the little whippersnapper!" he replied. "He knows full well what he's doing to mess things up."

I replied, "Look at the spirit inside you now. You're angry and frustrated and full of judgments. Do you think you can use some surface-level listening technique with your son and get him to open up? Do you think it's possible for you to talk to him or even look at him without somehow communicating all those negative things you're feeling deep inside? You've got to do much more private work inside your own mind and heart. You'll eventually learn to appreciate him and to love him unconditionally just the way he is rather than withholding your love until he shapes up. On the way, you'll learn to listen within his frame of reference and, if necessary, apologize for your judgments and past mistakes or do whatever it takes."

My friend caught the message. He could see that he had been trying to practice the technique at the surface but was not dealing with what would produce the power to practice it sincerely and consistently, regardless of the outcome.

So he returned to class for more learning and began to work on his feelings and motives, particularly the need to appreciate, respect and empathize. He soon started to sense a new attitude within himself. His feelings about his son turned more tender and sensitive and open. He became profoundly grateful for his son, simply because he sincerely wanted to understood and appreciate his son.

He finally said, "I'm ready. I'm going to try it again."

I said, "He'll test your sincerity again."

"It's all right, Stephen," he replied. "At this point I feel as if he could reject every overture I make, and it would be all right. I would just keep making them because it's the right thing to do, and he's worth it. I feel so grateful for him and for the hard learning."

That night he sat down with his son and said, "I know you feel as though I haven't tried to understand and appreciate you, but I want you to know that I am trying and will continue to try."

Again, the boy coldly replied, "you have never understood me." He stood up and started to walk out, but just as he reached the door, my friend said to his son, "Before you leave, I want to say that I'm really sorry for the way I embarrassed you in front of your friends the other night."

His son whipped around and said, "You have no idea how much that embarrassed me!" His eyes began to fill with tears.

"Stephen," he said to me later, "all the training and encouragement you gave me did not even begin to have the impact of that moment when I saw my son begin to tear up. I had no idea that he even cared, that he was that vulnerable. For the first time I really wanted to listen. My gratitude grew immensely."

And listen he did. The boy gradually began to open up. They talked until midnight, and when his wife came in and said, "It's time for bed," his son quickly replied, "We want to talk, don't we, Dad?" They continued to talk into the early morning hours.

The next day in the hallway of my office building, my friend, with tears in his eyes, said, "Stephen, I found my son again."

As my friend discovered, there are certain fundamental principles that govern in all human interactions, and living in harmony with those principles or natural laws is absolutely essential for quality family life. In this situation, for example, the principles my friend had been violating were the basic principles of gratitude, empathy and respect. The son also violated them. But this father's choice to live in harmony with that principle—to try to genuinely and empathically listen to and understand his son—dramatically changed the entire situation. The son also felt so grateful for his father and for the understanding they achieved. You change one element in any chemical formula and everything changes.

Exercising the principles of gratitude, empathy and respect and being to able to genuinely and empathically listen to another human being are among the habits of highly effective people in any walk of life. Can you imagine a truly effective individual who would not respect and appreciate others or who would not deeply listen and understand?

~Stephen R. Covey

The Girl in the Box

Enjoy the little things,
for one day you may look back
and realize they were the big things.
~Robert Brault

I stumbled upon the box one rainy afternoon while cleaning out the garage. Buried beneath an artificial Christmas tree and a clump of cobwebs, the box was just one of the many I hadn't had the energy to unpack since our move back to California. To my surprise, a pile of school yearbooks, old photographs, birthday cards, and trinkets greeted me as I plunged my hand inside. The contents of my life, all shoved into a ragged box that had survived one too many moves.

I set the lid back on the box, not sure I was really ready to tackle this stuff today. As the rain pounded down on the garage roof, I buried my face in my hands and let the tears fall. It wasn't the first time I'd cried today. The littlest things seemed to set me off these days... burning a piece of toast, losing my keys, my feeble macaroni and cheese dinner going unappreciated by four whiny kids. I felt like a ticking time bomb, ready to explode at any given second. What was wrong with me?!

Three years ago, we'd packed up the biggest U-Haul we could find and set off for Arizona, dreaming about a fresh start for our growing family. We had joined the "gold rush movement" out of California, purchasing our first home in a place we were assured was the "perfect family environment." Our new town boasted landscaped parks on every corner, sprawling new homes, and all the promise of a good life. When my husband secured a great job in the city, it seemed everything was truly falling into place. Our dreams were finally coming true!

The minute the four walls went up in our new home, however, everything inside of it seemed to crumble. My oldest son was diagnosed with Tourette syndrome, while my youngest suffered from extreme colic. My husband's job that had seemed so promising began to wear on him, while I tried to hold down the fort at home with what little energy I had left. To top it off, our finances took a nosedive, which baffled me to no end. Hadn't we moved out here for a better life?

One afternoon, things hit rock bottom. As the temperature peaked at 120 degrees, our brand new air conditioner went out, forcing us to drive to a hotel. My husband threw his work clothes into the trunk of the battered 1995 Ford Taurus he'd traded in his new car for, and looked down at me sadly. "I'm sorry," he whispered. "If I'd known things would turn out like this..."

Nearly three years after making our move, I found myself once again packing boxes. The tears I'd stored up for so long fell at last as I mourned our dreams. My husband's company had relocated, and he'd taken a position back in California. With the feeble real estate market, it looked as though we'd have to go through a foreclosure on our home. The home we'd saved for, dreamed about, built from the ground up. With a last glance at my coveted granite countertops, I hoisted the boxes into the moving truck and tried not to look back.

I put on a brave smile for the kids as we hiked up the steps of our "new" rental home in California. "Look at the view!" I gushed, trying to stay positive. But that night, as I tossed and turned, I felt anywhere but home. We'd tried so hard to make things work! How could we have failed?!

Within weeks of our return to California, I grew ill with a terrible virus, which left me debilitated for months. Too fatigued to get out and socialize, I became isolated and depressed. Any hope of trying to make a new life here went right out the window. On a good day, I managed to throw a chicken in the Crock-Pot and wash my hair. The vivacious woman who'd once been the type-A party planner, the leader, the social butterfly, was now hardly recognizable with her matted hair and dirty sweatpants.

It was on one of those days, when I hadn't managed to change out of my sweats or wash my hair, that I stumbled upon the box. Figuring I might as well tackle the daunting pile of stuff we hadn't unpacked since our move, I set up the kids with a cartoon video and busied myself in the garage. Three hours later, I'd polished off an entire bag of Cheetos but hadn't made a dent in the stuff. And then I opened the box.

At last, I took a deep breath and popped the lid off again. One by one, I pulled out the items. A photograph of me, smiling on my graduation day with a silly lei around my neck and my husband-to-be beaming proudly beside me. A card from my best friend, telling me how much it meant to her that I took the time for a good heart-to-heart. My daughter's first sonogram photo, on which I'd happily scrawled: "It's a girl!" A Valentine's card from my son, complete with a set of pink handprints. My high school yearbook, in which I boasted the world's worst perm. A dusty wooden plaque for participating in the state spelling bee. (I got out on the word "adjacent," which I'll never misspell again in my life!)

As I sifted through the things, the tears fell once again. All these precious things, gone untouched for years, just waiting for me like a sacred gift. Pieces of me, of my life... pieces I'd somehow lost along the way. Where was that smiling girl with the bad perm? (My hair hadn't improved much since then, but still... when was the last time I'd smiled like that?)

Glancing back down at a photo, I shook my head. Somehow along the way, I'd lost myself. In the hustle and bustle of life, I'd let myself, and everything that really mattered go. While pursuing the dreams the world told me to have, I'd missed out on the very things before my eyes. And when those dreams had been shattered, I'd forgotten how far I'd come, how much I'd been blessed.

That was the day I decided to start living again. I picked up that box, picked up those pieces, and instead of shutting the lid, I opened my heart. I lounged in bed on Saturday mornings with my kids instead of rushing off to do the laundry. I counted stars with my daughter on our steps one rare clear-skied night. I let my son lick the cookie batter out of the bowl without reprimanding him about germs. I rolled down the car windows and took the coastal route home, blasting Bon Jovi and drumming the steering wheel like a teenager. And for once, I didn't care what anyone thought about me.

I'm thankful for that girl in the box. She taught me that life is not always easy, but that at the end of the day, it's in the midst of these trials that we find ourselves, stronger than we thought we were, thankful for the simple things, celebrating the past, and looking forward.

~Karen Koczwara

An Unexpected Encounter

Our brightest blazes of gladness are commonly kindled
by unexpected sparks.
~Samuel Johnson

"**D**o you have time to participate in a ceremony?" a voice spoke from behind us in the trees.

My husband and I were on the road to the top of Mount Evans in Colorado, to see the changing aspens. We had stopped at a picnic area to go on a short walk. We were looking for clarity and strength, because the previous day the stock market had crashed. We didn't know how we were going to survive financially. We were both semi-retired. My husband, Dave, had a part-time job working at a golf course, and I was working only one morning a week teaching preschool. I had been laid off from my other part-time job, and Dave was not working at the time because his job was seasonal. We had been using the interest income from our investments, and we knew we were going to have to make some drastic changes in our finances. In the past, we had found that our trips to the mountains gave us perspective on things.

We looked back and saw a Native American standing in a small clearing on top of some rocks. He was tall, with an Indian headband tied around his silver hair. A decorated Indian blanket was draped over his shoulders, and he was barefoot. At his feet lay a plain red blanket covered with various objects.

"What kind of ceremony is it?" I asked.

"It is a ceremony to give thanks, and to ask for help for many people," he replied.

"Can we do it when we get back from our walk?"

"Well, I will probably be gone by then, as I have everything prepared to start now," he responded.

I wondered if this was some scheme to make money so I asked, "Is it free?"

"Of course," he answered. "But only participate if you want to."

My husband was not sure at first, but after finding out that the ceremony would only be about ten minutes, we both agreed and walked back to where he was standing. We introduced ourselves, and found out his name was Michael Bird Bear, and that he was a Native American medicine man for a Sioux tribe in South Dakota. He had been in Boulder, Colorado for a conference. Before his trip, he had promised several people that he would do this ceremony at this sacred spot in the mountains. He said that part of the ceremony would be in his native language, and part would be in English. He asked us to please not take any pictures, and we agreed.

"Can you tell us what all these objects on the blanket symbolize?" I asked.

"This piece of meteorite in my left hand is thousands of years old, and the crystal in my right hand has special properties too. The objects on the blanket stand for all the creatures from the very largest to the smallest. There is a bear paw with the claws attached, and a rattle made from the small skull of a muskrat. The snake skin stands for the renewal of all things, because snakes shed their skin to grow a new one. There is also a long piece of petrified wood, and a special rock. There are two tomahawks, one that is very ancient with beading on it, and a newer one, showing the transition of time."

Looking at a ball of tangled string with multicolored pom-poms on the ends, I questioned, "What is that?"

"Those are the prayers of the angels," he said. "You know there are always angels around you, and these stand for the prayers of thousands of people all over the world, not just in America. The angels tangled them up so that the prayers could not be undone."

He told us that first he would give thanks to the Great Spirit for all of our blessings, and then he would ask the Great Spirit to answer the prayers of the angels. He raised his arms to the sky, and quietly chanted in his native language, turning slowly to face each direction of the compass. Then he said in English, "Thank you for all things. Please answer the special prayers of David and Marna Jones," and he continued to name several other people and Native American families. He then completed the ceremony by chanting again in his native language.

"Is that the end of the ceremony?" my husband asked.

"Yes, I promised it would be short," Michael answered. He did not know that we were worried about money, but then he said, "You know the Great Spirit does not want people to live in poverty. It is okay to be financially secure."

I thought he was going to ask us for money to help his tribe, but instead he said, "Don't worry; things will be fine for you."

"How did you know this was a sacred spot?" I asked. "Was the location handed down?"

"Yes. You may wonder why it is so close to the outdoor bathroom. The sacred spot came first, and the bathroom was added later!" he answered, and we all laughed.

I told him that my husband really liked Native American culture, and that his father's family lived next to the reservation in Mission, South Dakota. I also said that I identified with the Native American concept that all things are connected.

"I believe the Great Spirit is in the spaces between the atoms," I explained.

"Exactly," said Michael. "Have you heard of Don Miguel Ruiz?"

"No," I answered.

"He has written a book that I think you would enjoy. It is called *The Four Agreements*."

"I will get it," I answered.

Dave and I thanked him for letting us be part of the ceremony, wished him good luck, and we all shook hands before saying good-bye. Dave and I walked back to the parking area, which was empty except for our car and Michael Bird Bear's. On the way home we talked about how strange it was that we had connected with him. We had never stopped at any of the picnic areas before, and if we had not also stopped to take pictures at a lake on the way up the mountain, our paths would not have crossed.

After we got home, we talked about our finances, realizing we would both need to work more. Dave got a job during the holidays working at RadioShack, and went back to his golf course job, where he appreciates the free golf included as part of his compensation. I got substitute teaching jobs at two schools, utilizing my degree in elementary education. I really enjoy teaching again, and participating in the development of young minds.

We are using some of our savings, and have scrunched our monthly budget, eliminating extras like eating out a lot, but we are doing all right. We appreciate small things even more, like our time together, and we are closer than ever now. Our ceremony with Michael Bird Bear reassured us, reinforced our connection, and gave us strength.

~Marna Malag Jones

The Lunch Hour

Time is an illusion, lunchtime doubly so.
~Douglas Adams

I clutched a yogurt in one hand as I tried to eat and catch up on customer e-mail during the noon hour. Even fifteen minutes in the employee lunchroom seemed too much of a luxury. My company, like many companies, had cut costs by not replacing people as they left. The survivors were expected to take up the slack.

For me, this meant no lunch hour, plus taking work home in the evening or on the weekends. I didn't feel I worked at a job; I felt I was my job. I wanted to quit, but given the economy, I felt I couldn't until I had another job in hand. Nice in theory, but given how cranky all the extra hours made me feel, it was difficult to convince potential employers to hire me. I felt trapped. Then a chance conversation with a stranger's six-year-old daughter changed my outlook. The young girl was positively bouncy, standing in line with her mom at the grocery store.

"Good day at school?" I asked.

A nod.

"What's your favorite subject?"

"Lunch."

I smiled at the answer. I remembered when that had been my answer. At lunch, there were no adults to tell you what to do and when to do it. You could sit and talk with your friends or play an exuberant game of four-square. You could draw pictures or swing on the monkey bars. The time was yours to do whatever you wanted. Sometimes we planned our time, bringing stickers to trade or Chinese jacks for a weeklong tournament. Sometimes we were more spontaneous, only deciding what to do while we were eating our peanut butter and jelly sandwiches and slurping our little paper cartons of milk.

That brief encounter left me wondering: What had happened to lunch?

I knew that by law I was entitled to a lunch break at work. So I decided to simply start taking it. The office was located in the downtown area of a small town and I set out to explore it. A few blocks away was a local art museum with free admission. At the end of another street, I was startled to discover some horses grazing in a field. A cute gift boutique made for pleasant and sometimes humorous browsing, particularly looking through the leftover holiday items and laughing at the sometimes funny things, like jack-o'-lantern sunglasses and temporary Santa tattoos that no one had the foresight to buy.

When the weather turned cold, I visited the used bookstore or public library. Near the library was a small man-made pond that attracted ducks and small children with their parents, all of whom provided much amusement as they demanded to be fed. Even running errands at lunch to the bank or the post office brought me a small measure of joy. Doing those errands during the week freed up some time on the weekends for fun activities.

When I decided to take back my lunch hour, I braced myself for catty remarks or stares from my co-workers, but they never materialized. In fact, I watched in amazement as some of my co-workers started to drift away occasionally from their own desks during lunch. We started inviting each other out for walks during good weather and discovered that we had other topics of conversation beyond the now common complaints about work.

I'm still looking for a new position, but with less stressed-out urgency than before. You can't always change your circumstances, but you can always change your perspective.

~Michelle Mach

Emergencies
of the Heart

We can do no great things,
only small things with great love.
~Mother Teresa

Accompanying a friend to the emergency room at our local hospital, I dreaded the hours of waiting I knew that I most likely faced. I had heard horror stories of people spending all day—eight or nine hours, maybe longer—just waiting. Still, my friend needed me to take her, so I went.

I settled myself into an uncomfortable chair and started flipping through the outdated magazines that were donated by the local churches. At one time, I would have sat there, oblivious to everyone around me. This time, for some reason, I looked restlessly around me, unable to focus on reading.

There was a young mother with three small children. One was a little girl of about seven with a dreadful rash on her legs. She got into everything, even though her harried mother tried to keep track of her. The two younger children, a toddler and an infant, cried continuously, the decibel level increasing with each passing minute.

A young woman, sitting next to them, leaned over and said something to the exhausted mother. Smiling gratefully, the mother nodded, and the young woman gently reached into the carrier and snuggled the baby into her arms. When she offered a bottle, the baby began to nurse hungrily.

The mother captured the toddler as he climbed over a chair in an attempt to reach the window. His screams were those of frustration from not being able to achieve his goal. The mother stood holding him, rocking side to side, as she pointed toward the window. The rain cascaded, tapping against the glass. The mother began to tap, tap, tap her hand on the toddler's back in time to the rain as she crooned softly. It wasn't long before his head began to bob and finally nestled between his mother's chin and shoulder. Wearily she sat down, gently resting her head on his as he slept.

By this time, the seven-year-old girl was engaged in a conversation with an elderly man who had a bloody bandage around his leg. She was entranced by the story of how he had fallen out of a tree while trying to rescue his cat, describing how the fire department had to come to his assistance. I smiled at this corny old story.

A hospital representative came out. "We are ready for you now," she said to the young mother. "Let me help you take the children back."

I was surprised when the young woman who had quieted the baby stayed behind.

"Aren't you allowed to go back with your friend?" I asked. If that was the rule, I understood, but was incredulous nonetheless.

"Oh, I don't know her," she responded. "I could see she just needed help with those children. I'm here because I'm pregnant and I may be losing my baby."

Her eyes misted and her lips trembled. Before I could respond she also was called to go back.

Taking a deep breath, I prayed that she and her baby would be all right.

Blinking, I looked around the small waiting room and realized that the only ones who remained were the elderly man who had entertained the little girl, a young man whom I had not noticed before, and me. I looked over at the elderly man and he smiled invitingly.

"You did a great job entertaining that little girl with your harrowing story," I laughed.

"Well, it always works on the little ones," he said sheepishly. "I do like kids, even though I don't have any of my own."

"How did you really hurt your leg?" I asked.

"Well, when Daniel here came over to get my dog," he responded, nodding his head toward the younger man, "I lost my footing and fell down an embankment. When Daniel tried to help, he fell right on top of me."

Just then, the hospital aide came into the waiting area and wheeled the old man back to see the doctor.

Looking at Daniel, I asked, "Can you finish the story?"

"Sure," he obliged. "Mr. C had his dog for about fifteen years. It just died of old age, I guess. But he loved that dog and he couldn't stand the thought of burying him and leaving. You see, he and Mrs. C are retiring and will be moving. He didn't have the heart to leave his best friend behind."

Daniel's eyes met mine. "So I was picking him up to have him cremated. That's what I do you see. I cremate people's pets."

At this point in the story, the hospital aide called Daniel's name.

"Darn the efficiency of this hospital," I muttered.

Alone now, I was left with my thoughts. I sat peacefully reflecting on my afternoon in the emergency room, of the many bittersweet stories here. Yet my spirit was uplifted and joyous because of them. I thought of the selflessness of the young woman who had put aside her own grief and fear over her unborn child to help a distressed mother care for her children, the elderly man who helped calm a little girl with his tall tales, while he sat bleeding and in pain, and the young man who, with such sensitivity, provided comfort to someone who had lost a beloved pet.

What happened that afternoon would inspire me for some time to come. I had waited, yes, but my time had not been wasted. At a time when there is so much focus on the dark side of life, my time in that emergency room was an unexpected blessing.

~Linda B. Breeden

Lesson from Everest

I have climbed my mountain, but I must still live my life.
~Tenzing Norgay

Phinjo and I cried with heaving sobs as we clutched each other tightly on the summit, the tears instantly freezing to our cheeks in the minus twenty-five degree air. Phi reverently removed a yellow kata scarf that he had painstakingly printed with our names and the date in English and Nepali and lashed it on to a strand of prayer flags snapping in the wind. The already brutal chill was intensifying and it penetrated and enveloped my body even in the cocoon of my down one-piece suit. I didn't dare remove my heavy gloves as I rummaged for my camera, knowing that my fingers would become frostbitten if I touched anything metallic in this incalculable wind-chill.

As I removed the tiny Canon from my insulated pocket I was alarmed to see it encased in ice. Evidently, dripping saliva from my oxygen apparatus had seeped into the pocket and frozen solid. I couldn't believe my luck as I hit the ON button and it came to life, needing only a little persuasion to open the lens cover.

As we took pictures of each other and radioed to Tuck and Jangbu at base camp, it was already time to go. After all the years of planning, training, and sacrifice we stood on the top of the world for a scant ten minutes. At a little past 5 A.M. on May 24, 2008, with one cramponed boot in Nepal and one in Tibet, Phi and I start the descent of Everest's southeast ridge route realizing full well that our journey was only half completed. We now had to get down with all our fingers, toes and a pulse.

The most dangerous part of this endeavor is the downclimbing, as often there is a psychological let-down of attention post-summit, leading to a missed clip or a stumble with the crampon points and either one can kill you quickly here. The debilitating effect of low oxygen pressure wreaks havoc on accurate decision-making and climbing technique and the more time spent in the "death zone" above 25,000 feet the more risk of cerebral edema, which often kills Himalayan climbers. One moment lucid and the next comatose.

Now bathed in full light of day there was no escaping the gut-tightening exposure as we descended past broken rock and corniced overhangs. The most pressing issue was that we had been running on pure adrenaline for hours as it was simply too dangerous to stop for an energy gel and a swig of water. At first we made good progress but then we had to pass two ascending climbers who were too exhausted to move to the side and give us rope. Time ticked by as we snaked by the down-clad figures bent over their ice axes with heaving lungs, oblivious to anything but their own suffering.

Finally, I follow Phi's lead, simply grabbed a handful of old ropes and swung down Tarzan-style past the last guy. A slip in any direction would have been our deaths as there was 7,000 feet of air on our right and 10,000 feet on our left. In fifteen years of climbing I had never taken such risks on any mountain and I chastised myself firmly. Passing other climbers on the Hillary Step and the South Summit was a shock, "Did I look this bad on the way up?" I asked myself, as people seemed to have a very tenuous grip on reality, and they still had hours to go. The precipices were beguiling and terrible. "No mistakes now, focus on every step and each clip, focus on every little movement, stay alive," I repeated in my mind.

The fatigue built as we clambered over the lesser south summit. The sun was out and no cloud was visible in the milky blue sky but it was frigid in the gusty wind and my hands alternated freezing as I maneuver the safety loop and carabiner around the anchors. My legs were fine but my arms were so wasted it took all I had to concentrate on these simple tasks which were my only connection to relative safety. We descended mindlessly for hours and I constantly tried to change arm muscles by using a cadre of friction techniques to get down the rope.

I repeated my mantra from other climbs and hikes when I am knackered with fatigue: "The trail never ends." For some reason this always gives me solace and hope. I had become sunburned here in the troposphere and the oxygen mask had rubbed my face raw in several places. With each labored respiration the mask ground itself into the wounds. My glacier glasses fogged badly, making it nearly impossible to get accurate depth perception. I was hot here and cold there and all at the same time. When I tried to vent a body part, another was chilled. I felt increasing anger and irritation. To top it off Phinjo was way ahead of me. Each step elicited a moan and an epithet.

Two climbers slid up behind me and I guessed they had enough because one of them said, "Dude, you summited, right?" I still did not recognize him in my altitude-addled mind when he said, "Hey, great place for a picture," and motioned for my camera. Finally in my hypoxic state I realized it was Walter, an Austrian mountain guide. The thought occured to me that I would never have stopped and looked around if Walter didn't shake my tree.

I focused more on moaning and groaning than looking at the amazing world that I was at the top of. Now I noticed the pristine day, the snow, ice, and rock of the world's biggest mountain under my boots; I saw Kanchenjunga, the third-highest mountain on the planet, was on my left, Makalu, the fifth-highest, was on my right. I would be safe! Tears came as I suddenly realized how lucky I was. "I will never be here again so I better look around," I reasoned.

The past was history and the future a dream and all that existed for me was that second. I was in a beautiful, fascinating place, having an extraordinary experience and I would not miss it. I reminded myself with every step to live in the moment and be aware. On the other hand, I could not linger as a lack of focus on the climbing could and would kill me. It's the yin and yang of Everest: extreme beauty and death can occupy nearly the same moment. I realized the source of mental irritation at myself and Phi: I was, and had been, utterly terrified. I explained this to Phi at the balcony at 27,500 feet as we shared the first gulp of water in many hours. Phinjo Sherpa, devout Buddhist and five-time Everest summiter nodded in wordless understanding.

~Dr. Timothy W. Warren

88

We're Saved!

We cannot live only for ourselves.
A thousand fibers connect us with our fellow men.
~Herman Melville

O ur neighborhood, Rancho Bernardo, was ablaze. We barely escaped, and fled to Qualcomm Stadium. Greedily we gulped fresh air. Water and hot dogs were proffered—balm to our stress.

We set up the portacrib in a handicap area and settled our six-month-old twin grandbabies, Joey and Lizzie, ash smudging their cheeks. TVs spewed a steady narration of the fire's advance. It snuck up the freeway, gobbled the hillside, then five homes along the eastern ridge. Historic Battle Mountain was stripped and blackened, but the white steel cross landmark persevered.

It hopped the freeway, and west of I-15 was burning too. Ten homes disappeared as firemen chased the flames with axes and hoses. Valiant firefighters on foot, infantrymen, could not keep up. Hurricane force winds rendered air cover impossible. Fire hopscotched up Aguamiel Road and took out twenty homes, as we gaped from our concrete bunker.

All around us, frantically, evacuees shared scraps of information, huddling over my husband Jim's BlackBerry, seeking which streets were burning. People were heroic even in their devastation—sharing food, drinks, news, comfort. Familiar faces floated by in the crowd and on the screen. Every once in a while a sob went up, "That's my house."

Our neighbors, the Kains, who followed us there, settled on the floor above, then encouraged us to join them—better for the babies. Jim went ahead to select a spot before we relinquished our seats, then summoned us by phone. Dragging the crib full of baby gear, we passed a growing tent city of sleeping bags, blankets, and pillows marking territory.

I pushed the stroller while the twins' mom, Linda, bumped the crib up the spiral ramp to the Club level. There were glass enclosed enclaves for seniors evacuated from retirement homes. We encamped between them on the concourse, near two TVs and the restroom. We strung chairs together as a fence around the baby bed, and hunkered down for the duration.

Volunteers poured in from churches and organizations, offering water, food, supplies, even a highchair and baby seat. We accepted only what we needed, leaving the rest for evacuees who escaped with just their lives.

As dark came on, we were exhausted. San Diego State University students arrived with blankets. On the concourse, we were out-doors—in October. A wind shield rose about three-quarters up the wall, but cold night air streamed in over the top. Constructed of concrete and steel, the temperatures inside and out were indistinguishable, but we felt safe from fire. We burrowed under blankets, and covered the mesh portacrib with comforters.

Steel-framed cots were delivered by the Army—they even set them up. It's amazing how territorial we became. Using chairs at the foot of each cot, we formed a perimeter, paranoid about the babies amidst 10,000 strangers. Jim sat up all night and guarded them while we slept, fitfully. I relieved him at dawn, and we all shared their care throughout the day.

Joey and Lizzie, blissful in their ignorance, cheered passersby. Everyone stopped for smiles and giggles, and the babies produced an endless stream of joy.

Nearby, in the club room, more than one hundred seniors received patient attention. Some were disoriented and fretful. Often, we would assist when they said, "I don't know how to get back" from the restrooms. Reporters tried to take their photos looking pathetic, but we sent them packing.

Increasingly, media arrived—local, then major networks, international reporters, even cubbies earning journalism degrees. The Border Patrol posted lists of homes burned. Insurance companies offered guidance. Farmers Insurance cooked pancakes, sausage, hot dogs. Starbucks served coffee. Local politicians manned booths. Telecommunications companies provided cell phone recharging, Internet access. Day three, showers were set up.

Entertainers came from the beginning: guitarists, singers, clowns, balloonists, face painters. Churches provided for children, with toys, bubbles, crayons, paints. Governor Schwarzenegger arrived by helicopter. I expected him to rappel down the side of the stadium.

We expanded from bewildered evacuees to include freeloaders and scamsters. I saw a woman selling the donations she'd gotten inside to a mother with children camped outside. Some people heard it was like Woodstock, so they came. We knew it was time to leave.

Jim left on the third morning to see if we could get into Westwood, the hardest hit area. National Guardsmen and police blocked every entrance. They were still checking for gas leaks and hot spots.

Exhausted, we hung back, having no safer harbor to go to. By noon, the mayor, senators, council members, the county supervisor, everyone, broadcast what the city was doing, but no word for us. I blocked the departure of the county supervisor and put the question to him. He sincerely advised that we stay put until we were specifically instructed to go back.

At two o'clock, I listened to the mayor and our councilman broadcasting from Westwood. There were conflicting reports about Westwood being open. I asked the reporter why she was telling the public something different than our councilman said minutes earlier. She grew as frustrated as we were at the conflicting information. We had to get out of there.

I called Linda from the growing circus below, told her to get the babies fed and changed—we were leaving. Upstairs, a strange woman held Joey. She'd heard about the evacuees and decided to sneak up to help. Paranoid, I took Joey from her and changed him, then laid him down on a comforter while I made them bottles. She picked him up, and sat beside Linda feeding Lizzie. I hastily assembled all of our stuff, leaving everything the volunteers had provided. Maybe I was just worn out, but I felt like this woman could run away with Joey into the crowd of now 20,000 people. Too much *Law & Order*, I guess.

The woman begged to help us carry out the babies, but I refused staunchly, nabbing one of the passing church volunteers, a big strapping fellow, to help us with the gear. Linda wheeled the babies in their stroller. I carried some belongings. We bee-lined to our cars, covered in ash.

Linda's mother had returned to her Escondido home, so Linda would take them there. Jim, worn out from his all-night vigils, went to the home of friends in Poway to shower, change, and rest. I had to see our neighborhood.

I was never so glad to leave anywhere, or so grateful. I can't thank Qualcomm Stadium or the City of San Diego enough. Likewise, the volunteers and businesses that donated an ocean of supplies. Even some of the Chargers came to offer comfort, like Clinton Hart.

At Westwood, I met blockades. Parking along the road I could peer over the block wall and see my house. I climbed on a transformer box, and there it was: The house we had fled in the dead of night, where I'd lived for twenty-five years, and raised my children.

That predawn escape seemed so long ago. Whenever we were allowed back in, I would go to the Crisis Center and volunteer to help those who were not so lucky. In all, 365 homes burned in Rancho Bernardo, about 1,500 in San Diego County. We will never stop counting this blessing.

~Nancy Canfield

Without a Warning

Rain showers my spirit and waters my soul.
~Emily Logan Decens

"Tomorrow is your thirtieth wedding anniversary and it's going to be unique because all three of your kids will be celebrating with you," remarks our daughter, Betsy, to Jim and me as she pulls into the Tampa airport to pick up her brother, Steve. Her sister, Lori, is unpacking at our home overlooking the Intracoastal Waterway. We plan to return there by midnight.

After greeting Steve at the baggage claim and exchanging hugs, we turn our attention to the announcement coming over the loud-speakers. "Those departing the airport are advised to drive with extreme caution as winds are over 100 miles per hour." A storm? We never received any warnings about a storm when we watched the news.

Outside, we're shocked at the weather as gale winds and driving rain threaten us. Betsy is nervous as she drives across the causeway spanning Tampa Bay, creeping along at five miles per hour with the emergency lights flashing. Angry gusts attempt to push us into deep water as Betsy clutches the wheel and struggles to keep the car on the road. Nobody speaks. We silently pray.

After a heart-thumping trip, Betsy pulls into our flooded drive-way strewn with palm fronds and oak limbs. Jim jumps out and yells to Steve, "Help me raise the boat on the davits! This storm surge will destroy it if we don't hurry." The girls and I hurry to rescue potted plants and deck furniture.

I fall into a fitful sleep until the roar of the pounding storm awakens me around 3:00 A.M. I go downstairs in the dark and find Steve staring at the boat through the glass sliding doors, as enormous waves push it high, then drop it with a punishing shudder. It's positioned like a torpedo ready for launch. "The boat can come crashing into the living room at any moment," says Steve. Then he adds, "Look, water is being forced under the doors and onto the tile."

Just then we hear a knock on the front door. When I open it, waves carry debris into the living room and I'm facing two drenched policemen. "We're here to tell you not to evacuate. Everything is flooded and there's no way out. Do the best you can. Good luck."

The rest of our family awakens and positions towel barricades at the doors to soak up water. The storm surge is over the sea wall and waves are crashing against the house. Jim and Steve struggle to carry heavy antiques upstairs and then return to elevate the downstairs furniture on bricks. With grim faces we watch as the violent water pounds our boat to death. The stern davit cable snaps, the inboard/outboard motor sinks to the bottom, and the front davit holds up the bow, making the boat look like a breaching whale.

Dawn streaks the leaden skies and the wind is finally out of breath. We venture outside and survey the damage to our boat, home, yard, and neighbors. Lori snaps pictures of the destruction for insurance purposes and our photo album. The knot in my stomach tells me I won't want to look at reminders of the storm.

A television news helicopter descends from nowhere and hovers over our dock while a cameraman films our damaged boat... details at six. Later, news reports question why people weren't warned about this deadly storm, on the night of March 13, 1993. It destroyed 18,000 homes and killed twenty-six people. Although it was a no-name hurricane, it is called the Storm of the Century that struck the eastern United States and produced a strong storm surge along the Gulf Coast of Florida.

Weary and sleep-deprived, our family begins to clean up the mess and put the house back together. Suddenly, Lori announces a cheery, "Happy Anniversary!" Startled that I had forgotten today was to be a celebration, I stop sweeping water out the door. Jim drops a pile of soaked towels and gives me a kiss in front of our grinning kids.

As I look at the faces of my husband of thirty years and the three wonderful children our marriage produced, I'm grateful we're safe and together. Betsy was right when she predicted this would be a unique anniversary I would always remember.

~Miriam Hill

90

Precious Moments

Life gives us brief moments with another...
but sometimes in those brief moments
we get memories that last a lifetime.
~Author Unknown

itting by my hospital window, I watched a sparrow hopping from branch to branch. How precious life is, I thought. It was Mother's Day and I marveled at my beautiful gift — my third child, Kimberly Ann. As I looked at my sleeping baby she made a sucking sound with her lips. Auburn curls on top of her head were highlighted with gold streaks.

"Kim, God gave you a frost job — a heavenly one," I whispered. Already, I treasured the precious moments spent with my baby, and looked forward to many more. Soon we'd be going home. I had dressed Kim in a pair of pink knit pajamas with small embroidered roses on the collar. She also wore a bib that said, "I love my daddy."

"Are my girls ready to go home?" I looked up into my husband's smiling face.

"Yes, we are."

As the nurse wheeled me out to the car, my son and daughter walked close by. Soon we were all secure in our family car. A short time later, Ted pulled into our driveway and parked. I announced, "We're home, baby girl."

As soon as we walked through our front door, Robbie asked, "Mom, can I hold Kim?"

"Yes, be careful to support her head." Robbie looked adoringly at Kim nestled in his arms.

My daughter, Linda exclaimed, "She is so small."

"Once upon a time, you were just as small," I replied.

"Mommy, look. She's holding onto my finger," Linda said excitedly. We sat close together on the couch for a few minutes. Then Kim started to cry, and Robbie handed her back to me.

During the next three months life revolved around our youngest member. Robbie loved to hold his sister. He struggled with a speech disorder, but when he held Kim she'd smile as he spoke to her. I overheard Robbie saying to Kim, "When you go to school no one had better tease you."

Linda loved to help me bathe Kim and pick out her outfits, "Mom," she'd ask excitedly, "when can we move Kim into my room?"

"Soon," I replied.

In preparation for that coming event we redecorated Linda's room—for the girls. We painted, and Linda peeked in and said, "You look funny with yellow paint on your nose."

"I bet I do. But do you like your room?"

"Yes. I love yellow."

Linda and I went shopping and bought a new bedspread for her bed, and a baby quilt with the same color scheme for Kim's crib.

One morning, I felt a deep need to hold Kim. She'd nuzzled close to my neck, and we shared a precious moment. After a busy morning I lay Kim down for her nap. I rubbed her back until she fell asleep. I tiptoed out of the room not realizing that Kim would never wake up from her nap. She died of Sudden Infant Death Syndrome.

The following days seemed like a dream that I kept trying to wake up from.

Friends and family surrounded us—food, cards, phone calls, all provided comfort. At Kim's funeral, beautiful roses lined the front of the church, and I felt comforted by the words in the hymns. Friends tried to comfort us by saying, "Kim's in a better place," or "She's one of God's angels."

But I wanted my daughter here with me. I wanted to watch her grow up. I found peace in those who put a value on Kim's short life. A close friend confided in me, "Kim's life has made me think about my own life. I want to help others."

As I stood at my daughter's graveside, a gentle breeze blew. It felt like someone touched my cheek, and within the breeze, I heard a gentle whisper, "treasure the memories." I looked around at Ted. My arms went around my children, and the four of us turned and walked away.

Grief was like an ocean tide. It flowed in and out. Its waves sometimes seemed gentle and at other times stormy. Soon Ted returned to work, and my children returned to school. I sat alone at home, wondering how I was supposed to face the future. There were times I thought I heard Kim cry, but her crib remained empty.

When Linda and Robbie came home from school they looked sad, and would go to their rooms. I realized that I needed to help my children grieve and move on.

I told them, "It's okay to cry. It's okay to miss Kim." By giving them permission to show their feelings I noticed that each day they seemed a little stronger, a little happier.

Before Kim had been born I'd run a daycare in my home. I had planned on starting that back up when she turned a year old. But after she died my grief had not allowed me to do this.

A year later, I decided to return to school. Not really knowing what I wanted to take, but needing something new to keep me busy, I signed up for a key punch course. At the end of my six-week course I received a certificate. I placed my certificate in a kitchen drawer and forgot about it. Then at the end of the week my sister called and said, "Karen, a position in our key punch department has opened up. Are you interested?"

"Yes, but first I need someone to watch Robbie and Linda for two hours after school." I asked my neighbor, Ginny. She agreed, and I decided to go for an interview. To my surprise I was hired.

As it turned out, my skills as a key punch operator were lacking. Eventually, my supervisor moved me to accounts payable. I worked on the book accounts of Corrie ten Boom, an evangelist who had lost her whole family in concentration camps during World War II. Yet, after the war ended, Corrie, at the age of fifty-two, stepped out in faith and traveled the world sharing a message of hope and forgiveness.

Over the next year, I met many evangelists and heard their stories of courage. Stories of people living through tough circumstances, yet who pressed forward—even when it hurt.

Gradually, I realized that I, too, had been moving forward one step at a time.

I found happiness in watching my children grow: Robbie earning his Boy Scout badges. Linda out growing her Barbie's, experimenting with make-up, becoming a beautiful young woman. Yes, life continued, with its good, bad, and sometimes outrageous moments.

Fifteen years later, I sat next to a hospital window and watched a sparrow pick a berry and fly away. My daughter, Linda smiled as her nurse walked in with a wee-bundle in her arms. She smiled and said, "An angel said this baby girl wants Grandma to hold her."

As I held my granddaughter, Breanna, I savored the moment. Looking into her sparkling eyes, I smiled and said, "Linda, she's so beautiful."

Four years later, I welcomed Breanna's sister, Staci. I am blessed. And my memories of Kim are like the sweet fragrance of a rose—often returning with a sense of joy.

~Karen Kosman

91

Five Open Hearts

It is only with the heart that one can see rightly;
what is essential is invisible to the eye.
~Antoine de Saint-Exupery

May 22nd, 2009 is a day I won't soon forget.

"Leigh Anne... telephone, it's your dad," my husband called to me at the kitchen table. I jumped up from an "exciting" game of *Go Fish* with my two young daughters.

"Hi Dad, what's up?" I asked happily, little knowing how, with his answer, my life would change. How my family's life would change. How everything would change.

"Your mom is in the hospital," my dad replied, his voice sounding distant and confused. "They are doing some tests on her heart."

Her heart?

"We aren't sure what is happening yet, but she had chest pains when we were hiking yesterday."

Chest pains? My mind raced. How long had she been having chest pains?

My dad continued to talk. I cannot recall what he said. He was trying to appear calm and in control, but deep down I knew he was shaken. Numerous thoughts and questions immediately flooded my mind. What was happening to my mom? What would the tests show? What if the unthinkable occurred?

I felt numb. Absolute disbelief; like one of those moments you read about where time stops, you completely disconnect. Almost an out-of-body experience. You hear something but can't absorb it. My dad had already told my younger sister and was about to call my twin sister, but I somehow I heard myself agreeing to do that.

To say we have a close family is an understatement. We always had dinner together as kids and still do when we get together for holidays or just regular weekend visits. We sang Gordon Lightfoot songs together on our weekend drives north to the cottage, and as teenagers we would even hang out with my parents on Friday nights playing board games or cards. Now that my sisters and I have our own families — lives away from Mom and Dad, we are still very connected and close. Not too many Fridays go by without our famous spaghetti and Caesar salad dinners, with whoever can make it. My parents are the center of those nights, high school sweethearts, still in love after all these years.

Mom has always been very healthy. She loves to walk the dog daily with my dad. They eat healthy food and she doesn't indulge too much in her sweet tooth. A dedicated personal counselor, she has listened, supported and guided others with their inner struggles for years. Such a big heart, one that we never thought would need any help with anything.

It never entered any of our minds that she would be having open-heart surgery.

The operation was a terrifying experience for us all. Five and a half hours of waiting. Intense waiting and praying and hoping... then more waiting. We sat there in the Cardiac Family Waiting Area as the seconds ticked slowly by. Three other families waited for their loved ones too. Connected by similar experiences, we didn't feel like strangers. I felt their worry and their hope. I waited with my family beside me. We were all there. My sisters, my dad and I, together, all supporting each other. We hugged each other and we prayed. The power of our desire for my mom's wellness was enormous. We were counting our blessings for the times we had already had. I thought about her love for my kids and her commitment to caring for my elder daughter when I was doing my internship. Her mentoring me through my private practice and encouraging me in all the times I needed her. The sound of her laugh.

After hours of waiting, her surgeon walked into the waiting area.

All the waiting and emotion crystallized into that moment. I was holding my breath—we all were. As we gripped each other's hands we heard the doctor say, "The surgery is over. She came through well, she's still in intensive care, but you are able to see her in several hours." Huge relief washed over us all. My dad reached out and shook the doctor's hand vigorously and held his grip a long, long time, his eyes welling. My sisters and I could not stop smiling and clinging to each other—we were like one person, sharing the same, surreal experience.

It wasn't long before my dad was on the phone to tell all of their friends and family that Wendy was "doing well."

My mom is still recovering from her surgery, but her heart was opened in more ways than one. All *five* of us opened our hearts that day and forever. My younger sister describes it as, "feeling layers of love I never knew I was capable of." My twin sister said that she hadn't ever truly appreciated the closeness of our family before this happened. My dad doesn't say much about it but he is softer, gentler and has a tenderness I hadn't seen or felt before. My mom has been given a second chance. Her gratitude is immeasurable.

As for me, the magnitude of what happened that day has changed me. I am more accepting, more appreciative of little things. I have stopped "doing" so much and have started listening to my children and husband more. I am now choosing to experience love and appreciation for people and things moment by moment.

On May 22nd, although my mother was the patient, her surgery opened *five hearts*, forever.

~Leigh Anne Saxe

Count Your Blessings

Having Faith

*God will not permit any troubles to come upon us,
unless He has a specific plan by which great blessing
can come out of the difficulty.*

~Peter Marshall

92

Give Thanks

Music's the medicine of the mind.
~John A. Logan

The sounds of the helicopter blades were deafening, but all I could hear in my heart and soul was myself singing "Give thanks with a grateful heart." Just hours before I had crawled away from a fiery inferno that once was our motor home. I had seen my skin melting off my arms and legs and felt excruciating pain from my back. The intense heat was literally melting me. The black billowing smoke blinded me as I looked for my husband and daughter. As I raced from the menacing flames I screamed, "Save my family! Save my family!"

Now, as I lingered in a fog, lying on a stretcher, all I could remember is the song that I was singing. I had been taken by ambulance to a nearby hospital to be stabilized. I was told that my family was alive. The nurses quickly cut the clothes off my charred body and the wedding ring off my swollen finger. I could hear my adult daughter screaming, "I want my mother" over and over from the room next to mine. I kept insisting that I needed to be with her, but three people working on me held me down. I had no idea how extreme my injuries were, and my heart was breaking with each one of her screams. They calmly kept telling me she was all right, and that they had taken my husband by helicopter to the burn center three hours away. That is when the song started playing in my head. My family is alive, and all I wanted to do was to praise God.

Now I was in the helicopter on my way to the burn center. "Give thanks with a grateful heart, give thanks to the Holy One, give thanks for what He has done for me." As they lifted me off the helicopter, one of my good friends was there to greet me. I was trying to lift my hands as I sang, and she gently helped me as she joined in. I kept saying "God is good." He kept us all alive.

That song kept me going through my darkest hours. Several days passed, and when I woke up in the burn unit, I recognized the enormity of the accident. Forty-eight percent of my body was burned and my back had been broken. Our daughter was thrown through the window away from the fire but broke many bones. My husband was lying in a coma two rooms from my own. He had fifteen fractures in his head and was sixty-eight percent burned with a nine percent chance of living.

I was trapped inside a severely burned body and the pain was ferocious. I had in fact become a prisoner within my uncontrollable shivering frame. Tears poured from my eyes, but my burned arms and hands could not reach to wipe them away.

My entire life had been full of challenges, and I knew my faith and music had always upheld me in the past. This time I would have to trust and allow them to carry me through this healing and restoring season. I had my son bring in a CD player and my praise worship music. The music played all through the day and gave me encouragement.

The song "Give Thanks" became my theme song for my bandage changes. Each day was full of extreme pain as I experienced two-hour bandage changes each morning and each night. I would ask my nurses to put my music on. As I tried to sing along, I would concentrate on each word, and the words would give me the hope I needed to get through. The nurses would sing along as they worked on me, and I found the music helped me with the pain management. Whenever I thought I could not go through another minute of the procedure, I would relocate into my music.

The melodies played on through the challenging and happy times of my life.

Thankfully, my husband and daughter survived. I now sing

happy songs to my grandchildren and life can't get much better. We've since made it our melody to share our success story with burn survivors and families all over the world, passing on the song of hope. I hope you too will find a song within the deep recesses of yourself to make it through life's challenging moments, knowing whatever your trial may be there is a brighter note to be sung.

~Susan Lugli

93

A True Friend, a Godsend

Two are better than one...
For if they fall, the one will lift up his fellow.
~Ecclesiastes

Not so long ago I was going through a real difficult time in my life that truly I could not have faced alone. Up until this point in life, I felt that I was finally getting a handle on things and was making some progress. My mindset was geared toward achieving success for the sake of my family. You see, I had all of my priorities wrong. I measured success in life based upon the amount of money I earned, the position I held, and the things I could afford for my family. I always thought that I was doing it for them. But then one day my wife walked out on me, taking our son with her. Two weeks later I lost my job; eventually I lost our home, car, and everything else I had worked so hard to attain. In desperation I called out to God, but it seemed I couldn't get an answer.

For days, weeks, and months, I cried and prayed, asking God "Why are these things happening to me? Lord, I have been faithful in attending church, tithing, and living a Godly life to the best of my understanding. So why am I experiencing the trouble I suddenly find myself facing?"

I have never had many friends who I could call true, close friends. Most were just social friends who I would go to lunch with on Sundays after morning service. Some would occasionally stop by our place, but usually this was only if we had invited them over for supper. But we never had someone who would just stop in to say, "Hi, are you okay? Are things going well? Haven't heard from you in a day or two and felt I needed to check on you."

However, a couple of years before this crisis, while working as the manager of a local bookstore, I met a gentleman who was interested in selling his book on consignment. So after reviewing his book, we accepted it. Over the next couple of months, Sam came by on several occasions to check on his book. Since it was his first book to be published, he was eager to make a sale. Each time he stopped by, we would talk about his writing and I would do my best to give him my insight on different publishers. During these conversations a friendship was born. At one point we began having lunch together. And over a period of a couple of years, our friendship developed to the point that we would confide in each other about things that were happening in our personal lives.

I didn't realize it at the time, but God was preparing me for what I was about to face later on. After my wife left, I was alone. I never had a strong relationship with my mother, brother, or sister. I love them, and we talked occasionally, but we did not have that close bond so that I could confide in them about my situation. But I had Sam. He would stop by on a regular basis just to check on me. At times he would bring food, or ask me to go to a restaurant with him. Of course, being unemployed I didn't have the funds to eat out, but he insisted that I go with him and that he would pay for it. He told me many times, "Don't worry about it. I enjoy the friendship and fellowship." Being a prideful person, I sometimes found it difficult to say yes. I felt that if I couldn't pay my own way, then I shouldn't be going. But God was teaching me a lesson in humility.

On several occasions I would get the blues and start feeling lonely. Then in prayer I would question, "God, why am I faced with this trial? I feel so alone." At times, I didn't have a dollar to my name and no gas in the car to go searching for a job. I had been unemployed for a couple of months. But then Sam would drop by and before leaving he would reach into his pocket and say, "I just felt that I should give you this." And he would stick money into my shirt pocket. In my stubborn prideful way, I wanted to say "No thanks!" But in reality, I truly needed it and was thankful.

What I didn't understand for some time was that God was caring for me through Sam. Sam was more than just someone who stopped by now and then. There were nights that he would sit and patiently listen to my sob story, while I whined and complained. Then he would give me some words of encouragement and advice. There were times when I was so frustrated that I couldn't focus on what I needed to do in order to find a job. He would sit down at my computer and spend two or three hours doing job searches online and submitting my résumé for me. I didn't have the motivation to do it. I had hit rock bottom. I had just about given up.

One evening in prayer, as I began to meditate and listen to God, he reminded me of a scripture in the Bible found in 1 Kings 17 verses 1-6. It says that God sent the prophet Elijah to the brook Cherith to stay there for a while. He drank the water from the brook and God sent ravens to bring him bread and meat every morning and night. That is when I got a clearer revelation about what was happening in my life.

From the beginning I had questioned God as to whether I had done something, or failed to do something, that caused his judgment to be pronounced upon me. I felt that maybe this trial was a curse from God for some sin in my life that I had failed to repent of. But that was not the case at all! God was teaching me to trust him for whatever provisions I needed for each day. He was teaching me that I couldn't stand alone as an Island, but that as a part of the body of Christ I need others to stand with me.

As for my daily sustenance, gas money, motivation, and encouragement, God sent my friend Sam on a regular basis. I thank Sam for being a true friend, and I thank God for the blessing of a true friend at a most crucial point in my life. It is my prayer that should I encounter someone who is in need of a friend, that I will be sensitive enough to recognize the need and humble enough to step up to the plate and fill that void in his or her life.

~Bob Arba

94

Blessed by More than Enough

*All I have seen teaches me
to trust the Creator for all I have not seen.*
~Ralph Waldo Emerson

The question was simple enough. "Do we have enough money to...?" My husband, Bob, asked that question each time he went to the store or filled up the truck with gas. It wasn't his question that put a huge knot in the middle of my stomach, but the answer I might have to give him.

Almost immediately after he purchased his dream truck the gas prices started to escalate. The new truck payment was a stretch for us. The higher gas prices and the rate at which this new vehicle drank the fuel was a potential budget breaker. It had already eaten the extra Bob allowed me to give to the church and was fast encroaching on what we considered staples of our lifestyle. The last fill-up cost sixty dollars. In a week the shiny red beauty would require another.

Because Bob was the only one making money, I felt guilt and shame when I had to tell him, no, we didn't have enough money in the bank for him to do something. His work schedule fluctuated, so if I did go to work the typical 8:00 to 5:00 office hours, we would not see each other. Neither of us wanted that. I stayed busy at home to compensate for my lack of earning power, but it was getting harder to justify staying home. Worse, the job market was dwindling while the gas prices soared.

Most days I checked the classifieds. I sent out résumés. I responded to interviews when I got a call. I did everything I knew to be a help to my husband. It seemed no one wanted me to work for them. I prayed for God to direct me.

One morning, in April of 2007, I sat down to read my Bible. It had opened to the fourteenth chapter of Matthew where Jesus fed a multitude of hungry people. He asked the disciples to take account of what they had. They tallied five loaves of bread and two fish—to feed five thousand men, not counting women and children. Matthew says Jesus looked toward Heaven and blessed the food. On another occasion, in the fifteenth chapter of Matthew, Jesus took the bread and the fish and gave thanks. He expressed gratitude for what he had.

What Jesus had was not enough. He didn't complain that it wasn't enough. There is no account written where he asked God for more. He took what he had, blessed it and gave thanks for it. Then he distributed it to those who had nothing and it was enough—no, it was more than enough. He got back twelve baskets more than he gave out.

I stopped reading and closed my eyes. I'd been complaining. I told Bob with every fill-up that we needed to get rid of that pig of a truck. I hadn't been thankful we were still able to fill it up, but instead, I worried that we wouldn't be able to next time. That was a far cry from what Jesus did with what He had.

I opened my eyes and deliberately looked for reasons to be thankful. I began to bless the Lord for what we had. I thanked God that He provided for us all we needed, and even some things we didn't need—like Bob's truck. The more I blessed and thanked, the more peace reigned in my heart.

At lunch, I told Bob about my epiphany. "I believe we need to bless God and give thanks for all we have. That word bless means to speak well of. I believe we should display more gratitude for what we have."

He didn't say anything, just furrowed his brow and looked away while continuing to eat his lunch. But the peace in my heart assured me I was right.

I spent that afternoon speaking gratitude. I blessed our family, our home—everything I could think of. I thanked God for his goodness toward us and his faithfulness. I went to bed that night feeling peace I hadn't felt in a long time.

The next morning I got a call from an acquaintance in the northern part of our state. Inez was part owner in a delivery service. They had an account with a bank located in the area where I live. The bank wanted to start a courier route in my area to service the banks in my town. Inez asked me to help her get it started.

I worked with her and the local bank to get the routes planned—all the day-to-day operations. She asked me to manage the route when we got the bid for it. I would be responsible for hiring employees, training, and scheduling. I took two of the routes myself and hired others to do the rest.

Without applying for a job, I had a job. I went from not having enough to having more than enough. This job was perfect for my husband's schedule. We could have dinner together every day. I was there when he got home from work and every weekend.

Inez blesses me continually—she's delighted with my work, and I in working with her. I praise the Lord for my job; I bless it and give thanks constantly. It is a miracle to me—a God-provision.

I know now, as I watch the jobless rate climb and our retirement plans dwindle, that God will provide. He has said he is willing. He has proven himself able. I refuse to worry.

My husband recently experienced deep cuts in his wages due to the economy. We now have an income substantially less than we had last month. But I continue to bless what we have and I am still so grateful for what God has provided. I take what we have and distribute it—and so far it has been enough. My trust is in God—not in the economy.

~Joie Fields

Lifestyle versus Life

I'm living my life, not buying a lifestyle.
~Barbara Kruger

The "perfect" lifestyle is never worth the cost of your life. If you have to sacrifice the quality of your family life or your spiritual life to keep up with your lifestyle ideals, you're cheating yourself. Society tells us if we just get that one more thing, we will be happy. Time after time, we give in only to find that we're still not really happy, so we go back to looking for that "one more thing."

One day two years ago, my husband, Scott, came home from work utterly depressed and burned out. The truth was that he'd been depressed for a couple of years. It is amazing what I could ignore in the busyness of our everyday lives. Just when you think you have everything together, life caves in on you. In all honesty, I panicked.

We lived in what I call "Stepford"—a very nice planned community for families. Little league under the lights, soccer fields, hiking trails, golf courses, you name it. We had a beautiful home, a great church, good schools for the kids, and a very comfortable lifestyle. We had the right cars, the right job, the right vacations. What we were lacking was a family life. Scott worked sixty to ninety hours a week. That's not a typo. That was our reality. He worked that crazy schedule for fifteen years. No wonder he was depressed.

Time isn't something you can ever earn back. Scott missed birthday parties and holidays and everything else in between for his career. I was raising our kids alone and also getting burned out—I wasn't doing it well, because I was doing it alone. In reality, our family didn't make a very pretty picture even though it was wrapped up in a beautiful package.

That month of our reckoning with reality, we faced some tough questions.

Is the time away from family worth the money Scott is making? If he quits his job, will we be able to provide for our four kids? When we began to talk about our current finances (which I was in charge of at the time), Scott asked me if I might have a gambling problem. "Of course not!" I said huffily. But then I realized the truth: our lifestyle was supported by credit cards. Our community was expensive. Keeping up with the Joneses never seemed to be at the forefront of our goals, but it certainly always lurked in the shadows.

We finally came to the same conclusion. Scott could not keep working at the same pace and survive. I could not keep raising our children alone and survive. What should we do? Tough questions require tough answers.

We prayed, our church prayed, our friends prayed, and then we prayed some more. Then we made the tough decision: we would move back to Scott's home state and live with his mother until our house sold. He would look for a job that would support our new goal of working together to raise our kids and nourish our marriage.

We thought the process would take under six months; it actually took a year and a half. That's a long time to be in limbo—and I didn't like it at all. I got angry and stubborn and bitter. Why shouldn't I have a nice house? Why shouldn't we have nice clothes and a vacation and all those wonderful things? I still wanted my lifestyle. I liked the nice house, the pool, the golf course. There I was stuck in a house I didn't even own, with not one thing of my own around me—and for what?

Needless to say, that year was our stretching year. We were stretched, our marriage was stretched, our kids were stretched. But was the lifestyle we gave up worth the price of my marriage, my children's happiness, and my authentic happiness? I came to realize that the answer to this question was an easy one. No. Never.

The "perfect" lifestyle is never worth the cost of your life.

When we began to ask the tough questions and pray about what we knew would be tough answers, we began to put our priorities in order. But I had a lot to learn, and my heart didn't change overnight. I came to realize that while I may have been caring for my kids 24/7 all those years, I had also been selfish. In many ways, I had put my wants and needs above those of my family. To be selfish is to be human, but when I look back, I know I was most miserable while I was separating myself from God by prioritizing my lifestyle over the life He wanted for me.

In our new fish-out-of-water living arrangement, I finally picked up my dusty Bible and began to re-establish my faith life. Then I took a good hard look at my heart and chose to bloom where God had planted me. I began re-connecting with God. While our circumstances haven't changed much, I am truly content. Our current "lifestyle" would be laughable by my old standards, but our family has never been closer—or more engaged in our faith lives.

I think I can sum it up with a conversation I had in the car one day with my fourteen-year-old son. I was trying to explain that while we didn't have as much "stuff" as we had in Arizona, his dad and I had made these decisions so that we could have a closer family. Tyler simply stated, "You know what, Mom? I think I saw Dad more in the first year we lived here than in the previous twelve years of my life."

That alone made every day of stretching ourselves worth it. The truth is, we may have given up everything we used to identify ourselves by, but what we got in exchange was priceless: we got our lives back.

~Kay Klebba

My Name
Is Nannymom

You don't choose your family.
They are God's gift to you, as you are to them.
~Desmond Tutu

When I turned forty, I went through some life-changing events.

My youngest child graduated from high school, my twenty-year marriage ended, I left my job as editor of a small newspaper, we had several deaths in my family, I moved twice, and I became a grandmother for the first time.

The announcement of the approaching baby was not met with fanfare. My daughter would be a single mom and at the time my marriage was shaky to say the least. But when I saw the sonogram, heard the heartbeat, and felt this precious life move for the first time, my heart filled with joy.

God never makes mistakes.

I knew the birth of this child would be a blessing, and twelve years later, he is my gift.

When he was six months old, I began the journey of raising this child on my own. Well, not entirely on my own—God has always been there and my wonderful mother has stood by me through thick and thin.

Mimi says her reason for living is this boy. He is our joy. He has a loving spirit, a great sense of humor—much to his great-grandmother's dismay—is an honor roll student, loves church, fishing, playing computer games, building things, working puzzles, reading, and he is a big help to me at home and even at work.

I can't think of my life without him. Some people say it's not fair for me to have to raise this child, but I say it's an honor.

It hasn't always been easy. We've had to face some difficult situations, but my faith in God and His direction has always pulled me through.

This year I will turn fifty-three and my grandson will be thirteen—a teenager! Luckily, I can still keep up with him. I can ride go-carts, fly kites, play putt-putt, take long walks, camp, and take him on fun outings. I have some tough roads ahead and sometimes I do get scared—can I do this alone? But, then I remember I'm never alone. God is with me. I have my family, my church and many, many friends. This precious boy is my first priority when I'm at work, volunteering in my community, and at home. His contagious smile sincerely radiates his love for family and in the spur of a moment he is always willing to lend a hand.

My grandson calls me his nanny, and he knows my daughter is his biological mother, but sometimes he simply refers to me as "Nannymom," and I wear that name with pride!

~Glenda Lee

97

God's Faithfulness

Faith is the virtue by which,
clinging to the faithfulness of God,
we lean upon him,
so that we may obtain what he gives to us.
~William Ames

In the five years since my husband started working at the church we attend, he was rarely absent. He had a long commute five days a week. His work was mentally exhausting, but Joseph was happy. Then circumstances changed. My husband lost his job.

"I was sure God was preparing me for a future there. Now I'm no longer needed." Joseph's voice shook with emotion as he put his head in his hands.

Joseph's disappointment was keen and his spirit crushed and he began to feel that God was displeased with him. This became a nagging and recurring thought.

Friends and co-workers from our church called to express their disappointment. He assisted them with their questions as they learned their new responsibilities in a changed environment.

"I've failed in some way or else I'd still be working there," he confided to me.

My husband's emotional wellbeing became as important as how we were going to manage financially, especially when he asked questions like, "What did I do wrong?" or "Now what?"

To get us through this crisis, I knew I needed God's help. I prayed for us. Then I began to see the hand of God in our situation.

We discovered that under the pension plan Joseph was enrolled in with a former employer, he could apply for early retirement benefits. This was our first indication that God was working on our behalf.

I've been a full time homemaker since our sons were born fifteen years ago. I decided to claim Social Security benefits this year when I reached age sixty-two. I learned at the time I applied that our boys were eligible for children's benefits as well. The Lord is faithful. He was providing for us.

A major concern was our children's education. It was re-enrollment time once again at their school. Would we be able to continue to provide them with the schooling we had committed to giving them? After applying for financial assistance, we were given a forty percent reduction on the following year's tuition. We were overjoyed!

And then there was the matter of health insurance coverage for us all. After some inquiries and searching the Internet, I learned that my husband and I were eligible for low-cost health insurance coverage. Our boys have free coverage under our state's children's health insurance program. God continued to meet our needs.

We now live more frugally on a lower, fixed income. Fortunately, our home is mortgage-free. But the high cost of utilities was another concern. I applied for financial help with those costs and received discounts on our electric and heating bills.

Since my husband's unemployment, the blessings have been many. I felt disappointed that Ben and Tim only got to see their dad a short time each day when he worked full time at our church. Now their father sees them off to school in the morning and picks them up later. He is free to go on field trips and youth group outings. But most important, my husband now has the time to sit and talk with our boys. They are witnesses to God's faithfulness to our family during a time of crisis.

Until his employment ended, I was concerned about Joseph's long hours and how they were affecting his health. Now we spend time together during the day and he seems more relaxed.

"Maybe I could help at the school. Do they still need volunteers for grounds work?" Joseph asked our son recently. Many projects left unfinished at home are now getting completed, too.

I've seen my husband's disappointment gradually vanish. We are continually experiencing God's faithfulness and seeing new mercies in our changed situation.

I will continue to believe good things of God.

~Pat Jeanne Davis

98

This Very Day

May you live every day of your life.
~Jonathan Swift

It would take many pages to explain the challenges my husband and I have faced. I have kept a journal for thirty years to help me keep my perspective. Recently I wrote this:

Lord, this very day I awoke, alive, here, now—this day. This day I will treat my body with respect. Nourish it well, clean it, protect it. A warm shower, a healthy meal, fastening my seat belt, wearing comfortable shoes... these will be my little acts of respect for this body You gave me—this body You breathed life into at birth and each day including this very day.

This very day I awoke, not alone, but unique as I am, a part of all mankind, each single person also unique. Let me respect the body of humanity and treat each single member as well as I treat my hands, my face, my feet. As I nourish my body let me nourish also the greater body. As I pour milk on my breakfast cereal, let me remember also to pour the milk of kindness on my family, my neighbors and colleagues, the stranger in traffic and souls in distant lands with prayers of compassion and thoughts of understanding.

This very day Lord, I will no doubt feel grains of irritation. Let me, with my degrees, my skills, my "knowledge of life," not overlook the simple wisdom of the oyster. Let me turn those parasites that would invade my attitude with bitterness or despair into pearls to shimmer in my world, gems to offer others proof that life and hope can conquer depression and fear.

This very day Lord, let me remember to smile, to laugh, to sing, to dance, even if my knees hurt. Let me remember to watch the doves winging past my window, to see the coppery glint of sun on a squirrel's tail, to listen to the puppy lapping water from his dish. Let me notice the bright vermillion blossom in the ditch even if it is just a "weed." Let me be amused by bumper stickers on trucks decked in shiny chrome and fat backpacks on skinny teens. Let me, as I walk to the post office, be delighted by babies cooing in strollers and fussing matrons in flowered frocks and the aroma of hot cinnamon buns from the local bakery.

Since I am alive this very day, let me live it!

~Phyllis McKinley

The Blessing of a Friend

There is one word
which may serve as a rule of practice for all one's life —
reciprocity.
~Confucius

For weeks on end, I waited to receive the call that I had lost my job due to cutbacks. Times were tough and I worked part-time at a private Christian school. All the employees were aware that problems in the economy had reduced enrollment. We were also aware that other local Christian schools had recently cut the number of classes and one had even closed. It was only a matter of time till I had no job at all.

When our school mentioned having to make cuts, such as not replacing some people who were leaving, freezing raises, and cutting non-essential personnel, I was sure I would be one of the first employees let go. After all, I had only been working at the school one year and shared a secretarial job with another woman who had been at the school many years. I worked the morning shift and she worked the afternoon shift. If they had to cut our position back to one person part-time, I was lowest on the totem pole. My husband and I loved the school and wanted our children to continue attending, but we knew it would be financially difficult, if not impossible, to keep three children there without me working.

All of our kids were well adjusted in the school and doing well academically. They were sharing with us the Bible lessons they were learning from their once a week chapel and from their daily Bible instruction in each of their classes. They had all made many friends, and the thought of making them change schools or become home-schooled again was unpleasant at best.

Because I was part-time I didn't work in the summer, but I checked in with the full-time people often to see how things were going. News was bad. Enrollment was not going up very fast. Jobs were being cut. Teachers lost their aides. Some grades went from two classes to one, so even some teachers lost their jobs. My income was not supporting the family but it did allow my children to attend. I prayed daily for those people at the school who needed their jobs to pay their bills and feed their families. But then I also prayed that my kids could keep attending. At the end of each prayer I prayed for God's will, knowing that He knows better than we do what we need.

The woman I job-shared with had worked at the school while her own children had attended, clear through to graduation. She was like a mentor to me. I often went to her with questions because she knew our position so much better than I did. If I lost my job, I'd miss not only the income, but working with her and the other ladies in my office. But as I said earlier, I knew God would take care of my situation.

The call came. My position had been cut from two part-time people to one. I was prepared to walk away, but what I wasn't pre-pared for was that my job-share partner had voluntarily given up her job so that I could keep mine. God was working in a way I had not expected.

This wonderful woman blessed me and my family by helping my kids to stay at the school. On the phone one day she told me, "I wanted to give your kids the same chance to stay through graduation that my girls had."

Not only did this wonderful friend give up her job for me, but she now fills in whenever I need a day off. I have had to call her many times at the last minute because of sick kids or other needs and she has been right there to work for me. I pray good things for her often and tell her that she has been a huge blessing for my family during these tough times.

Ultimately it's God that helps us through the tough times. In many cases, like this one, it's evident how He does it. Through the sacrificial love of others.

~Angel Ford

Election Day
Setback

To succeed in life, you need three things:
a wishbone, a backbone and a funnybone.
~Reba McEntire

I'd just driven away from my elderly client's home late in the afternoon when I noticed I had a missed call on my cell phone. It was from my husband. "Uh-oh," I groaned. That could mean only one thing. I waited until I arrived home to call him back.

"Hi honey," I said as cheerfully as I could when he answered. "Sorry I missed your call. What's up?" I had a feeling down deep in my gut that I knew what he was going to say. He'd been having trouble at work for several months. Ever since a new set of managers took over his department. Men who seemed bent on getting rid of him.

"It's over."

I think my heart stopped beating for a second or two. "It is?"

"Yep. I'm unemployed."

On that crisp November day—the same day Barack Obama made history by being elected the first black president of the United States—my husband was fired from a company he'd been with for more than twenty-three years. He'd worked there since he graduated from college. Since before we were married.

Somehow I didn't collapse in a puddle of tears right there on the kitchen floor. He certainly didn't need to deal with a hysterical wife. "Why don't you take some time to yourself before you come home," I suggested, knowing he probably wouldn't feel like facing the boys or me just then. He took me up on my offer and we hung up.

My heart was racing as I stared out the window to the backyard. Anxious, angry thoughts whirled through my mind.

That stupid, stupid company! Those stupid, stupid people!

One person in particular came to mind. My husband's former supervisor was also a longtime friend. How could he have been involved in this? How could they fire my husband, without so much as a penny of severance? After twenty-three years of being a dependable, hard-working, trustworthy employee, this is what he gets? The whole thing was simply too surreal to fathom just then, yet there were some very real matters we needed to face.

Like telling our two teenage sons.

I called the boys into the living room. I thought it best to prepare them before my husband came home. He wouldn't exactly be in the mood to explain things in a calm, soothing manner.

"Boys," I said, taking a deep breath. "We need to talk."

They both stared at me. It was obvious they knew something was wrong.

"Did Grandma die?" my fifteen-year-old asked, referring to my eighty-two-year-old mother who suffered from Alzheimer's disease and was not doing well.

I shook my head. "No, no. It's nothing like that." Although, in a way it was. The feelings and emotions that come with losing a job are very similar to those we experience when a death occurs. Sadness. Anger. Depression. Add to that the feelings of betrayal, and you've got a whopper of emotional baggage to sort through.

The boys kept staring at me. I decided to just blurt it out. "Dad was fired today."

Silence.

"We'll be okay," I reassured, knowing in my heart we would, but at the same time wondering how things would play out in the coming months. I work part-time. My husband was the main breadwinner. His job also provided our health and life insurance policies. What would we do now?

"Will we have to move?" Again, my youngest son, the worrier, voiced the question. My seventeen-year-old son, the one who rarely shows his emotions, stayed quiet. Much too quiet.

"No, we aren't going to have to move," came my firm, certain answer.

I hope not anyway, I worried silently, but who knows what might happen in the next few months. Our area hadn't suffered as many job losses as the rest of the country, but there are no guarantees when it comes to unemployment and securing a new job. I didn't share that concern with my sons though. There was no need to put unfounded fears on the table just yet. With both boys in high school, the prospect of moving was not something anyone in our family wanted. It made me sad they had to worry about such things now.

The tears came then. I hated to cry in front of the boys and I reined in the traitorous wetness fairly quickly, but it was obvious to them that I was worried. And hurt. But I also tried to be as optimistic as possible.

"Dad will find a new job. You know I've wanted him to leave that company for a while now. Maybe this is God's way of giving him something new. A better job. A job where he'll be appreciated."

With all my heart, I prayed that was true. The boys went back to their rooms and I waited for my husband to come home. When he walked in the door a short time later, I put on a brave smile to greet him. I even had some confetti to toss at him as he came into the kitchen.

"Hooray! Welcome home! You're free! Free! Free at last!"

He gave a slight chuckle. I'm sure he thinks he's married to a loon. "I'm free, all right. Free and unemployed."

Later that night we grew more serious. We talked about the immediate future and how we planned to make ends meet. We talked about résumés. We talked about the boys. We talked about all kinds of things.

And we prayed. God has a plan in all of this. Years down the road we'll look back and see how it all worked for our good. Right now, however, it didn't feel so good. It felt scary. Like being lost in a pitch-black cave without a flashlight. I don't like being scared, so I shoved thoughts of uncertainty away.

"Well," I said, trying to lighten the mood in the room. "Look at the bright side."

"What's that?" my husband asked.

"You don't have to get up at 4:45 A.M. anymore. You can sleep in!"

He actually smiled about that.

I found a few more things to add to the bright side list. He wouldn't have to eat leftovers for lunch every day. He'd save gallons and gallons of gas since he wouldn't have to commute into the city. And he'd be home a lot more, which was good for me and for the boys. He'd worked so hard for so many years, he'd missed a lot of time with the family. It would be nice to have him around.

"You know," I said as I gave him a big hug and settled in for the night. "I think I'm going to enjoy your unemployment. Just think of all the things you can do around the house while you're home. The yard needs some new mulch, and the trees need to be trimmed, and the bedroom ceiling needs to be repaired, and..."

He got the idea. "I hope I find a new job before you work me to death."

"Yeah," I grinned. "You will. But until then, you're all mine!"

~Michelle Shocklee

Drinking from Ola's Cup

Find yourself a cup of tea;
the teapot is behind you.
Now tell me about hundreds of things.
~Saki

It never failed. As I sipped the hot raspberry tea from the fragile china cup, I could almost see my sweet friend, Ola, sitting across the table once again. My fingers traced the delicate wildflowers painted on the cup she had given me. Once more, I was filled with gratefulness as I mulled over our unlikely friendship.

Ola was a tiny, frail wisp of a woman in her eighties who spent most of her time in a wheelchair. Under ordinary circumstances we might not have become such close friends. I was a thirty-six-year-old mother of four children. Who would think we had much in common? But we shared a bond that drew us closer than most. We met at a grief support group that met every Monday night. Both of our husbands had died recently. We were both seeking relief from the deep pain that threatened to consume us.

Naturally, there was a lot of sorrow and weeping in our group. There were some whose spouse had died, some whose parents had recently passed away, and a few who were there because of the death of a child. Some had experienced a long lingering illness with their loved one, while others were going through the shock of a traumatic accident that had taken their loved one without warning. Needless to say, our meetings were filled with much pain and anguish. Our group was a place where others really understood what you were going through.

Some group members were quiet and withdrawn, barely holding back their emotions. There were those who wallowed in self-pity, repeatedly asking why this terrible thing had happened to them. A few regulars were like pressure cookers, their rage ready to blow at the slightest nudge. Then there was Ola.

Every week her daughter wheeled her into the room. There wasn't anything to make you sit up and take notice of Ola. She was just a tiny white-haired old lady in a wheelchair. Her physical frailties were deceiving, though. Inside that withered little body of hers lived a strong determined spirit. Each week revealed more of it.

For such a feeble thing, Ola had an outspoken personality. She was always ready to share a joke to lighten the grief. But she shared more. Her age gave her the right to offer us guidance and encouragement. We all listened, knowing she had survived many hard times in her life. She and her four children had been abandoned by her first husband. After she married again, she discovered her second husband was an alcoholic. Later he was in an explosion which left him severely deformed. Two of her children died at an early age.

One thing she shared with us stood out above everything else. In a group of people whose lives were devastated, Ola consistently reminded us to think of things to be thankful for. She promised us that our hearts would be lifted if we did. Ola told us if we couldn't think of anything else, we should at least thank God for the air that we breathe. Through her wrinkled face glowed a light of wisdom and faith that had been born from a long and difficult journey. Before each meeting ended, Ola would begin thanking God for specific things. Some tried to follow her lead. It was amazing to see the hope in people's faces when they joined in.

Sadly, others were too angry or blinded by pain to think of anything to be thankful for. All they could see was their own tragic heartache. They remained bitter and overwhelmed by their grief.

I chose to follow Ola's lead. If she could be thankful despite all her hard times, I could certainly try. My heart longed to feel the hope that I saw in Ola. At first it was difficult. My loss seemed so great, I didn't know if I would ever smile again. Though it was tempting to feel sorry for myself, I was determined to be grateful.

I decided to begin by thanking God for the wonderful gift of having Steve in my life for twenty years. I would have loved more years, but that's longer than what some people have. And what a great twenty years it had been! My mind wandered as I thought about what my life would have been like if I had not known him. Before long, sweet memories flooded over me giving me more reasons to thank God: the walks through fields of wildflowers, exploring old abandoned houses together, the soothing sounds of Steve's guitar filling the house every night.

Then I thought of our four children who depended on me. How empty my life would be without them. They would carry pieces of their dad throughout the rest of their lives. How grateful I was for each child and the time they got to spend with their dad.

I thanked God for my fifteen-year-old daughter, who had her dad's zest for adventure and his fun easygoing way with people. I thanked God for our oldest son, who had learned from his dad how to stand tall as a man of loyalty and responsibility. Then I thanked God for my quiet seven-year-old son who had seen more suffering through his dad's illness than most people see in a lifetime. I knew his deep compassion would be used in the future. Of course, I had to thank God for our two-year-old son who came as a total shock in the midst of acute emergencies and hospital stays.

Then I thought of all the doctors and nurses who had showed us such kindness during Steve's long illness. I also had to thank God for our friends and family who had given us gifts of time, money and prayers during the hard times.

As I thought of the difficult battle we had gone through with Steve's illness, I had to thank God for the strength that He had given us both. We had withstood something that was impossible to handle on our own.

Though I would miss my husband terribly, I had to thank God

that he was finally free from the grip of daily suffering. I tried to imagine what it will be like some day when we are reunited in eternal life and I paused to thank God for the promise of that life to come which will be free from all sickness, death and hard times.

I suddenly realized that I was filled with a peaceful feeling of quiet joy! It had sprung from my grateful heart. My future shone brighter and full of hope. I knew I could go on. I knew I would never be alone. I felt so blessed!

My sweet friend Ola has since passed from this life. Every time I drink from the cup she gave me, I count my blessings. No matter what's going on, it's not long before I feel blessed beyond words. It has been said that a pessimist looks at his cup and sees it half empty, and that an optimist sees his cup half full. As I hold Ola's cup in my hands and find things to thank God for, I realize that my cup overflows!!

~Eva Juliuson

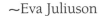

Chicken Soup for the Soul

Count Your Blessings

Meet Our Contributors
Meet Our Authors
Thank You
About Chicken Soup
Share with Us

Meet Our Contributors

Rachel Allord lives and writes in central Wisconsin. Apart from hanging out with her two great kids and one awesome husband, she loves hopping on planes and traveling just about anywhere to take in the culture, sights, and most importantly, the food. She is currently working on a novel.

Linda Apple is enjoying her "second" career as an inspirational writer and motivational speaker. Her first book, *Inspire! Writing from the Soul*, an instructional guide to inspirational writing, has recently been published. Please visit her website at www.lindacapple.com.

Bob Arba was ordained a minister in 1997. He has been involved in Lay Ministry, Music Ministry and Youth Ministry for the past seventeen years. Bob enjoys playing music, reading, writing poetry and Christian fiction. Bob is working on his second fiction book. You may contact Bob at Arba2722@yahoo.com.

Dan Bain is an award-winning features and humor writer from Raleigh, North Carolina. He's been writing for others' entertainment since the "Kick Me" incident of second grade, and hopes one day to prove to his beleaguered ex-teachers that yes, he amounted to something. Please see www.danbain.net for more damaging information.

Carol Band is a humor columnist and author whose work appears in publications around the country. E-mail her at carol@carolband.com or read her blog at www.carolband.wordpress.com.

Rob L. Berry received his Bachelor of Arts from California State

University, Bakersfield and continues to reside in Bakersfield with his wife Keri and son Ethan. Rob is a member of Writers of Kern and enjoys cycling, travelling, and spending time with his family. He can be reached at berrys@bak.rr.com.

Laura L. Bradford enjoys encouraging others with stories about faith and family. Her writings have appeared in: *Life Savors*, *A Cup of Comfort*, and *Chicken Soup for the Soul* book compilations, as well as in the *Oregon Christian Writers Newsletter*.

Linda Breeden, an inspiring writer, lives in Georgia and holds a Masters in Human Resources. Her stories have appeared in magazines such as *Simple Joy*, *Guideposts*, and *Redbook*. She is a popular speaker, which mirrors her writing style, leaving audiences with optimism and the desire to laugh right out loud!

Connie Sturm Cameron has been married to Chuck for thirty years. Together they have two children, Chase (Elizabeth), Chelsea (Matt), a stepdaughter Lori and three grandchildren. Connie is a speaker and the author of *God's Gentle Nudges*. Contact her at www.conniecameron.com.

Barbara Canale is a freelance writer and columnist for *The Catholic Sun*. She has been published in *Chicken Soup for the Veteran's Soul* and *Chicken Soup for the Adopted Soul*, and is the author of *Our Labor of Love; A Romanian Adoption Chronicle*. She enjoys biking, skiing, and gardening.

Nancy Canfield is married and has two children, four stepchildren, and five grandchildren. Two of her grandbabies live with her, as their mom is in the Navy. Nancy is the author of *Home Kids: The Story of St. Agatha Home for Children*. Learn more about *Home Kids* at www.StAgathaHome.org or contact her at ncanf@san.rr.com.

Leah M. Cano has written for *Transitions Abroad*, *MAMM* magazine, *Chicken Soup for the Breast Cancer Survivor's Soul* and *Chicken Soup for the*

Soul: Tough Times, Tough People. She is a Foreign Language teacher living in Laguna Beach, CA. You can e-mail her at leahmc@hotmail.com.

Kristen Clark is the founder of His Witness Ministries and contributing author to *New Beginnings Marriage Ministry*. Kristen has contributed stories to various publications including *Out of the Clueless Pit*, a compilation of faith stories from the women of Windwood Presbyterian Church. She lives in Texas with her husband, Lawrence.

Carly Collins is currently a high school sophomore. Her favorite subjects are English and Psychology. Carly enjoys reading, horseback riding, running, and color guard. She hopes to attend Georgetown University and to become a journalist.

Harriet Cooper is a freelance writer and instructor. She specializes in writing creative nonfiction and articles. Her work has appeared in several *Chicken Soup for the Soul* anthologies, as well as in newspapers, magazines, newsletters and websites. She often writes about health, nutrition, family, cats and the environment.

Stephen R. Covey is the bestselling author of *The 7 Habits of Highly Effective People* and *The 8th Habit: From Effectiveness to Greatness*. His latest book is *The Leader in Me: How Schools and Parents around the World Are Inspiring Greatness, One Child at a Time*. Join the Stephen Covey Community at www.stephencovey.com.

Jennifer Crites is a Honolulu-based photographer and writer whose words and images exploring travel, contemporary lifestyles, food, education and science have been published in magazines and books worldwide. She invites readers to visit her website at www. jennifercritesphotography.com.

Priscilla Dann-Courtney is a freelance writer, clinical psychologist and married mother of three. Her essays have appeared in numerous newspapers and magazines and she frequently reads her stories on local public radio. She is working on a book which is a collection of her essays. She loves running, skiing, yoga and baking and anything else that keeps her sane.

Pat Jeanne Davis is a homemaker and writer living in Philadelphia, PA with her husband and two sons. Her articles and short stories have appeared in regional and national publications. Pat has completed an historical inspirational novel. She can be reached at patjeannedavis@verizon.net or visit at www.patjeannedavis.com.

Susie Dinsmore's passion for writing came at a very early age, starting with short animal stories. She's a student of the Institute of Children's Literature. Her interests include the camera with a recently self-published venture, *A Part Of My Life*. She plans to continue writing inspirational stories and books. Please e-mail her at susie@mrunphoto.com.

Drema Sizemore Drudge received her Bachelor of Arts from Manchester College in 2008. She works for the Learn More Center. Drema is a graduate student in Spalding University's MFA program. She is working on her first novel. Drema is married to Barry and is the mother of two, Mia and Zack.

Anne Dunne is an award-winning author whose work appears in many *Chicken Soup for the Soul* anthologies, as well as various other anthologies and magazines. She is grateful every day for her countless blessings; marrying her high school sweetheart, her health and many family and friends.

Christina Dymock earned her Bachelor of Science Degree in Mass Communications from the University of Utah. She has worked as an editor and taught Marketing at the local community college. She is currently learning to cross country ski.

Britteny Elrick attended Regents College in London, where she began her writing career. Since then, she has traveled the world, started her own business, and grown increasingly perplexed about the male gender. Britteny is an aspiring author of nonfiction. You can find her at www.wordsbybrit.com or read her blog www.bluntdelivery.com.

Maria Victoria Espinosa-Peterson was born in Argentina. In 1999, she graduated from law school and moved to the capital city of Buenos Aires. There she met her husband Jeremy. They and their two children currently live in Arlington, VA, where she works as a yoga teacher. Contact her via e-mail at marichy007@hotmail.com.

Andrea Fecik has been living in New York City since 1995 when she began her studies in Interior Design at the Fashion Institute of Technology. Aside from her job in design she enjoys writing and is working on getting her first novel published. She also blogs at www.galinthecity.wordpress.com.

Joie Fields is author of the online BibleStudyNotes e-mail group at yahoo groups, as well as articles purchased by *Faith and Friends* and *War Cry* magazines and *Seasoned Cooking* e-zine. She and her husband, Bob, have two children and two grandchildren. They reside in Oklahoma.

Angel Ford is a wife and mother of three. She enjoys ministry, missions' related travel, spending time with her family and friends, and writing. She is currently working on a book and considering a master's degree. Please e-mail her at secretaryforhim@yahoo.com.

Betsy S. Franz is a freelance writer and photographer specializing in the Green movement, nature, wildlife, the environment and both humorous and inspirational human interest topics. She lives in Melbourne, FL with her husband Tom. Visit Betsy on the web at: www.naturesdetails.net.

Elaine K. Green is a freelance writer, native New Orleanian and Katrina survivor. Please e-mail her at ekgreen@hotmail.com.

Peter J. Green was born in Toronto, Canada and now resides in Western New York. He is a musician and songwriter specializing in music of faith. He hopes to continue his career as a writer, providing encouragement and inspiration.

Karen H. Gros is a freelance writer and has been published in national magazines. She contributes to Associated Content, where she is a "Top 1000" writer. Karen is an avid LSU sports fan and enjoys the outdoors and spending time with family. She can be reached via e-mail at lsu_is_number_1@yahoo.com.

Sheoli V. Gunaratne is a thirteen-year-old middle school student. Her family originates from the tropical island of Sri Lanka. She enjoys writing stories, poetry, and playing with her puppy Coco. She plans to continue her free-spirited writing.

Sarah Hamaker is a freelance writer and editor, and author of *Hired@ Home*, a guide to unlocking women's work-from-home potential. She has a Master's degree in Literature and Language from Marymount University. Sarah lives in Virginia with her husband and four children. Visit her online at www.sarahhamaker.com.

The writing journey **Debbie Harrell** began at age eight continues in Michigan where she enjoys the privilege of helping others tell their stories. Her passion is capturing the positive messages often learned in the midst of life's negatives. She welcomes your thoughts at deb@pricelesstreasures.org.

Miriam Hill is co-author of *Fabulous Florida* and a frequent contributor to *Chicken Soup for the Soul* books. She's been published in *The Christian Science Monitor*, *Grit*, *St. Petersburg Times*, *Sacramento Bee* and *Poynter Online*. Miriam's manuscript received Honorable Mention for Inspirational Writing in a Writer's Digest Writing Competition.

Rebecca Hill's father, "Dr. Don" was a teaching missionary in Africa, a mathematics professor at FAMU, a devoted member of Deer Lake UMC and the best father a girl could ask for. Rebecca is reaching out to museums to find a permanent home for Dr. Don's African Art Collection. bohoembassy@verizon.net.

Cara Holman is thankful that her cancer diagnosis three years ago led her to join a writing group, rekindling her writing aspirations. She lives in Portland, Oregon with her husband and the youngest of their three children. Her writings have appeared online, in an anthology and on her blog: http://caraholman.wordpress.com.

Mandy Houk lives in Colorado with her husband and two daughters. Her work has been published in national magazines and two previous editions of *Chicken Soup for the Soul*. She's the editor for the bimonthly *Pikes Peak Writers NewsMag*, and is working on selling her first novel and writing the second. www.mandyhouk.com.

Kelley Hunsicker is a wife, mother, and grandmother, and in her spare time she writes from her home in South Carolina. Visit her at www.kelleyhunsicker.com.

A lifelong athlete and never a smoker, **David Hyman** has been battling stage IV lung cancer since 2008. He finds blessing in whatever life sends his way and is strengthened by his wife, Ruth, and children. David is writing a book for couples on building a great, fulfilling marriage.

Rose M. Jackson, a teacher and speaker, has written books with Dr. Walt Kallestad and Donna Partow. She enjoys camping and hiking, and especially loves sharing from her life and insights at women's retreats and events. Read more of her devotional messages at www. rospiration.blogspot.com or contact Rose at ecrmjackson@msn.com.

While sipping her favorite mocha latte, **Rebecca Jay** edits and writes for various publications. She reads and writes every day, always trying to improve her craft. Rebecca is also a Bible teacher and is currently learning Mandarin. She has a grown son and lives with an elderly cat.

Marna Malag Jones raised a family, and retired early from personnel placement work. She has presented career seminars and is researching information for a seminar about caring for aging parents. Her first story, "Finding Lost Love," is in *Chicken Soup for the Father & Daughter Soul*. Contact her at marnakj@hotmail.com.

Mother of seven, grandmother of nine, "prayer cheerleader" **Eva Juliuson** shares God's love through writing, teaching, and working with kids. For seven years, she's sent out short e-mail prayers to help jump-start others into a deeper personal prayer life with God. To receive them, e-mail her at evajuliuson@hotmail.com.

Tammy L. Justice was born and raised in Columbus/Newark, Ohio. She has been writing poems and stories since age seven. She is currently self-employed in a profession that caters to the elderly. She has two wonderful children: David Phillips III and Samantha Shinn. You can e-mail her at justice1964@yahoo.com.

Marilyn Kentz has coauthored three books to both empower women and give them a reason to laugh at life with her. She has been facilitating women's support groups for the last six years and can't think of a better way to go through midlife. Contact her at marilynkentz@aol.com or learn more at www.fearless-aging.com or www.themommies.com.

Kay Klebba is happily married to Scott and the mother of four incredible children including one with special needs. Kay's passion is speaking and writing to women about the hilarity of our blessings. Please visit her blog at http://kayklebba.blogspot.com or e-mail her at kayklebba@gmail.com.

Mimi Greenwood Knight is a freelance writer and frequent *Chicken Soup for the Soul* contributor living in South Louisiana with her husband, David, and their four children, Haley O'Hara, Holly, Hewson and David Jonah. She's currently seeking a publisher for her first novel. (Hello out there!) Visit her blog at blog.nola.com/faith/mimi_greenwood_knight.

Karen Koczwara obtained an English degree from Chico State University in 2000. She taught high school English before staying home to raise her four children. Karen resides in Southern California, and enjoys hitting the beach, watching old movies, and baking (while trying not to burn!) batches of chocolate chip cookies.

Karen Kosman is an inspirational speaker and author of *Wounded by Words* (New Hope Publishers, 2007). Karen's joy and zest for life warms hearts. She has authored stories in several compilations and magazine articles. She can be reached via e-mail at ComKosman@aol.com.

Michele H. Lacina received her BA in Communications from Glassboro State in 1973. She has been published in *Country Woman*, *NJ Lifestyles*, *The Girls' Book of Success*, and *Chicken Soup for the Soul in Menopause*. She continues to work on publishing a mystery. She can be reached at mandj59021@earthlink.net.

Glenda Lee is an advertising director for a direct mail magazine. She is a published author of two bulletin board idea books, numerous magazine articles and poems. She enjoys writing, reading, gardening, fishing, spending time with her family and volunteer work. Please e-mail her at nanmom1@gmail.com.

Janeen A. Lewis is a freelance writer living in Kentucky with her husband Jesse and son Andrew. She graduated from Eastern Kentucky University with degrees in Journalism and Elementary Education. Lewis loves writing, caring for children and spending time with her family.

Patricia Lorenz is an art-of-living writer and speaker and the author of eleven books including *The 5 Things We Need to Be Happy* and *Life's Too Short to Fold Your Underwear*. She's one of the top contributing writers to the *Chicken Soup for the Soul* books with stories in nearly fifty of them so far. Visit her website at www.PatriciaLorenz.com.

Susan Lugli is a Christian speaker and author. Her stories have been published in *Chicken Soup for the Christian Woman's Soul*, *Chicken Soup for the Caregiver's Soul*, *Today's Christian Woman* magazine and many others. She is an advocate for burn survivors and speaks on their behalf. E-mail her at suenrusty@aol.com.

Natalia K. Lusinski created her first newspaper, "Nat's Neat News Notes," at age ten. Since then, she has worked as a writers' assistant on several TV shows, and recently associate produced a documentary for The History Channel. She also writes film and TV scripts, and short stories. E-mail her at writenataliainla@yahoo.com.

Michelle Mach is a freelance writer in Colorado. Her stories have appeared several anthologies, including *Chicken Soup for the Shopper's Soul* and *Chicken Soup for the Coffee Lover's Soul*. Visit her website at www.michellemach.com.

Cheryl Maguire graduated from Boston College with Bachelor's and Master's degrees in Counseling Psychology. Prior to becoming a mom, she worked as a counselor. Cheryl runs a website Swap Savers www.swapsavers.com, a social network for frugal folks. On her website she writes a money saving blog. E-mail: swapsavers@hotmail.com.

Ginger Manley received her BSN and MSN from Vanderbilt University. She is an Associate in Psychiatry at Vanderbilt Medical Center. She is researching a nonfiction book, entitled *Praying for Gloves*, the inspiring story of two nurses and the ways they have enabled change in Central Kenya. Her e-mail is manleygt@aol.com.

Judith Marks-White's award-winning "The Light Touch" column has appeared in the *Westport News* (CT) for twenty-five years. She is the author of two novels: *Seducing Harry* and *Bachelor Degree* published by Random House/Ballantine. Judith also teaches Humor Writing at Norwalk Community College in Norwalk, CT.

M. Sean Marshall is part of a rising generation in the field of social entrepreneurism. He works with CureDuchenne, a California based non-profit that funds research to cure Muscular Dystrophy. Sean enjoys a "curiously happy" family life with his wife and two girls. Please e-mail him at: sean@mseanmarshall.com.

Patrick Matthews is the president of Live Oak Games, and designer of the award-winning game *StoryTellers*. He's also the author of "DaddyTales," a newspaper column about his life as a dad.

Phyllis McKinley has four books of poetry published and is the author of the children's book *Do Clouds Have Feet?* Her work has received multiple awards and has been published in Canada, the USA and the UK. She lives in southwest Florida with her husband Dr. Hanford Brace. E-mail her at leafybough@hotmail.com.

Tasha Mitchell currently resides in Northwest Georgia with her husband and young son. She is a full time student pursing a nursing degree. Tasha enjoys traveling, dancing, reading and creative writing. She plans to finish her first book in the near future. Please e-mail her at tashakmitchell@yahoo.com.

Meg Werner Moreta has been a registered dietitian since 1992. Her journey started at Cal Poly, San Luis Obispo, California, where she learned their "learn by doing" philosophy. After finishing her Masters, Meg followed her passion to work in diabetes at her private practice in Beverly Hills. Meg enjoys life!

Risa Nye is a San Francisco Bay Area writer. She is co-editor of the anthology *Writin' on Empty: Parents Reveal the Upside, Downside, and*

Everything in Between When Children Leave the Nest. Her essays and articles have been published in several newspapers, magazines, and anthologies, including two *Chicken Soup for the Soul* books.

Emeri B. O'Brien is a native of Lake Charles, LA. She is a graduate of Grambling State University and the University of Maryland. She has worked as a reporter and a copy editor at various publications. She is now evening editor for MSN.com. Please e-mail her at emeriobrien@hotmail.com.

Author and motivational speaker, **Jennifer Oliver**, hails from Copperas Cove, Texas, where she and househubby are raising four magnificent creative life forces. Her stories have appeared in several *Chicken Soup for the Soul* books and other heartwarming publications.

LaVerne Otis loves to write and is presently taking her first writing class at a local community college. She has been published in *Country* and *Birds and Blooms* magazines. Other hobbies include photography, bird watching, gardening and spending lots of time with her family. She can be contacted at lotiswrites@msn.com.

Chantal Panozzo is a writer and advertising copywriter. Her articles and essays have appeared in *The Christian Science Monitor*, *National Geographic Glimpse*, and other publications, and she recently received the Rosalie Fleming Memorial Humor Prize. An American expatriate, Chantal travels extensively in Europe and lives in Zurich, Switzerland. (www.chantalpanozzo.com).

Laraine Paquette and her husband, Ken, have a Language School in the Boston area. Besides teaching English, Laraine does children's entertainment (story-telling, magic, music, balloon-sculpture and face-painting). She is a mother of six children and a grandmother of eleven. She holds a BA in English Literature. E-mail her at lpaquette@ learneslnow.com.

Ava Pennington is a writer, speaker, and Bible teacher. She has published magazine articles and contributed to fifteen anthologies, including twelve *Chicken Soup for the Soul* books. She is also author of *A Year Alone with God*—a 366-day devotional guide to the names and attributes of God. Learn more at www.avawrites.com.

Susan W. Peters graduated from the University of Kansas and lived and worked in a number of countries before returning to her Midwestern roots in 2006. She writes short stories and poetry, and teaches academic writing at a local community college. She can be contacted at swpetersksusa@yahoo.com.

Joe Rector is the community editor for the *Karns/Hardin Valley Shopper News*. Joe also does freelance writing, and his work has appeared in other *Chicken Soup for the Soul* books, as well as magazines and books. He hopes to find a publisher for his work. Please e-mail Joe at joerector@comcast.net.

Theresa Sanders contributes frequently to *Chicken Soup for the Soul*. Before turning to creative writing, she was an award-winning technical writer and consultant, and has been published in trade journals. A Springfield, Missouri native and a University of Maryland graduate, she has four grown children and lives with her husband in suburban St. Louis.

Leigh Anne Saxe is a Happiness Coach, Inspirational Speaker and Radio Host. Creator and founder of Living In The Moment (livinginthemoment.ca) Leigh Anne is committed to helping others find joy in the moment. Leigh Anne has her MA in Counseling Psychology from the Adler School of Professional Psychology in Toronto.

Heather Simms Schichtel is a writer, advocate and full time mom to Samantha. She lives in Colorado with her family, enjoying the sun, snow and mountains. You can follow their story at www.samsmom-heathers.blogspot.com or e-mail Heather at heather.schichtel@gmail.com.

Jacqueline Seewald has taught creative, expository and technical writing at the university level, and also worked as an academic librarian and educational media specialist. Her short stories, poems, essays, reviews and articles have appeared in diverse publications. Eight of her books have been published. Her most recent novel is *The Drowning Pool*.

Michelle Shocklee lives with her family in Central Texas. She writes historical fiction and is a member of American Christian Fiction Writers. Michelle enjoys movie dates with her husband, laughing with her sons, and reading, especially research material for her novels. Visit her Blog at: michelleshocklee.blogspot.com.

Dayle Allen Shockley is an award-winning writer whose by-line has appeared in dozens of publications. She is the author of three books and a contributor to many other works, including the *Chicken Soup for the Soul* series. E-mail her at dayle@dayleshockley.com.

Dena Slater received a Bachelor of Arts with honors and then earned a Master of Science. She taught English for twenty-seven years in Rockland Country, NY before retiring in New Jersey. She loves travel, bridge, and is a prolific reader.

Alaina Smith enjoys composing short stories and is a contributor to multiple volumes of two anthology series, *Chocolate for Women* and *A Cup of Comfort*. She also likes working for nonprofit organizations, volunteering for progressive causes, and spending time with her husband, Frank. E-mail her at writersmith@yahoo.com.

Sherri A. Stanczak is a freelance writer for several magazines, newsletters and online publications. Sherri writes regularly for a local website www.riverbills.com. She is also the author of two books. She enjoys spending time with family, boating, flying and writing. Please e-mail her at sherri0526@aol.com.

Diane Stark is a former teacher turned stay-at-home mom and freelance writer. She loves to write about the things that are most important to her, her family and her faith. Her first book, a devotional for teachers, was released in the fall of 2009. Diane can be reached at DianeStark19@yahoo.com.

Helen Stein lives with her husband, Ken, in the Great Lakes state of Michigan. They have four children and five energetic grandchildren. For eighteen years she edited and wrote safety articles for a motor carrier. She spends time with family, assists her parents, tends her perennial garden and plays tennis.

Joyce E. Sudbeck retired from Liguori Publications in 2008. She has been previously published in *Chicken Soup for the Soul* and *Liguorian Magazine*, and recently won first prize in a poetry contest. She writes short stories, poetry, and plans to start her first novel.

Annmarie B. Tait lives in Conshohocken, PA with her husband Joe and Sammy the "Wonder Yorkie." Annmarie has contributed several stories to the *Chicken Soup for the Soul* series. When not writing, Annmarie also enjoys cooking along with singing and recording American and Irish folk songs. E-mail her at irishbloom@aol.com.

B.J. Taylor is an award-winning author whose work has appeared in *Guideposts*, more than a dozen *Chicken Soup for the Soul* books, and numerous magazines and newspapers. She has a wonderful husband, four children and two grandsons. You can reach B.J. through her website at www.bjtayloronline.com.

Terri Tiffany counseled adults for seventeen years before owning a Christian bookstore. She resides in Florida with her husband where she writes full time. Her stories have appeared in Sunday school take-home papers, magazines and numerous anthologies. Please visit her at http://terri-treasures.blogspot.com.

Paula Maugiri Tindall, RN, writes her stories and finds her inspiration from personal life experiences and through nature while overlooking the lake where she resides in Florida, completing her first book. Her work has been previously published in *Chicken Soup for the Grandma's Soul*. She can be reached at lucylu54@aol.com.

Beverly F. Walker enjoys writing, photography, scrapbooking, and being with her grandchildren. She monitors a grief recovery group on line, and her stories appear in many *Chicken Soup for the Soul* books and in *Angel Cats: Divine Messengers of Comfort*.

Dr. Timothy Warren has operated a successful family chiropractic office in Warwick, RI since 1987. He is a lifelong athlete and has been mountaineering for the last fifteen years. He has summitted the highest mountain on four continents, most recently Mt. Everest. He lives deep in the woods with RoseMarie. www.drtimwarren.com.

Bill Wetterman is a retired Search Consultant from Oklahoma. He is a member of the American Christian Fiction Writers and a graduate of Ohio University. Bill and his wife, Pam, have taught Sunday school at their church for over twenty years. Please e-mail him at bwetterman@cox.net.

Valerie Whisenand, writing as Valerie Hansen, is the author of many Christian novels. When she moved to the Ozarks, she found her calling as well as a beautiful atmosphere filled with loving, caring people. She's been married to her high school sweetheart for a gazillion years! E-mail her at val@valeriehansen.com.

Woody Woodburn lives and writes in Ventura, California. A former national award-winning sports columnist and the co-author of *Raising Your Child to Be a Champion in Athletics, Arts and Academics*, he is working on two new books. He can be contacted at Woodycolum@aol.com.

Ashley Young is studying writing and hopes to work for a newspaper and write children's books when she graduates. Ashley was diagnosed with cancer when she was fourteen and has been in remission now for six years. Please e-mail her at pirategirl1588@aol.com.

Meet Our Authors

Jack Canfield is the co-creator of the *Chicken Soup for the Soul* series, which *Time* magazine has called "the publishing phenomenon of the decade." Jack is also the co-author of eight other bestselling books.

Jack is the CEO of the Canfield Training Group in Santa Barbara, California, and founder of the Foundation for Self-Esteem in Culver City, California. He has conducted intensive personal and professional development seminars on the principles of success for more than a million people in twenty-three countries. Jack is a dynamic keynote speaker and he has spoken to hundreds of thousands of people at more than 1,000 corporations, universities, professional conferences and conventions, and has been seen by millions more on national television shows such as *The Today Show*, *Fox and Friends*, *Inside Edition*, *Hard Copy*, CNN's *Talk Back Live*, *20/20*, *Eye to Eye*, the *NBC Nightly News* and the *CBS Evening News*.

Jack has received many awards and honors, including three honorary doctorates and a Guinness World Records Certificate for having seven books from the *Chicken Soup for the Soul* series appearing on the New York Times bestseller list on May 24, 1998.

You can reach Jack at:

Jack Canfield
P.O. Box 30880 • Santa Barbara, CA 93130
phone: 805-563-2935 • fax: 805-563-2945
www.jackcanfield.com

Mark Victor Hansen is the co-founder of Chicken Soup for the Soul, along with Jack Canfield. He is a sought-after keynote speaker, best-selling author, and marketing maven. Mark's powerful messages of possibility, opportunity, and action have created powerful change in thousands of organizations and millions of individuals worldwide.

Mark is a prolific writer with many bestselling books in addition to the *Chicken Soup for the Soul* series. Mark has had a profound influence in the field of human potential through his library of audios, videos, and articles in the areas of big thinking, sales achievement, wealth building, publishing success, and personal and professional development. He is also the founder of the MEGA Seminar Series.

He has appeared on *Oprah*, CNN, and *The Today Show*. He has been quoted in *Time*, *U. S. News & World Report*, *USA Today*, *The New York Times*, and *Entrepreneur* and has given countless radio interviews, assuring our planet's people that "You can easily create the life you deserve."

Mark has received numerous awards that honor his entrepreneurial spirit, philanthropic heart, and business acumen. He is a lifetime member of the Horatio Alger Association of Distinguished Americans.

You can reach Mark at:

Mark Victor Hansen & Associates, Inc.
P.O. Box 7665 • Newport Beach, CA 92658
phone: 949-764-2640 • fax: 949-722-6912
www.markvictorhansen.com

Amy Newmark is the publisher of Chicken Soup for the Soul, after a thirty-year career as a writer, speaker, financial analyst, and business executive in the worlds of finance and telecommunications. Amy is a *magna cum laude* graduate of Harvard College, where she majored in Portuguese, minored in French, and traveled extensively. She is also the mother of two children in college and two grown stepchildren who are recent college graduates.

After a long career writing books on telecommunications, voluminous financial reports, business plans, and corporate press releases, Chicken Soup for the Soul is a breath of fresh air for Amy. She has fallen in love with Chicken Soup for the Soul and its life-changing books, and really enjoys putting these books together for Chicken Soup's wonderful readers.

You can reach Amy and the rest of the Chicken Soup for the Soul team via e-mail through webmaster@chickensoupforthesoul.com.

Game inventor **Laura Robinson** often says she has been "selling laughter for over twenty years." She is the co-inventor of the best-selling classic bluffing game *Balderdash* (over 15 million copies sold worldwide). Along with business partner Elizabeth Bryan, Laura invented the *Count Your Blessings* game, based on an earlier game concept created with Los Angeles-based writer Rachel Naples. Known as one of the "Thomas Edisons of the Toy Industry," Laura also launched *Identity Crisis, the Funniest Game about Famous Names* in 2007. She is featured in the 2005 book *Women Invent* and has been a keynote speaker at various inventors' symposiums.

Laura is also an actor/musician and has enjoyed a successful career in film and television both in Los Angeles and Toronto. She was a regular on the CBS crime series *Night Heat*, and guest starred on many popular television shows, including *Frasier* and *Cheers* and just completed filming a music reality show, called *Big Voice* scheduled to air on a major U.S. network, spring 2010.

Laura lives in Toronto with her husband and two children. She is a "mom with a mission," committed to creating "good message" games and products that celebrate the transformational power of gratitude. With Bryan, Robinson is also launching *Win-Win*, a family game inspired by "The 7 Habits" series of books.

Robinson is honored and grateful to be involved with the Chicken Soup for the Soul team and their inspiring books.

You can reach Laura at: www.countyourblessingsgame.com or visit www.identitycrisisgame.com.

Elizabeth Bryan is a parent/artist/writer with a mission of sharing the message of gratitude through all things creative. With business partner and *Balderdash* inventor Laura Robinson, Bryan developed the current *Chicken Soup for the Soul: Count Your Blessings* game, which was inspired by an earlier version developed with writer Rachel Naples.

Elizabeth and Laura are committed to creating good-message games that bring families together through joy and play. They are also set to release a family game with Franklin Covey entitled *Win-Win*, based on the bestselling "7 Habits" series of books.

Elizabeth has enjoyed a successful career as an artist and has work in collections throughout the United States. She is also known for her unique clothing designs which have been worn by numerous celebrities, appeared in *Vanity Fair*, and have been sold by Wynn Resorts in Las Vegas.

Her passions also extend to helping others access their creative genius. She has been honored by various organizations for her charitable art projects and is also the founder of G.I.F.T. (www.giftproject. net), a non-profit organization committed to creating and marketing products that raise awareness for various causes. G.I.F.T. stands for Gratitude, Inspiration, Focus and Trust—Elizabeth believes that accessing and practicing these four qualities can help all of us reach our fullest potential.

Elizabeth is incredibly grateful and honored to share *Chicken Soup for the Soul: Count Your Blessings* with the Chicken Soup for the Soul audience.

You can reach Elizabeth through www.countyourblessingsgame. com, or www.elizabethbryanstudio.com.

Thank You

We owe huge thanks to all of our contributors. We know that you pour your hearts and souls into the thousands of stories and poems that you share with us, and ultimately with each other. We appreciate your willingness to open up your lives to other Chicken Soup for the Soul readers.

We can only publish a small percentage of the stories that are submitted, but we read every single one and even the ones that do not appear in the book have an influence on us and on the final manuscript.

We want to thank Chicken Soup for the Soul editor Kristiana Glavin for her assistance with the final manuscript and proofreading. We also want to thank our assistant publisher, D'ette Corona, and our editor and webmaster Barbara LoMonaco for their expert editorial, proofreading, and organizational assistance, as well as Leigh Holmes, who keeps our office running smoothly.

We owe a very special thanks to our creative director and book producer, Brian Taylor at Pneuma Books, for his brilliant vision for our covers and interiors. Finally, none of this would be possible without the business and creative leadership of our CEO, Bill Rouhana, and our president, Bob Jacobs.

Improving Your Life Every Day

Real people sharing real stories—for fifteen years. Now, Chicken Soup for the Soul has gone beyond the bookstore to become a world leader in life improvement. Through books, movies, DVDs, online resources and other partnerships, we bring hope, courage, inspiration and love to hundreds of millions of people around the world. Chicken Soup for the Soul's writers and readers belong to a one-of-a-kind global community, sharing advice, support, guidance, comfort, and knowledge.

Chicken Soup for the Soul stories have been translated into more than forty languages and can be found in more than one hundred countries. Every day, millions of people experience a Chicken Soup for the Soul story in a book, magazine, newspaper or online. As we share our life experiences through these stories, we offer hope, comfort and inspiration to one another. The stories travel from person to person, and from country to country, helping to improve lives everywhere.

Share with Us

We all have had Chicken Soup for the Soul moments in our lives. If you would like to share your story or poem with millions of people around the world, go to chickensoup.com and click on "Submit Your Story." You may be able to help another reader, and become a published author at the same time. Some of our past contributors have launched writing and speaking careers from the publication of their stories in our books!

Our submission volume has been increasing steadily—the quality and quantity of your submissions has been fabulous. Starting in 2010, we will only accept story submissions via our website. They will no longer be accepted via mail or fax.

To contact us regarding other matters, please send us an e-mail through webmaster@chickensoupforthesoul.com, or fax or write us at:

Chicken Soup for the Soul
P.O. Box 700
Cos Cob, CT 06807-0700
Fax: 203-861-7194

One more note from your friends at Chicken Soup for the Soul: Occasionally, we receive an unsolicited book manuscript from one of our readers, and we would like to respectfully inform you that we do not accept unsolicited manuscripts and we must discard the ones that appear.

Every cloud really *does* have a silver lining. And, once you start to play this insightful and often hilarious new game with your family and friends, you'll go from frazzled to dazzled, tired to inspired and stressed to blessed! Visit www.countyourblessingsgame.com for game info and other fun.

Now you can play the Board Game!

Chicken Soup for the Soul®

Tough Times, Tough People

TOUGH TIMES WON'T LAST BUT TOUGH PEOPLE WILL

101 Stories about Overcoming the Economic Crisis and Other Challenges

Jack Canfield, Mark Victor Hansen & Amy Newmark

Tough times won't last, but tough people will. Many people have lost money, and many are losing their jobs, homes, or at least making cutbacks. Others have faced life-changing natural disasters, such as hurricanes and fires, as well as health and family difficulties. Yhis book is all about overcoming adversity, pulling together, making do with less, facing challenges, and finding new joys in a simpler life. Stories address downsizing, getting out of debt, managing chronic health problems, dealing with loss, having faith, blessings in disguise, and finding new perspectives. Anyone going through a difficult time will find encouragement, inspiration, and support.

978-1-935096-35-1

More Inspiration
& Encouragement

Chicken Soup
for the Soul
www.ChickenSoup.com